The Greatest Among You:

Unleashing the Power of Servant Leadership in Life, Business, and Faith

Lee Burchett

Dedication

To Grand Canyon University
and the Colangelo College of Business—

Thank you for changing my life.

In my years as a Lope, I didn't just earn degrees, I found my calling. The lessons you taught me extended far beyond textbooks and lectures. They reached deep into my heart, awakened my purpose, and anchored my leadership in faith.

At GCU, servant leadership became more than a concept, it became a conviction. Through every class, every challenge, and every moment of reflection, my vision was sharpened and my spirit strengthened. I discovered that greatness isn't about status, it's about service.

I will never take this knowledge or my newfound purpose for granted.

Thank you for giving me the tools to lead with humility, love, and boldness—and for reminding me that the greatest among us will always be the servant.

Lopes Up—Always.

"For even the Son of Man did not come to be served, but to serve,
and to give his life as a ransom for many." — Mark 10:45 (NIV)

To every student searching for purpose—this is proof that God can take your education and turn it into a mission. GCU didn't just prepare me for a career, it prepared me to make an eternal impact.

Copyright Page:

The Greatest Among You

© 2025 by Lee Burchett

All rights reserved. No part of this publication may be reproduced, stored in a retrieval system, or transmitted in any form or by any means—electronic, mechanical, photocopy, recording, or otherwise—without the prior written permission of the publisher, except for brief quotations used in reviews or scholarly works.

This book is a work of original thought, leadership insight, and creative storytelling. Any resemblance to actual people, living or dead, is purely coincidental unless otherwise noted by the author.

For information, inquiries, or permission requests, please contact:
Lee@vykanlegacy.com

ISBN: 979-8-9992797-4-3

Published by Vykan Legacy Press

Cover design & Interior layout by Vykan Legacy Press

First edition, 2025

Table of Contents

The Leadership Crisis and the Call to Serve............i

    The Burnout Epidemic: When Leadership Fails and People Pay the Price......................vii

    The Trust Deficit in Organizations: When Belief Dies and Chaos Reigns........................xvii

    Why Servant Leadership Is the Answer: The Strategy That Outlasts the Storm....................xxix

    The Example of Christ (Philippians 2:3–8): The Blueprint for Greatness................xxxiii

    The Model That Changes Everything......... xxxvii

CHAPTER 1: What Is Servant Leadership—Really?..1

    The World Got It Backwards..............1

    Servant Leadership Begins with the Heart.........2

    Authority Doesn't Disappear—It Gets Rebuilt 4

    It's Not a Leadership Style—It's a Lifestyle........6

    Servant Leaders Build, They Don't Break..........8

    This Isn't About Titles—It's About Impact....10

    You Carry Their Wins, Not Just Their Work..12

This Kind of Leadership Changes Everything 13

Definition and Core Principles: The DNA of Servant Leadership 15

The Core Foundation: It Starts with Love, Not Leverage 17

When These Principles Come Alive, So Does Your Culture 22

Robert Greenleaf's Original Concept: The Spark That Lit a Movement 23

The Servant-Leader Test: His Defining Standard 25

He Didn't Just Create a Model—He Created a Mirror 27

Why It's Still So Relevant Today 28

The Business World Started Listening 29

The Legacy Lives On—Through You 30

Jesus: The Ultimate Servant Leader 31

The Towel Over the Title 32

He Led From Among, Not Above 34

He Gave Everything—Not for Applause, But for People 36

His Model Wasn't Temporary—It Was Transformational 37

The Cross Was the Ultimate Act of Servant Leadership 37

His Legacy Was Multiplication, Not Control .. 38

Call to Action: Chapter 1 — Rise and Serve 39

CHAPTER 2: The Business Case for Servant Leadership 45

Stop the Eye Roll—Start the Awakening 45

Higher Engagement = Higher Profits 46

Low Turnover Isn't Luck—It's Leadership 48

Innovation Thrives in Safety 49

Customer Satisfaction Starts With Employee Loyalty 51

Servant Leaders Multiply Leadership 52

Servant Leadership Future-Proofs Your Culture 54

Stop Managing. Start Building. 55

The Numbers Don't Lie—They Roar 57

Performance Gets Supercharged 58

Culture Isn't Fluff—It's Firepower 59

Retention Skyrockets with Servant Leadership 61

The Greenleaf Effect in Action 62

Psychological Safety = Innovation and Risk-Taking 64

Servant Leadership Boosts Emotional Intelligence and Purpose 65

When the Data Matches the Spirit, You've Got a Revolution 67

The Lie of the Bottom Line 68

When You Prioritize People, You Multiply Performance 70

Loyalty You Can Bank On 71

Servant Leadership Turns Employees Into Advocates 72

Healthier Teams = Healthier Bottom Line 74

Innovation Explodes Where People Are Empowered 75

Every System Gets Better When People Come First 76

You Can't Afford Not to Lead This Way 78

Call to Action: Chapter 2 — Step into the Revolution 80

CHAPTER 3: Servant Leadership in Action 85

The Stage Is Set—Now Let's Walk It Out 85

Leadership That Looks Like Jesus 87

The Battlefield Is Boardrooms and Break Rooms 88

Leading with Both Courage and Compassion . 90

The Stories That Prove It Works 92

You'll Face Resistance—Lead Anyway 93

The Fruit That Follows Obedience 95

The Towel Is Waiting—Pick It Up 96

Leading with Humility and Courage 98

Humility Isn't Weakness—It's Unstoppable Strength 100

Humility Builds Unshakable Trust 100

Courage Isn't Loud—It's Loyal 102

Courage and Humility Together Change Everything 104

Leadership Is Not About Being Liked—It's About Being Real... 105

The Greatest Leaders Lead from Their Knees 107

The Call: Kneel Lower. Stand Taller. 109

Real Stories from Faith-Based Leaders and CEOs.. 109

A Luxury Brand Built on Human Dignity 111

A Car Dealer Who Led Like a Pastor............ 112

Giving It All Back... 113

When Profit Meets Purpose............................ 115

My Story in the Trenches 116

Servant Leadership Is Already Winning......... 117

This Is YOUR Moment................................... 118

Challenges Faced and Victories Won 119

Servant Leaders Get Hit Hard—But They Don't Break 120

The Cost of Courage.. 122

Turning Betrayal into Breakthrough............... 123

The Battle of Burnout...................................... 124

The Vindication of Vision 126

The Rewards You Can't Quantify 127

The Fire Refines the Faithful 128

The Divine Blueprint for Leadership............ 129

Act Justly: Leading With Righteous Conviction 131

Love Mercy: Lead With Grace, Not Guilt 132

Walk Humbly With Your God: The Posture of True Greatness 133

Shepherd the Flock—Not Dominate the People 134

Willing Hearts Win the War 135

Leadership Without Lording......................... 136

Set the Example, Ignite the Movement 138

7-DAY SERVANT LEADERSHIP ACTION CHALLENGE.. 139

CHAPTER 4: Servant Leadership and Organizational Culture... 145

Culture Isn't a Perk—It's the Pulse................ 145

Leaders Are the Thermostat, Not the Thermometer.. 147

Culture Begins in the Soul of the Leader 148

Your Values Mean Nothing Without Action 150

From Vision to Vibe: How Servant Leadership Shapes Every Corner 151

Culture as Your Greatest Asset—or Your Greatest Liability 153

God Cares About Your Culture 155

The Movement Starts With You 157

How Values Become Behaviors 158

Values Require Consistent Modeling 160

From Beliefs to Habits 162

Small Decisions Shape Deep Culture 164

People Repeat What's Rewarded 165

Accountability Is Not Optional 167

Build Rituals Around What You Believe 169

Values That Flow from the Throne 170

Servant Leadership as a System, not a Slogan 172

If It's Not Built into the System, It Doesn't Exist 172

Leadership Is a System of Influence 173

Embedding the Mission in Every Layer 175

Hiring and Firing by the Values 177

Training the Servant Way 179

Accountability that Honors the Mission 180

Servant Systems Produce Scalable Impact 182

The Metrics That Actually Matter 184

Evaluation the Servant Way 186

Designing Feedback Loops That Build, Not Break 188

This Is the Infrastructure of Revival 190

Building Psychological Safety and Mission Alignment 192

Fear-Based Leadership Is a Silent Killer 193

The Gospel Calls for Radical Safety 195

Safety Leads to Alignment 196

Alignment Is Clarity Plus Purpose 198

Safe Cultures Call Out the Best 199

Guardrails for Alignment: Systems That Call Us Back 201

Innovation and Risk-Taking 203

Safety Multiplies Risk-Taking and Innovation 206

The Culture of the Kingdom 208

Kingdom Culture Is Counterculture 209

Honor Over Ego 211

Devotion Is the Fuel of Service 213

Galatians 5:13 — Freedom That Serves 215

Humility Isn't a Weakness—It's a Weapon ... 217

Love That Moves 219

Systems of Honor Create Movements 220

Leadership that Reflects Heaven 222

Call to Action — Chapter 4: Light the Fire in the Culture 224

Final Rally: 231

CHAPTER 5: Building Systems That Scale 233

Culture Without Systems is Just a Mood 233

Scale is the Real Test of Leadership 234

Systems Are Not the Enemy of the Spirit 236

From the Boardroom to the Break Room 237

What Gets Repeated Gets Reinforced............ 239

Systems Multiply the Mission, Not the Man. 241

Systems Are the Bridge from Vision to Victory 243

Buckle Up—It's Time to Build....................... 245

Servant Leadership Must Be Everywhere...... 247

Culture Is Caught, Not Just Taught 250

Hierarchies Don't Create Movements—
Servants Do... 254

Every Level Needs the Language 258

Coaches, Not Commanders 260

Pipelines of Purpose 262

From Jesus to Jack Welch............................... 264

Ready to Equip a Revolution 267

Creating Servant Leaders at Every Level....... 269

Leadership Isn't a Title—It's a Posture 271

Culture is Carried, Not Just Created 274

Culture Carrier Toolbox................................. 276

The Power of the First Follower 277

You Don't Have to Wait to Lead.................... 280

Develop People, Don't Just Deploy Them ... 283

Accountability with Compassion 286

Structure Must Support Servant Leadership . 290

Innovation No One's Talking About: The Inverted Scorecard 291

How You Build a Structure That Supports Servant Leadership 292

Next-Level Practice: The Legacy Table.......... 294

Final Word.. 294

The Movement Starts with You 295

Leadership Is Caught Before It's Taught........ 296

Modeling Drives Culture 297

Coaching Your Team to Serve Others 299

Start with" Heartset", Not Just Skillset 300

Use the I-Do, We-Do, You-Do Model.......... 301

Create Feedback Loops that Build Culture.... 301

Develop Peer Coaches to Multiply the Mission 302

Turn Every Touchpoint into a Teaching Moment 303

Bottom Line 304

Coaching Isn't Correcting—It's Cultivating . 304

From Feedback to Formation 305

See the Seed, Not Just the Soil 306

Coaching Requires Rhythms, Not Randomness 307

Coach With Fire and Grace 308

Coach to the Whole Person, Not Just the Performer 308

Final Charge 309

Model Before You Mentor 310

Create a Culture of Coaching 310

Coach the Why, Not Just the What 311

Reframe Every Task Through Purpose 312

Make "Why" Part of the Rhythm 312

Coaching Framework: The "WHY-WHAT-HOW" Model 313

Why Coaching the Why Builds Leaders 314

Final Charge 315

Use Story as a Coaching Tool 315

Why Story Works in Servant Leadership 316

How to Use Story to Build Servant Leaders .. 317

Make Your Culture Legendary 318

How to Make Your Culture Legendary Through Story 320

Tactical Coaching Strategy: Story-Driven Culture Loops 322

Jesus Wasn't Just a Teacher—He Was a Master Storyteller 323

Final Charge 324

Encourage Progress, Not Perfection 324

Call Out the Climb 325

Don't Just Praise—Be Precise 329

The Jesus Model 330

Final Charge 331

Make Coaching an Expectation, Not a Favor 331

Coaching Creates a Chain Reaction 332

How to Build a Servant-First Pipeline 333

Create a Culture of Mentorship 334

Rotate and Expose 334

Build in Feedback Loops 335

Create Small Leadership Labs 335

Celebrate Pipeline Progress 335

Build It To Outlive You 336

From the Sermon to the System 340

Discipline Builds Disciples 343

Light the Fuse — Build the Movement 344

CHAPTER 6: The Faith Factor 347

Why Christ-Centered Leadership Changes Everything 350

Integrating Prayer, Purpose, and People 353

Living Out the Gospel Through Service 356

This Is the Way 362

CHAPTER 7: Obstacles to Servant Leadership 365

Ego, Control, and Fear 367

Toxic Cultures and How to Detox Them 370

How to Build a Legendary Servant Culture .. 373

Why Servant Leadership Is the Only Model That Works 376

The Courage to Serve When It's Inconvenient 377

Rally Cry: We Serve—And We Never Surrender 380

CHAPTER 8: Servant Leadership in Schools, Sports, and Nonprofits 383

Building Future Leaders Through Education and Coaching 386

Creating Purpose-Driven Environments for Youth 389

Stories from Life: Coaching, Teaching, and Leading 392

Building Future Leaders Through Education and Coaching 397

Creating Purpose-Driven Environments for Youth 400

Rally Cry: Raise the Standard, Light the Fire . 405

14-Day Plan: Building Future Leaders Through Education and Coaching 406

CHAPTER 9: Leaving a Legacy of Service 415

Servant Leadership That Outlives the Leader 417

Mentorship, Multiplication, and Mission 419

Finishing Well 420

Leaving a Legacy of Service 424

Ignite the Movement of Servant Leadership 426

CHAPTER 10: The Greatest Among You 429

The Legacy of Impact: Building What Outlives You 431

Multiplying the Mission: Disciples Who Make Disciples 433

The Invitation to Greatness: Will You Answer the Call? 435

THE REVOLUTION STARTS WITH YOU
.... 437

A Challenge to the Reader 438

Prayer of Commissioning 439

30 Days to a Servant-Led Culture: The Challenge 441

The Leadership Crisis and the Call to Serve

"Whoever wants to become great among you must be your servant."
— *Jesus, Matthew 20:26 (NIV)*

The Crisis No One Can Ignore

There's a leadership crisis happening right now—and it's not subtle. It's loud. It echoes in burned-out workplaces, crumbling team cultures, broken school systems, and organizations chasing profit over people. We see it in politicians who serve themselves instead of their constituents, executives who treat employees like numbers, and coaches who prioritize records over relationships. Trust in leadership is at an all-time low—not because we expect too much, but because we've been sold something shallow.

We've been told that leadership is about image. That power is about presence. That influence comes from charisma, title, and control. But we're waking up. We're realizing that leadership built on ego is fragile. It cracks under pressure. It can win attention—but it can't win hearts.

So what happens when the world sees through the illusion? What do you do when the emperor has no clothes and the "experts" don't have answers? You go back. Back to something ancient. Back to something tested. You return to the kind of leadership that doesn't collapse when it's challenged—the kind that bends low, lifts others, and leads with love. That's what this book is about. That's what the world is crying out for.

A Better Way Is Waiting

There is a better way to lead—one that doesn't compromise results, but multiplies them. It's not soft. It's not passive. It's not weak. It's servant leadership—and it is the most powerful, transformational leadership model the world has ever known. Jesus didn't build an empire with a sword. He built a Kingdom with a towel. He didn't stand above His followers; He knelt to wash their feet.

This model of leadership isn't just spiritual—it's strategic. The best companies in the world are adopting it. The healthiest teams are shaped by it. The most resilient cultures are built on it. Research backs it. Results prove it. And the greatest leader the world has ever known lived it. That's not coincidence—that's a calling.

What if you didn't have to choose between high expectations and a healthy team? What if you could drive results and build people at the same time? What if you could lead with strength *and* compassion, clarity *and* humility, purpose *and* performance? You can. And it starts here.

Why This Book Matters Now

This book is not about theory—it's about a revolution in how we lead. It's about showing up to work, practice, or the boardroom and choosing to put people first every single time. It's about redefining strength—not as domination, but as dedication. Not as loudness, but as consistency. Not as control, but as trust earned through service.

We live in a world that rewards image, performance, and speed. But real leadership is not about how fast you climb—it's about how well you carry others as you go. Servant leadership turns the world's leadership model upside down. It invites us to trade power plays for empathy, status for stewardship, and pressure for peace. This isn't soft leadership—it's steel-wrapped-in-love leadership.

The truth is this: the most impactful leaders aren't always the ones you notice first. They're the ones who show up when it's hard. They sacrifice without applause. They build others in silence, only to watch them shine. That's what the greatest among us do. And it's exactly what Jesus meant when He said the way up is down.

From Experience, Not Just Insight

I've seen this model work in places most leadership books don't reach. In the classroom. On the sidelines. In small businesses with no budget and high burnout. In failing teams that needed culture change more than new policies. I've lived this—not just read about it. And I've watched as it breathed life into places that were dying.

This book will walk you through practical, powerful steps to embed servant leadership into your culture. It will give you stories, tools, action plans, and Scripture. But more importantly, it will show you what it looks like to lead like Jesus—and win in life, business, and faith because of it.

You don't need to be a pastor to lead this way. You don't need to have a pulpit. You don't need a fancy title. You need heart. You need humility. And you need the willingness to serve before you're ever served. That's what separates the good from the great. That's what will change your life—and everyone you lead.

A Call to the Brave

If you're holding this book, it means something in you is already ready. You've tasted the emptiness of positional leadership. You've watched the burnout. You've seen talent wasted under poor guidance. And something in you knows there has to be more. There has to be a way to lead that doesn't break people—but builds them. That doesn't demand from the front—but lifts from behind.

This isn't a call to sit down. It's a call to kneel—and rise up stronger because of it. It's a call to flip the script, rewrite the rules, and bring heaven's mindset to earth's leadership problems. It's a call to become more than a manager, more than a boss, more than a figurehead. It's a call to become a builder of people. A steward of trust. A firestarter of culture.

Are you ready? Because once you step into this, there's no going back. The world will look different. Your influence will grow. But more importantly—your soul will be anchored. And so will theirs.

Let's Start a Movement

The pages that follow are not about perfection—they're about pursuit. The pursuit of leadership that reflects Jesus. The pursuit of systems that scale culture, not just profit. The pursuit of leaving people better than you found them—every single time.

This is not a quick-fix leadership hack. It's not

a motivational poster. It's a war cry for leaders who are ready to serve with strength, lead with love, and finish well. If that's you, then welcome. You've found your tribe.

Now let's build something that lasts. Something that multiplies. Something that honors God and elevates people.
Let's start the movement.

The Burnout Epidemic: When Leadership Fails and People Pay the Price

The Fire's Out — and We Know Who Killed It

Burnout is not just a buzzword. It's a crisis. And let's be real: it's not caused by "lazy employees" or "entitled workers." It's caused by weak, selfish, insecure bosses who think leadership is about control instead of contribution. I've been working since I was 15 years old, and I've seen the worst of them. People who wore the title like a crown, not a calling. People who believed they were God's gift to the workplace just because they had a bigger office and a louder voice.

And here's the part that makes my blood boil: these so-called "leaders" hide behind buzzwords and leadership seminars, but they wouldn't last a day leading with integrity. They weaponize authority and punish authenticity. They crush initiative under the weight of their insecurity. The fire didn't burn out because the team got tired. It burned out because the people trusted to protect it were too obsessed with preserving their image to actually protect their people. Let's stop pretending burnout is a mystery—it's a direct result of cowardly leadership that confuses fear with respect and silence with loyalty.

But we're flipping the script—right here, right now. We're calling out the lie that domination equals leadership. True leaders don't steal energy—they give it. They don't hoard credit—they multiply it. The kind of leader who revives a culture is the one who walks into the room and fans the flame back to life, not with noise, but with presence. With consistency. With love. Servant leadership doesn't just relight the fire—it guards it with everything it has. And when that fire comes back? Watch the entire team rise with it—fueled by purpose, led by heart, and unstoppable in unity.

The Tyrants in Office Chairs

You know the type. They don't coach—they command. They don't inspire—they intimidate. These are the bosses who bark orders from behind their desk like Caesar on a throne, never lifting a finger to help, never getting their hands dirty, and never actually *leading*. They crush creativity with their fragile egos—because the only good ideas are the ones they thought of first. If you dare to think for yourself, you're a threat. If you dare to care, you're "too soft." These people aren't leaders. They're toxic. And they're everywhere.

They lead through fear because deep down, they're terrified themselves—terrified someone smarter, kinder, or braver might expose how hollow their authority really is. So they build walls of control instead of bridges of trust. They cancel creativity with condescension. They laugh at vulnerability because they've never had the guts to be real. Their meetings feel like interrogations, not inspiration. Their feedback is a weapon, not a gift. And every room they walk into gets quieter—not because they command respect, but because they kill it.

But guess what? That reign is ending. A new breed of leader is rising—one that doesn't need a throne to lead. One that knows leadership isn't about barking orders, but about building people. Real leaders aren't afraid of good ideas—they celebrate them. They don't feel threatened by passion—they ignite it. Servant leaders don't silence voices—they create space for them to be heard, seen, and unleashed. That's the future. That's the movement. And if you've ever worked under a tyrant and thought, *"There has to be more than this..."*—you're dang right there is. And you're the one who's going to bring it.

The Cost of Cowardice

Here's what those kinds of "leaders" never see: their people are drowning. Their teams are exhausted, disillusioned, and disengaged. They wonder why performance is down, why turnover is up, why morale is in the basement—when the answer is staring at them in the mirror. It's not the job that burns people out. It's the **absence of leadership**. When people don't feel seen, heard, or valued—they stop showing up with heart. First emotionally. Then physically. Then permanently.

They preach "accountability," but never take ownership. They quote leadership books, but don't live a single principle. And they sit in corner offices wondering why their "vision" isn't catching on—when the only thing they've passed down is fear. Cowardice in leadership doesn't just cause confusion—it breeds chaos. It creates cultures where survival replaces strategy, where apathy replaces excellence, and where even the most passionate people lose their flame. And when that flame dies, it doesn't come back easy.

Because people don't quit jobs—they quit being invisible. They quit feeling like a number. They quit giving their all to someone who wouldn't notice if they disappeared tomorrow. The cost of cowardice isn't just missed deadlines or botched meetings. It's talent lost. Potential buried. Purpose wasted. And the sickest part? Most of these so-called "leaders" will never even realize what they had—until it's already gone. And by then, the damage is done, the team is broken, and the culture is bleeding out. But not on our watch.

Not anymore.

I've Lived It

I've worked under bosses who treated every workday like a warzone—and every suggestion like treason. The kind who scream when they're stressed and disappear when it matters. They never asked how you were doing. They never said "thank you." Their entire identity was wrapped up in being in charge. Power was their drug. And when you work under people like that, burnout isn't an "if"—it's a **when**. You start hating the sound of your alarm. You stop caring about your work. You call out, show up late, or sit at your desk wondering what it's all for.

Burnout Doesn't Just Break Workers—It Breaks Cultures

Burnout kills innovation. It kills momentum. It kills loyalty. People stop believing that what they do matters. They start doing the bare minimum, not because they're lazy, but because they're trying to survive. And survival mode is not where greatness lives. You can't build excellence in a battlefield of fear. You can't create joy in a culture of shame. And you can't call yourself a leader if your people are burning out in silence while you bask in the glow of your own ego.

The Lie We've Been Sold

We've been told that leadership is about control. That strong leaders don't bend. That you can't care and still command respect. But that's garbage. That lie is exactly what's driven millions of people to the edge of mental and emotional collapse. The truth? People don't burn out because they're weak. They burn out because they're **carrying too much alone, for too long, with too little care.** They burn out under leaders who see them as tools, not humans. And I don't know about you—but I'm done watching it happen.

You've been lied to. Sold a version of leadership that worships dominance and punishes compassion. Told that empathy is weakness and that silence is strength. But real strength doesn't come from barking orders or wielding power—it comes from standing in the fire with your people, from lifting them when they fall, from choosing love when control would be easier. The lie says leadership is about being feared. But the truth? The greatest leaders are followed because they are trusted, not because they are feared.

That lie has cost us brilliant minds, dedicated workers, inspired teams, and thriving cultures. It has left hallways full of resignation letters and breakrooms full of broken spirits. We're not just losing employees—we're losing people who once believed they mattered. And it's all because a few insecure leaders were too proud to bend, too fragile to serve, and too blind to care. That ends here. That ends with us. It's time to rewrite the script. To raise a new kind of leader—one who doesn't lead from above, but from beside. One who doesn't crush, but calls up. One who knows the truth: **you don't have to choose between love and leadership. The real ones live both.**

Enough Is Enough

We need a new generation of leaders who don't hide behind titles. Leaders who don't micromanage or manipulate. We need leaders who show up, lean in, and fight for their people—not against them. We need men and women who are brave enough to *serve*—

because servant leadership doesn't produce burnout, it prevents it. It creates belonging. It builds teams that last. And when people feel seen and supported, they don't just perform—they **thrive**.

Enough is enough. We're done watching fake leaders chase applause while their teams bleed out behind them. We're done tolerating cowards who hide behind their title like it's a bulletproof vest, who weaponize fear because they've never learned how to earn trust. This isn't leadership—it's laziness wrapped in arrogance. And we're not bowing to it anymore. We're raising up a new kind of leader—bold, humble, unshakable in character, and relentless in their love for their people.

This generation of leaders will not be forged in boardrooms—they'll be born in the trenches. They'll be the ones who say, "Put the title down and pick the people up." They'll sacrifice comfort for culture, abandon ego for empathy, and trade manipulation for mission. These are the leaders who will restore the workplace, reimagine our schools, and rebuild what broken systems tried to destroy. **Because when servant leadership rises,** burnout dies. When people feel seen, they soar. When they're supported, they shine. And when they're led with purpose—they set the world on fire.

Light the Fire Again

Burnout happens when leadership forgets its purpose. But servant leadership fans the flame back to life. It reminds people why they started. It builds trust instead of tearing it down. It says, "I'm here with you," not "I'm above you." And the second that kind of leader shows up, people start rising again. They start caring again. They start believing again. And just like that—the fire returns.

Servant leadership doesn't just fix what's broken—it resurrects what was dead. It steps into the ashes of burnout and breathes purpose back into tired souls. It's the leader who walks in, sees the pain, and refuses to walk out until the flame is lit again. They don't need a microphone or a mandate—they lead by presence. They reignite belief in people who thought they were done. And that belief? It spreads like wildfire.

Because once people feel seen, supported, and *valued*—they don't just show up, they show out. They innovate. They lead. They serve each other. They become torchbearers of the culture you dared to ignite. And before long, that one flame becomes a blaze that burns down fear, silences doubt, and turns ordinary workplaces into purpose-driven battlegrounds of greatness. This is how movements begin. This is how revival starts. Not with noise—but with a servant's heart and a soul set on fire.

The Trust Deficit in Organizations: When Belief Dies and Chaos Reigns

The Great Collapse

If burnout is the fire that burns people out, then broken trust is the match that lights it. Let's not sugarcoat it—**most people don't trust their leaders.** And they have every reason not to. We've watched leaders say one thing and do another. We've seen decisions made in backrooms that sabotage front-line workers. We've felt the sting of promises broken, credit stolen, and concerns ignored.

Trust has become a luxury instead of a standard—and that's a leadership failure of the highest order.

This isn't a minor crack—it's a catastrophic cave-in. When trust crumbles, everything else follows. Loyalty? Gone. Creativity? Gutted. Morale? Buried. Leaders who say one thing and do another don't just damage credibility—they detonate it. And when trust explodes, it takes with it every ounce of belief your team had in the mission. You can't build greatness on broken promises. You can't rally a movement with a crooked compass.

Trust isn't a bonus—it's the oxygen of every thriving culture. And when it's gone, people don't just whisper in the breakroom—they check out in silence. They stop speaking up. They stop believing anything will change. And then? They leave. Sometimes physically. Sometimes emotionally. But always for good. The collapse isn't caused by competition or pressure. It's caused by leaders who traded integrity for image—and lost everything that mattered most.

The Fallout of Faking It

When leaders fake it, cut corners, play favorites, or lead with fear instead of integrity, people notice. They may not say it out loud—but they see everything. They see who gets protected and who gets punished. They see who gets heard and who gets shut down. And what they see sends a message: **"You can't trust this place. You can't trust this leader. You're on your own."** And once that message lands, morale isn't just low—it's shattered.

Fake leadership is a virus—and the symptoms are everywhere. You can smell it in closed-door meetings. You can hear it in the forced laughs and fake affirmations. You can feel it in the silence when no one dares speak truth to power. When leaders pretend to care, people learn to pretend back. And that's when the culture rots. Not from rebellion—but from resignation. From a deep, soul-crushing realization that authenticity isn't welcome here. That survival means silence.

And make no mistake—your team sees it all. They see who gets the credit and who gets the crumbs. They see who's untouchable and who's disposable. They see the double standards, the favoritism, the fear-based decisions dressed up as "strategy." And every time they do, a piece of belief dies. One crack becomes a chasm. And suddenly, the team that once burned with purpose is numb, guarded, and gone. That's the real fallout: not loud rebellion—but quiet surrender. And it's the kind of damage that no performance review can fix.

Trust Isn't Given—It's Earned and Lived

Here's the truth: trust is built in a thousand small moments. It's built when a leader follows through. When they show up on time. When they apologize with sincerity. When they defend their team instead of throwing them under the bus. When they live what they preach. People don't expect perfection from leaders—but they do expect **honesty, consistency, and courage**. When they don't get it? The foundation cracks.

Trust is not a perk. It's not a benefit. It's not something you're handed just because you sit in the big chair. Trust is war-forged. It's blood-earned. It's sweat-drenched. It's built when a leader *shows up*—when they *speak truth even when it costs them*, when they *stay when it's messy*, and when they *own the hard decisions without scapegoating someone else*. Trust is forged in the fire—and you can't fake fire. Not one damn spark.

People don't demand perfection—but they are begging for *real*. They want leaders who aren't scared of vulnerability. Leaders who don't bail when things break. Leaders who bleed beside them, not just bark from above. Every broken promise, every ignored voice, every cowardly dodge of accountability? That's one more sledgehammer blow to the foundation. And once trust cracks—it's not a slow leak. It's a cave-in. You don't get trust because you say the right things. You get it when you *live* the right things, consistently, especially when no one's watching. That's where real leadership begins.

I've Seen It with My Own Eyes

I've been part of organizations where the mission statement was painted in gold on the walls but **ignored in the halls.** Where leaders said all the right things on stage but left destruction in their wake behind the scenes. Where staff was told they were a "family," only to be discarded when things got hard. Trust was dead—and no spreadsheet or slogan could save it. That kind of environment doesn't just hurt people—it **repels greatness**.

I've watched it happen—felt it in my bones. I've stood in buildings where mission statements were carved into the walls like scripture, but where integrity was buried six feet under in the breakroom. Where the words *vision, excellence, and family* were echoed in marketing videos and keynote speeches, while behind the curtain, fear and favoritism ruled the day. Where the ones who gave everything—heart, sweat, loyalty—were tossed aside the moment they became inconvenient. I've seen leaders smile for the crowd, then slash trust like a knife behind closed doors. That isn't leadership—it's betrayal wrapped in branding.

You know what it feels like. To walk into a space that *says* all the right things, but *bleeds* all the wrong energy. You feel it in your gut before anyone says a word. The heaviness. The performance. The politics. And the worst part? Everyone knows. The employees whisper it. The hallway tension screams it. But no one dares call it out—because they've seen what happens to the ones who do. And in that kind of culture, trust doesn't just erode—it implodes. Greatness doesn't grow in that soil. It rots. It retreats. Because no one can build their best under a roof that's leaking with hypocrisy.

No Trust, No Buy-In

Let me make this clear: you cannot lead people who don't trust you. You can manage them. You can manipulate them. You might even coerce them for a while. But you will never unleash their full potential. You will never earn their loyalty. You will never get their heart. Without trust, there is no team—just terrified individuals protecting themselves. And that is the **graveyard of every culture that once had potential.**

Trust is the fuel of every lasting movement. It's the unseen currency that pays for effort, sacrifice, and belief. Without it, leaders are left dragging their people through mud instead of watching them run with vision. With it, even ordinary teams do extraordinary things. Trust turns managers into mentors, employees into advocates, and culture into a competitive advantage. But here's the catch—you can't demand it. You have to earn it every single day.

And that's what so many leaders miss. They chase compliance instead of commitment, results instead of relationships. They build systems without soul. But people don't buy into systems—they buy into leaders. They follow heart before hierarchy. Grand Canyon University drives this truth home: "True servant leadership builds trust because it is rooted in authenticity, humility, and the consistent pursuit of what is best for others" (Colangelo, 2022). That's the secret sauce. That's what separates the leaders people remember from the ones they tolerate.

People Don't Leave Jobs—They Leave Leaders

The number one reason people quit isn't money. It's not hours. It's not lack of perks. It's **toxic leadership** and broken trust. When people don't trust their leader, they don't stay. They don't invest. They don't speak up. They sit in meetings with fake smiles and dead eyes, counting the minutes until they can leave. That's the cost of a trust deficit. And it's **costing companies billions—and costing**

people their joy.

Poor leadership is the silent killer of workplace culture. It robs people of purpose and strips organizations of loyalty. It turns vibrant teams into ghost towns. You can add perks, raise salaries, and launch wellness campaigns—but if your leadership is toxic, your people will leave or shut down emotionally long before they hand in their badge. The reality is brutal: a paycheck can't fix a broken spirit, and no mission survives without trust.

And research backs it up. Gallup found that 70% of the variance in team engagement is directly attributable to the manager (Harter et al., 2020). That means the quality of your leadership—not the brand, not the office perks, not the mission statement—determines whether your people stay or leave. So if you're serious about retention, performance, and legacy, start by fixing what's behind the desk.

Servant Leadership Rebuilds What Was Lost

But there's hope. There's a better way. Servant leadership doesn't demand trust—it **earns it.** It earns it by putting others first. By keeping promises. By staying consistent even when it's inconvenient. By leading with humility, not pride. A servant leader says, "I'm not here to be served—I'm here to serve you." And suddenly, people breathe again. Walls fall. Trust grows. And the entire culture begins to heal.

Servant leadership shows up like oxygen in a suffocating room. It doesn't roar—it revives. When people see their leader walk in with integrity, with kindness, with backbone and heart, something shifts. The fog starts to lift. People sit up straighter. They speak more boldly. They create with courage again. They risk, because someone finally made it safe to trust again. That's what servant leadership does—it gives people their fight back.

It's not just a healing mechanism—it's a rebuilding strategy. Servant leadership isn't here to slap a motivational band-aid over dysfunction. It's here to uproot the rot, reset the foundation, and raise a culture where people feel worthy, wanted, and wildly alive. And let me tell you—when that happens?

Loyalty explodes. Innovation ignites. And the culture that once felt fractured becomes a family built on faith, trust, and fire. As Grand Canyon University affirms, servant leadership empowers individuals to flourish in purpose-driven environments where excellence and integrity become the cultural norm (Colangelo, 2022).

The Revival of Belief

The most powerful thing a leader can do is **create an environment where trust thrives.** Where people feel safe enough to speak, brave enough to try, and valued enough to stay. That's the kind of leader the world is starving for. That's the kind of leader *you* were born to be. Servant leadership doesn't just restore trust—it multiplies it. And when that happens? Performance soars. Loyalty explodes. And culture catches fire with purpose.

Because belief isn't built through speeches—it's built through sacrifice. It's built by the leader who doesn't just say "I've got your back," but proves it day after day in the trenches. It's the leader who shows up early, checks in when no one's looking, and never makes trust a transaction. Servant leadership creates more than momentum—it creates movement. It flips the script, silences fear, and raises up voices that used to stay silent. And when people *believe* again, they *build* again—with energy that doesn't fade and faith that doesn't fracture.

This is what leadership is meant to do—not to control people, but to *ignite* them. To awaken the fire they thought they lost. To look them in the eyes and say, "You are safe. You are seen. And we will rise together." This kind of leadership doesn't just make headlines—it makes history. And it starts with one leader. One choice. One commitment to lead with courage and serve with soul. As Grand Canyon University declares, servant leadership is not only a foundation—it is a transformational force that unleashes purpose and fosters unwavering belief (Grand Canyon University, n.d.).

Why Servant Leadership Is the Answer: The Strategy That Outlasts the Storm

"When the storm hits, titles blow away—but servant leaders stand firm, not because they command the wind, but because they anchor others in the middle of it."

Let's Be Honest—What We're Doing Isn't Working

The modern leadership playbook is broken. We've built empires on performance metrics while our people suffer in silence. We've elevated charisma over character, speed over sustainability, and ego over empathy. The result? Cultures that are efficient—but empty. Companies that are productive—but purposeless. Organizations that chase success—but never stop to ask if they're actually making lives better. We don't need more perks or performance reviews—we need a complete reset.

The Most Underrated Competitive Advantage on Earth

Servant leadership is not soft—it's savage. It's bold enough to care when others stay cold. It's courageous enough to listen, to admit fault, to lift others up when it's easier to push down. It's the **single most underrated competitive advantage on earth**—because when people are seen, supported, and empowered, they produce at a level no fear-driven team ever could. Servant leadership doesn't just feel good. It **performs**. It *wins*. And the data proves it.

Chick-fil-A Doesn't Just Sell Chicken

Let's talk facts. The most respected brands in the world—Chick-fil-A, Southwest Airlines, Patagonia—didn't build greatness through ruthless command. They built it through cultures of care. They created environments where employees were treated like people, not pawns. Where leadership was a position of responsibility, not privilege. Their secret weapon? Servant leadership. And that's why their people stay, their customers return, and their impact endures (Hunter, 2004).

The CEO That Gets Off the Stage and Gets in the Trenches

The servant leader doesn't need the spotlight—they need the mission to move forward. They show up early, stay late, and leave their title at the door when the team needs them. They don't measure success by how much applause they get—but by how much progress others make because of their influence. That's the kind of CEO who doesn't just lead a company—they lead a **movement.** And let me tell you: people don't forget leaders like that. They talk about them at weddings. They name their kids after them. They change lives.

Real Leadership Isn't Loud—It's Loyal

Anyone can demand attention. Anyone can enforce authority. But not everyone can inspire trust. **Servant leaders don't shout instructions from above—they roll up their sleeves and get in the grind with you.**
They're not too big for the break room. They don't hide when things go wrong. They show up. They stay late. They lean in. That kind of loyalty from a leader creates loyalty in return—and loyalty is the glue that no amount of money or title can replace.

The Death of the "Boss" and the Rise of the Builder

Let's say it plainly: the era of the "boss" is over. People don't want a boss. They want a builder. Someone who helps them grow, who coaches them, who believes in their potential more than they believe in their own excuses. Servant leaders don't hoard wisdom—they multiply it. They don't protect their seat at the table—they make space for others to sit down. And when that happens? You don't just build a business. You build legacy (Hunter, 2004).

Servant Leadership Isn't Weak—It's Warrior-Level Strength

You want to know what's weak? Yelling when you're insecure. Avoiding feedback. Hiding behind your title. You want to know what's strong? Sitting with your people in their pain. Owning your mistakes. Lifting others while you're still climbing. **That's the grit of servant leadership.** That's the kind of strength that doesn't just command rooms—it transforms them. It's what separates influencers from *impact makers*.

The Future Belongs to Servants

The companies that last, the teams that win, the cultures that thrive—they will all be led by servant leaders. The future of leadership is not top-down—it's *people-first*. It's not about control—it's about **catalyzing others** to greatness. If you want short-term results, scream louder. If you want long-term greatness, serve deeper. The greatest leaders are not those who demand to be followed—they're the ones people would **walk through fire for** (Parris & Peachey, 2013).That's the promise of servant leadership. And that's what this book will teach you how to become.

The Example of Christ (Philippians 2:3–8): The Blueprint for Greatness

The Greatest Among Us Got Low

Let's start with this: Jesus had *every* right to claim the highest seat in the house—but He chose the lowest one. The Son of God—eternal, holy, flawless—stepped out of heaven and wrapped Himself in the dusty skin of man. Why? Because **serving wasn't beneath Him.** It was His mission. Philippians 2 doesn't just describe humility. It **defines** greatness. *"Do nothing out of selfish ambition or vain conceit. Rather, in humility value others above yourselves."* That's not just Scripture. That's the **framework for world-shifting leadership.**

Leadership Is a Descent, not a Pedestal

Too many leaders think success means climbing higher. Jesus flipped the ladder upside down. Philippians says He "made Himself nothing." Let that sit. The One who breathed the stars into existence *made Himself nothing*—not because He had to, but because greatness demands it. If the King of Glory didn't see Himself as "too important" to wash feet, **you better believe we have no excuse.** You want to lead like Christ? Then learn to go low.

Pride Breaks Cultures. Humility Builds Empires.

Most of what's wrong with leadership today

comes down to pride. Pride is what keeps leaders from apologizing. It keeps them from listening. It keeps them from admitting when they're wrong. And it's the **cancer** that slowly eats away at influence, trust, and legacy. Jesus had no pride to protect—only people to redeem. That's why His name is still on people's lips 2,000 years later. That's not charisma. That's **character.**

Jesus Didn't Manage—He Modeled

Philippians 2:7 says Jesus "took the very nature of a servant." It doesn't say He acted like one—it says He **became** one. This wasn't performance. It was identity. He didn't serve when it was convenient or strategic—He served because it was **who He was.** That's what sets servant leaders apart. They don't shift gears when it's time to lead—they stay locked into a posture of service because it's written into their DNA.

Obedience Over Optics

Jesus didn't chase attention. He chased obedience. While leaders today chase likes, followers, and approval, Christ chased the cross. He was obedient even "to death on a cross." That wasn't convenient leadership. That was **sacrificial, costly, and eternal.** If your leadership only shows up when it benefits you, it's not leadership—it's manipulation. But if your leadership is rooted in obedience to God and service to others? It will bear fruit that never dies.

Strength Isn't Stoic—It's Sacrificial

The world says strong leaders don't show weakness. But Jesus wept. He sweat blood. He got tired. He let Himself *feel*—not because He was fragile, but because He was **fierce in His humanity.** Real leaders don't hide behind stoicism—they lean into sacrifice. Servant leadership doesn't avoid pain. It **absorbs** it so others can be free. That's not soft. That's supernatural strength.

God Exalts the Humble

Philippians 2 ends with a promise: "Therefore God exalted Him to the highest place..." That "therefore" is critical. Jesus went low—**so God raised Him up.** That's the secret no ego-driven leader understands: when you make yourself low, God makes your impact high. The way up is always down. You don't have to claw for recognition when Heaven has already approved your posture.

The Model That Changes Everything

If Jesus is the standard—and He is—then servant leadership isn't optional. It's **foundational.** It's the kind of leadership that breaks cycles of fear, restores trust, and turns toxic cultures into thriving ones. You want your leadership to last? You want your influence to mean something? Then get on your knees. Pick up a towel. And follow the only Leader who ever had every crown—and still chose a cross.

This is the blueprint. This is the model. And from this point forward, every chapter in this book is going to help you lead more like **Him**.

This isn't just a framework—it's a fire. One that burns away pride, selfish ambition, and surface-level leadership. When Jesus picked up the towel, He wasn't just cleaning feet—He was cleaning house on every broken model of power the world had known. He showed us that greatness doesn't sit at the head of the table—it kneels beside the hurting. That kind of leadership doesn't fade with trends or collapse under pressure. It multiplies in the dark. It rises in the trenches. It sets a new standard, not just for leaders in churches—but for leaders in schools, locker rooms, businesses, and homes.

So don't just admire the model—become it. Don't just quote it—live it. Every time you humble yourself, listen with compassion, lift someone who's fallen, or put people before position, you're echoing the life of the greatest Leader to ever walk this earth. And make no mistake: when you lead like Jesus, you don't just change organizations—you change eternities. Now let's dig deep, gear up, and get to work—because the blueprint is in your hands, and the world is waiting for the builder.

Foreword

Every now and then, a book finds you at just the right moment—like a light cutting through the fog, like a compass pointing true north when the world spins wildly. *The Greatest Among You* is that kind of book.

What you hold in your hands isn't just a leadership manual. It's a call to war against ego, against shallow influence, against everything broken in the way we've been taught to lead. This is a manifesto of something ancient and eternal—something Jesus taught with a towel, not a throne.

Lee Burchett doesn't write these words from a distance. He has lived them. From the sidelines of soccer fields to classrooms, boardrooms, and battlefields of belief, his journey through faith, education, and fierce reflection is inked into every chapter. His voice is bold. His message is grounded. His vision is clear: leadership must return to its original design—humble, sacrificial, servant-first.

I've watched Lee's passion ignite movements, his voice rally the discouraged, and his faith shape the atmosphere of every room he walks into. He writes not just as a thinker, but as a practitioner. As someone who has failed, learned, lifted others, and now offers a blueprint that blends business acumen, biblical truth, and deeply human purpose.

This book does more than challenge you. It trains you. It stretches your imagination of what's possible when leaders lead like Jesus. It offers a system, a standard, and a spirit—a way forward for companies, classrooms, churches, and communities alike.

So read every page with expectation. Underline the parts that make you pause. And then—go live it.

Because the greatest among you will always be the one who serves.

CHAPTER 1: What Is Servant Leadership—Really?

At Grand Canyon University, President Brian Mueller explained the university's purpose clearly: **"Teaching from a Christian worldview perspective produces graduates who are known for their integrity, servant leadership and ability to solve problems in a collaborative environment"** (Mueller, 2024). That ethos isn't just educational—they're lived values. And everything in this book is meant to help you live out those same values in every aspect of leadership.

The World Got It Backwards

The world told us leadership is about being first. It's about climbing ladders, claiming titles, barking orders, and standing tall while **others** kneel. But *real* leadership—**servant leadership**—flips that script. It's not about being above people. It's about *getting beneath them to lift them up.* Servant leadership isn't weakness. It's the most courageous, sacrificial, and radical form of leadership the world has ever seen—and very few are bold enough to live it.

We've been taught to chase power instead of purpose, image instead of integrity. We glorify dominance and dismiss humility as soft—but humility is the steel backbone of every servant leader. The world elevates the loudest voice in the room, but the greatest leaders are often the ones willing to **stoop, listen, and serve in silence.** We don't need more heroes in suits—we need **warriors in aprons.** The world doesn't need more bosses—it's starving for builders. And the ones who will rebuild what's been broken? They lead with heart.

We've glorified the grind but forgotten the grace. We applaud the ones who win at all costs, even if the cost is people's dignity. But servant leadership doesn't play that game. It doesn't step on people to rise—it kneels to raise others. In a world obsessed with visibility, servant leaders are busy doing the invisible work that actually changes lives. They don't need spotlights because they carry the light. They don't demand followers—they create freedom.

That's why this kind of leadership has to begin in the heart. Because no policy, program, or platform can fake real care. You can't Google it. You can't script it. And you sure as hell can't outsource it. Servant leadership isn't a skill you master—it's a spirit you carry. If your heart isn't aligned, your impact won't last. Because the foundation of every servant leader isn't ambition—it's love.

Servant Leadership Begins with the Heart

At its core, servant leadership is not a strategy—it's a posture. It begins in the **heart** before it ever shows up in your habits. It's not about pretending to be humble—it's

CHAPTER 1: What Is Servant Leadership—Really?

about actually caring more about the mission and the people than your own ego. As Jerry Colangelo—namesake of the Colangelo College of Business at Grand Canyon University—once said, "Leadership, to me, is about making a difference in someone else's life. It's about putting others first" (Colangelo, 2022). Servant leadership says, "My purpose isn't to be celebrated—it's to build others who will be." You don't become a servant leader to be liked. You become one because you believe **serving is leading.**

But a heart posture isn't enough by itself—it has to translate into action, into how you carry your authority, how you guide, how you build trust. Because servant leadership doesn't mean abandoning influence—it means redefining it. Your authority doesn't vanish when you serve—it gets **reconstructed into something people will follow without fear.** The heart is where it starts, but it's what you do with your position next that defines whether you're building a movement—or just a moment. That brings us to the next truth: real leadership doesn't disappear when you bend low—it gets *stronger*. Because...

The heart of a servant leader is a forge—where conviction gets hammered into courage, and love gets shaped into leadership. It's not weak. It's not passive. It's power under control. When you lead from the heart, you lead with empathy that doesn't just feel—but acts. You stand in the trenches with your people. You celebrate their wins louder than your own. And when they fail, you're the first to say, "We'll get back up together." That's not strategy. That's sacrifice. And sacrifice is the highest form of leadership.

But here's the raw truth: if the heart doesn't shape how you use your authority, it will corrupt how you carry it. Power that isn't grounded in service becomes poison. But power that flows from a servant's heart? That power builds trust, unlocks potential, and fuels movements that last. So no, servant leadership doesn't make you less powerful—it makes your power trustworthy. The moment you choose to lead with love is the moment your leadership begins to multiply. Because in this new kind of leadership, bending low doesn't break your authority—it rebuilds it into something far stronger.

SIDEBAR: The Heart Is the Headquarters

Servant leadership doesn't originate in a manual—it starts in your **motives**. You don't fake your way into servant leadership. You **feel** your way into it—through conviction, compassion, and courage. It's not about technique—it's about truth. People don't follow leaders who are perfect. They follow leaders who **genuinely care**. And that kind of care? It always starts in the heart.

"If your heart's not in it, your leadership has no pulse."

Authority Doesn't Disappear—It Gets Rebuilt

Let's be clear: servant leadership doesn't mean

CHAPTER 1: What Is Servant Leadership—Really?

abandoning authority. It means **redefining** it. It means using your position, power, and influence to empower others—not control them. You don't lead from the front to be seen—you lead from the center so you can connect. You coach, you mentor, you encourage, you guide. A servant leader doesn't throw weight around—they carry the weight *with* their team.

This kind of authority doesn't demand respect—it earns it daily in the trenches. It's not about flexing titles; it's about flexing trust. Servant leaders understand that the real power isn't in a corner office—it's in the courage to **show up with humility**. They don't operate from fear of losing control—they operate from faith in lifting others. That's why servant leadership isn't just a theory—it's a **lifestyle** that transforms every space it enters.

When you lead like this, your title stops being your identity and starts being your tool. You don't wield it like a sword—you use it like a bridge. Because real servant leaders don't just sit at the table—they set the table. They invite others in, pull out chairs, and say, "Let's build something together." This isn't authority that intimidates—it activates. It breathes life into tired teams and reminds people that leadership isn't about being important—it's about making others feel that they are.

That's the kind of authority the world is starving for. Not positional power that rules from above—but personal integrity that lifts from within. Servant leadership rebuilds authority into something people don't just submit to—

they believe in. They trust it, follow it, and most importantly—they grow under it. Because when people know you care more about their development than your dominance, they don't just follow orders—they follow you through fire. That's when you know this isn't some leadership tactic you turn on and off.

That's when you realize...

IT'S NOT A LEADERSHIP STYLE—IT'S A LIFESTYLE.

SIDEBAR: Power, Rewritten

True authority isn't loud—it's **steady**. It doesn't need a megaphone. It needs **character**. Servant leaders don't command from the top—they **connect from the middle**. They don't protect power—they **multiply purpose**. When your leadership lifts others, your influence multiplies beyond anything a title could ever guarantee.

"Real authority doesn't push people down—it pulls people up."

It's Not a Leadership Style—It's a Lifestyle

This isn't a strategy you apply during team meetings or throw into a mission statement. **Servant leadership is a way of life.** It follows you into every conversation, every decision, every conflict, every win, and every loss. You don't switch it on and off. It's who you are. It affects how

CHAPTER 1: What Is Servant Leadership—Really?

you listen, how you correct, how you reward, and how you recover. Servant leaders don't fake empathy—they live it, breathe it, and bleed it.

It shows up in how you treat the receptionist and the custodian—not just the CEO. It's in the unseen moments—when no one's watching, when credit's up for grabs, when the spotlight shines elsewhere. That's when lifestyle leadership speaks the loudest. Servant leaders don't just lead during office hours—they **live the mission 24/7**. And when your leadership is this real, this relentless, and this rooted in love—you don't just manage people, you build them.

This is the kind of leadership that doesn't punch a clock—it punches through walls. It shows up early, stays late, and fights through fatigue because it's not driven by ego—it's driven by purpose. You don't just wear servant leadership like a name tag—you bleed it into every fiber of your culture. From how you write an email to how you handle conflict, the posture of service permeates everything. It's not something you *do*—it's someone you *become*.

And when you *become* that kind of leader, everything around you changes. Toxicity shrinks. Trust expands. Growth multiplies. Why? Because people can tell the difference between a leader who's performing—and one who's planted. And a lifestyle of servant leadership? That's leadership planted in something deeper than ambition. It's rooted in values that won't bend when the heat rises or when pressure hits. That's when the building begins.

And that leads us to the next truth that every servant leader must own:

SERVANT LEADERS BUILD, THEY DON'T BREAK.

SIDEBAR: The Lifestyle Litmus Test

Ask yourself this: *Would your team describe your leadership the same way your family would?* If not, it's not a lifestyle—it's an act. Servant leadership is consistent across the boardroom, the living room, and the locker room. **It doesn't shift with mood or setting—it stands firm in character.**

"Leadership that lasts is leadership that lives beyond the job description."

Servant Leaders Build, They Don't Break

Servant leaders don't use people—they *build* people. They see potential in places no one else is looking. They coach in the shadows, celebrate in the spotlight, and take blame before passing it down. They don't lead by fear—they lead by **trust and truth.** And when mistakes happen (because they will), servant leaders lean in instead of lashing out. They ask what went wrong and how they can help. Because they know the goal isn't

CHAPTER 1: What Is Servant Leadership—Really?

control—it's **growth.**

That's what separates pretenders from purpose-driven powerhouses. Most leaders are obsessed with what people can produce—**but servant leaders are obsessed with who people can become.** They don't just manage behavior—they develop identity. They don't react with punishment—they respond with partnership. They see every failure as an opportunity to grow something greater. And that's why their leadership leaves a mark that lasts long after the meeting ends.

They're not addicted to being right—they're committed to getting it right. That means owning mistakes, listening with humility, and choosing growth over ego every time. Servant leaders know that broken moments can build unbreakable people—*if someone has the courage to lead them through it.* They don't just stand beside their team in victory—they show up shoulder-to-shoulder in the valley. That's where credibility is forged. That's where loyalty is born. And that's why the people they lead don't just follow—they *believe*.

You want to know what defines the greatest among us? It's not a title on a door or letters after your name. It's how many lives you've built—how many people you've lifted—how many futures you've helped shape. That's the currency of true leadership. And that brings us to a truth every leader must confront: **this has never been about titles. It's always been about impact.** Because in the end, it won't be your position that's remembered—it'll be your presence.

SIDEBAR: From Breakdown to Breakthrough

Servant leaders turn conflict into coaching, breakdown into breakthrough, and blame into belief.
They don't pile on pressure—they help carry the weight.

> **"Servant leaders don't use people to build empires—they build people to change the world."**

This Isn't About Titles—It's About Impact

You don't need a title to be a servant leader. You don't need an office, a badge, or a microphone. You just need a mindset that says, "I'm here to serve others into greatness." The janitor can be a servant leader. So can the CEO. So can the assistant coach, the school secretary, the shift supervisor. It's not about *where* you sit—it's about *how* you serve. And servant leaders? They lead from **anywhere.**

This is the secret sauce most organizations miss: **true leadership is not conferred—it's cultivated.** It's not about hierarchy—it's about influence earned through humility and action. Servant leaders don't wait for permission to lead—they see a need, they serve, and that's where the ripple effect begins. Great cultures are built by people who carry influence without needing a

CHAPTER 1: What Is Servant Leadership—Really?

nameplate to prove it. Because when you lead from the heart, your impact outshines any title on your door.

Real leadership is lived, not labeled. It's in the way you notice, uplift, and call greatness out of others before they even see it in themselves. It's how you show up on the hard days, how you lead when no one's looking, and how you treat the people who can do nothing for you. And here's the truth: titles can be stripped, but legacy cannot. When your leadership is rooted in purpose, not position, you stop chasing validation and start creating transformation (Hunter, 2004).

The best servant leaders don't need the corner office—they lead from the break room, the bus stop, the bench. They show up when others check out. They bring their full heart, not because they have to, but because they believe it matters. And guess what? That kind of influence—quiet, consistent, compassionate—moves the culture more than any memo ever will. Because servant leadership isn't about controlling people's hands. It's about igniting their hearts.

SIDEBAR: No Title Required

The most powerful leaders are often the ones no one sees coming.
They don't chase the spotlight—they carry the torch in the dark.

> "Leadership isn't where you sit. It's how you show up."

You Carry Their Wins, Not Just Their Work

Here's what most leaders miss: servant leadership isn't about taking burdens—it's about **multiplying breakthroughs.** You don't just help people with tasks. You help them **become.** You see who they could be five years from now and help pull that future forward. You remember birthdays. You notice patterns. You affirm the small steps. Because servant leadership isn't about results alone—it's about **raising people up to reach their full potential.**

The greatest servant leaders don't just focus on performance—they focus on **people in process.** They recognize progress over perfection and understand that breakthrough moments don't always happen in boardrooms—they happen in conversations, in encouragement, in that one moment when someone feels seen. Servant leadership says, "Your success is my success. Your win is my reward." And that's when trust deepens. That's when people stop working for a paycheck—and start working with passion.

This is where servant leadership flips the entire paradigm: it's not about what people produce—it's about who they become in the process. When you celebrate identity over output, you don't just get results—you get revival. You create a culture where people bring their full selves, not just their skillsets. That kind of culture isn't

CHAPTER 1: What Is Servant Leadership—Really?

built in spreadsheets—it's built in the trenches with leaders who see greatness before it's obvious and believe in people when they're struggling to believe in themselves (Van Dierendonck, 2011).

And here's the kicker: when people feel known, believed in, and championed—they rise. They don't rise because they're pushed. They rise because they're seen. That's the sacred weight of servant leadership: to carry not just someone's workload, but their self-worth. To say, "I see more in you than you see in yourself—and I'm going to walk with you until you believe it too." And when that becomes the norm, cultures don't just shift—they ignite.

SIDEBAR: Win Multipliers

Servant leaders don't carry just the load—they carry the vision.
They don't chase credit—they chase transformation.

"A servant leader doesn't just measure what gets done. They celebrate who's becoming."

This Kind of Leadership Changes Everything

When servant leadership takes root, cultures heal. Teams unite. Innovation thrives. Trust is rebuilt. Turnover drops. Ownership rises. People don't just show up—they show up *with fire*. Because they're not working for a paycheck—they're working **with purpose** under someone who *actually gives a rip*. Servant leadership isn't a theory—it's a revolution. And the moment you choose it? **Everything changes.**

This isn't leadership for the faint-hearted. This is leadership forged in the trenches of sacrifice and lit by the torch of conviction. It's not about looking good in a boardroom—it's about showing up when the cameras are off and your team is running on fumes. It's about speaking life when doubt is loudest. It's about turning cubicles into communities, locker rooms into legacies, and staff meetings into strategy sessions for transformation. The world doesn't need more polished talkers. It needs more purpose-driven warriors. And servant leaders? We build from the inside out—with love that leads and truth that ignites.

Because when servant leadership walks into the room, everything starts to rise. Engagement spikes. Ownership deepens. Morale transforms. Why? Because people finally feel safe to bring their full selves. They don't just execute—they create. They don't just comply—they believe. That's not fluff. That's the fruit of leading like Jesus. It's not a one-time motivational moment—it's a living, breathing movement that shifts the atmosphere and writes legacy into the walls. This is what it means to lead with heart. **This is what it means to lead like Him.**

That's **what servant leadership really is**. Not a trend. Not a tactic. A way of life that **redefines greatness**.

CHAPTER 1: What Is Servant Leadership—Really?

Gallup research shows that companies in the top quartile of employee engagement are 21% more profitable and experience 59% less turnover (Gallup, 2020). Why? Because when people feel valued, heard, and supported, they don't just perform—they pour themselves into the mission. Servant leaders create this kind of engagement by investing in people first. When you shift the focus from control to connection, from title to trust, everything begins to rise: morale, performance, and loyalty. That's the seismic shift of servant leadership—and it never returns void.

SIDEBAR: The Culture Multiplier

Servant leadership doesn't just fix broken culture—it creates unstoppable momentum.
When leaders serve, people believe again. And when people believe, they build like never before.

> "Servant leadership isn't a theory—it's a revolution."

Definition and Core Principles: The DNA of Servant Leadership

What Is Servant Leadership?

Servant leadership is the unwavering decision to put *people before power*. It's leadership that doesn't seek to be impressive—it seeks to be impactful. It's the belief that the **true measure of a leader is not how many serve them, but how many they serve into strength.** It's not about taking the spotlight. It's about lighting the path. Servant leaders walk into every room asking, *"Who needs lifted? Who needs seen? Who needs equipped?"*—and they build cultures where greatness multiplies from the ground up.

And that question—"Who needs equipped?"—isn't just philosophical. It's foundational. It shapes how decisions are made, how meetings are run, and how people are developed. Servant leadership shifts the culture from top-down command to bottom-up empowerment. It changes the very *definition* of influence—from manipulation to multiplication. At its core, servant leadership isn't about doing more for people—it's about drawing more out of them (Greenleaf, 1970; Spears, 1995).

SIDEBAR: The Leadership Lens

If your leadership isn't lifting people higher, it's not servant leadership.
True servant leaders walk in asking, *"Who can I build today?"* not *"Who can build me?"*

> **"It's not about taking the spotlight—it's about lighting the path."**

When your default posture is service, your impact becomes unstoppable.

CHAPTER 1: What Is Servant Leadership—Really?

The Core Foundation: It Starts with Love, Not Leverage

At the center of servant leadership is **love**—not leverage. That word might scare the boardroom, but it shouldn't. Because love doesn't mean being soft—it means being *invested*. Love shows up in accountability, in encouragement, in honest conversations, in real presence. Servant leaders love the people they lead so much they refuse to let them settle for average. They push—but they also protect. They challenge—but they also cheer. That's not weakness. That's *warrior-level love*.

When love becomes the foundation of leadership, it changes everything. Love listens before it lectures. It elevates people above politics. It fights for excellence, not perfection. And when leaders lead with love, teams stop performing out of fear—and start producing out of passion. Robert Greenleaf understood this when he said, *"The servant-leader is servant first..."*—not manager, not figurehead, not boss—*"servant first"* (Greenleaf, 1970). That's what sets the stage for the next principle: **People Over Position.**

SIDEBAR: The Foundation That Never Cracks

Love isn't weak—it's the strongest force in leadership. It's what makes teams believe, cultures rise, and greatness multiply.

"Love doesn't coddle—it compels. It doesn't

control—it calls people higher."

The First Principle: People Over Position

You want a core principle that changes everything? Here it is: **Your people are not a means to your success. They are your mission.** Servant leaders don't climb over people to get higher. They *lift people* so the entire team rises. Your position might give you authority, but it's how you treat people that gives you **influence.** And if you treat people like tools, don't be surprised when they walk away the moment they find someone who treats them like humans.

People are never obstacles—they're opportunities. When a leader values the person more than the position, trust flourishes. Teams begin to feel like families. Work becomes more than a job—it becomes a place where people grow. According to Greenleaf (1970), the servant leader's test is simple: *"Do those served grow as persons?"* That growth begins the moment they feel seen, heard, and valued—and it all starts with listening.

SIDEBAR: Mission Over Metrics

People aren't just part of the plan—they *are* the plan. When you serve your people, success follows them—and you.

> **"If you treat people like tools, don't cry when your culture breaks."**

The Second Principle: Listening Over Lecturing

Servant leaders listen with the intent to understand—not just the intent to reply. They don't dominate every meeting, every Zoom call, every decision. They create space. They ask real questions. They make eye contact. They silence their ego long enough to hear the heartbeat of their team. Because the people closest to the problems often have the most powerful solutions—but only *if you're humble enough to listen*.

Listening isn't passive—it's powerful. It communicates value. It creates safety. And it cultivates innovation. Greenleaf (1970) identified listening as one of the ten core characteristics of a servant leader, because it transforms communication from one-way monologue into meaningful dialogue. It says, "I care about more than your output—I care about your voice." And when leaders truly listen, people rise.

SIDEBAR: The Power of Presence

The greatest gift you can give your team is your full attention.
Your silence speaks louder than your status.

> "You can't lead the people if you don't listen to the pulse."

The Third Principle: Empowerment Over Control

You can't micromanage people into greatness. You have to **empower** them. Servant leaders equip their teams to think, create, solve, and own. They give away responsibility like seeds, not shackles. They build leaders, not followers. Because control creates compliance—but empowerment creates **ownership.** And people who feel ownership don't need to be pushed... they *run with the vision*.

Greenleaf (1970) emphasized that the best test of servant leadership is whether people grow and become "more autonomous, more likely themselves to become servants." Empowerment is not about removing structure; it's about removing fear. It's about fostering environments where people are free to take initiative, explore new solutions, and grow into their calling. Servant leaders don't hoard authority—they transfer it with trust. That's not just good leadership—it's transformational leadership.

SIDEBAR: Growth Happens When You Let Go

The tighter you grip control, the more potential you choke.
Empowerment isn't risky—it's revolutionary.

> **"Control creates followers. Empowerment creates leaders."**

The Fourth Principle: Sacrifice Over Spotlight

The best leaders don't need their name on the banner—

CHAPTER 1: What Is Servant Leadership—Really?

they're happy to see others celebrated. They take the hit when things go wrong and give the glory when things go right. Servant leaders sacrifice ego, comfort, and sometimes recognition—because their leadership isn't about applause. It's about **alignment.** They live to make sure the mission moves forward, not to make sure they look good in the process. And in doing so, they earn something better than attention: **loyalty.**

True servant leaders understand that legacy is built on sacrifice, not self-promotion. Greenleaf (1970) argued that servant leaders are "sharply different from the person who is leader first," because their focus is not on status or power—it's on people and purpose. These leaders lay down comfort to pick up commitment. They embrace hard decisions, uncomfortable conversations, and behind-the-scenes work that rarely gets noticed but always moves the mission forward. In doing so, they set a standard that others want to follow—not because they demand it, but because they model it.

SIDEBAR: Mission Over Me

Great leaders don't chase the spotlight.
They become the reason someone else shines.

"Applause fades. Alignment lasts."

The Fifth Principle: Character Over Charisma

Servant leadership isn't about how loud you speak. It's about **how well you live.** You don't need to be the most charismatic person in the room—you need to be the most *consistent*. Your team isn't looking for someone flashy. They're looking for someone *trustworthy*. Someone whose actions match their words. Someone who's the same in private as they are in public. That's character—and it's the **core currency of servant leadership.**

In a world where charisma often gets mistaken for competence, servant leaders quietly stand out through character that cannot be shaken. Robert Greenleaf emphasized that "the servant-leader is servant first," and that servanthood springs from a desire to lead by integrity, not image (Greenleaf, 1970). You don't need to wow the room with speeches—you need to walk the room with integrity. Leadership that lasts is not built on hype. It's built on habits. And your character is the bedrock that sustains a culture long after the excitement wears off. Trust isn't given because you inspire—it's earned because you're real.

SIDEBAR: Trust Isn't Flashy

Charisma starts the fire.
Character keeps it burning.

"Consistency beats charisma—every time."

When These Principles Come Alive, So Does Your Culture

When servant leadership takes hold, everything begins to

CHAPTER 1: What Is Servant Leadership—Really?

change. The breakroom sounds different. Meetings feel different. Turnover drops. Engagement rises. People bring their full selves—not just their skill sets. Why? Because servant leadership creates a culture of safety, ownership, purpose, and **fire**. It tells every employee, "You matter. Your growth matters. Your voice matters." And when people believe that? They build things that last.

That's the **definition and DNA** of servant leadership: It's people-first, purpose-driven, powerfully humble, and **absolutely unstoppable.**

Robert Greenleaf's Original Concept: The Spark That Lit a Movement

The Man Who Dared to Redefine Leadership

In 1970, a retired AT&T executive named **Robert K. Greenleaf** released a game-changing essay titled **"The Servant as Leader."** It wasn't just a paper—it was a declaration of war against the command-and-control mindset that had poisoned leadership for decades. Greenleaf didn't come from a monastery—he came from the **corporate world.** He saw firsthand how top-down, power-driven leadership models were burning people out and draining purpose from organizations. So, he asked a radical question: *What if the leader's first job was to serve* (Greenleaf, 1970)?

The One Line That Changed Everything

Greenleaf's philosophy can be boiled down to one unforgettable sentence:

"The servant-leader is servant first."

He didn't mean a servant in title, or a servant in branding. He meant someone whose *primary motivation* for leading was to serve others—to *elevate* people, not manipulate them. It wasn't about being nice. It was about being **effective through empathy, humility, and vision.** That one sentence kicked off a global movement and inspired leaders in business, education, nonprofits, and government to completely rethink what greatness looks like.

He Saw What Others Missed

Greenleaf had the vision to see what most business leaders were blind to: **that service multiplies, but control corrodes.** He believed that leadership wasn't about status—it was about *stewardship* (Greenleaf, 1970). In his writings, he warned that many institutions were collapsing not from lack of strategy, but from **a failure of moral responsibility.** His idea wasn't rooted in religion, but in **human dignity and social responsibility**—which is why it caught fire across industries, sectors, and belief systems.

CHAPTER 1: What Is Servant Leadership—Really?

Greenleaf didn't just observe the problem—he exposed it with the force of a prophet. He ripped the mask off empty leadership and dared to say what others wouldn't: **control is not leadership—it's fear dressed in a suit.** He saw that real power lies in the courage to uplift others, not in the convenience of barking commands. While the world applauded the loudest voices in the room, Greenleaf was listening for the quiet ones—those who led with heart, who carried water instead of wielding whips, who built legacy through love, not leverage.

And here's the truth: **his words didn't whisper—they roared.** They struck a nerve in boardrooms, classrooms, and churches. He wasn't pitching a feel-good idea—he was throwing down a gauntlet. Greenleaf dared leaders to step off their pedestals and into the trenches. He knew that when leaders stopped clinging to authority and started cultivating it through service, the ripple effect could shake the foundations of every broken institution. He didn't just see the future—**he sparked it.** And now it's on us to carry the torch.

The Servant-Leader Test: His Defining Standard

Greenleaf laid down a clear standard for what qualifies someone as a servant-leader. It's not title. It's not performance. It's one simple question:

> "Do those served grow as persons... while being

> served, do they, while being served, become healthier, wiser, freer, more autonomous, more likely themselves to become servants?"

That question is **the litmus test**. If your leadership doesn't help people grow—it's not servant leadership. If it's about your gain at their expense, you've missed the mark. That one idea? It still holds up as the most *practical and piercing test* of leadership we've ever seen.

That question isn't just a reflection of leadership—it's a **revelation.** It stops you in your tracks and forces you to look in the mirror: Are your people stronger, wiser, and more courageous because of your leadership? Or are they shrinking under the weight of your ego? Greenleaf didn't hand us a checklist—he handed us a **measuring stick for the soul** of leadership. And make no mistake: if your influence doesn't lift others into their potential, then you're not leading—you're **leeching.**

And here's where it hits hardest—**this test is ongoing.** It's not passed once with a motivational speech or a quarterly review. It's passed in the ordinary, the unseen, the daily decisions where a leader chooses service over spotlight, development over domination. Real servant leadership multiplies leaders, not minions. It replicates strength, not dependence. And if your people aren't rising higher, owning more, dreaming bigger—then it's time to ask yourself: **Who am I really serving?**

He Didn't Just Create a Model—He Created a Mirror

Greenleaf didn't just offer a model. He handed leaders a **mirror** and said, "Look again." His writings challenge us to ask hard questions: Are my people better because I lead them? Or just busier? Am I producing excellence—or just extracting it? Am I building a team—or building *my brand*? The power of his work isn't in its complexity—it's in its **honesty.** He forces you to confront whether you're using your team to build your ego or using your influence to build their lives.

Greenleaf didn't write from a pedestal—he wrote from the trenches. He knew leadership wasn't about building kingdoms. It was about **building people.** His mirror is unrelenting, but it's also **liberating.** Because the moment you stop hiding behind metrics and titles and finally ask yourself, "Am I making them better?"—you unlock a whole new level of purpose. It's not about perfection. It's about pursuit. The pursuit of leaving people **stronger, bolder, freer** than you found them.

This mirror doesn't flatter—it **frees.** It frees you from performative leadership. It frees you from pretending. It frees you from the shallow chase of approval and drags you into the depth of accountability. Greenleaf's model gives you the blueprint, but his mirror gives you the **conviction.** And the truth is, when leaders have the guts to look honestly and lead humbly—teams heal, cultures transform, and movements ignite.

Why It's Still So Relevant Today

Decades later, Greenleaf's ideas are more relevant than ever. Why? Because people are waking up. Employees, students, athletes—they don't want to follow tyrants. They want leaders who *see* them. Support them. Believe in them. Greenleaf predicted it. He said, *"The servant-leader is one who begins by asking, 'How can I serve?' and not, 'How can I lead?'"* (Greenleaf, 1970). That shift? It's not just a leadership trend. It's a **cultural tidal wave**. And servant leaders are the ones riding the crest.

Because here's the truth: every generation hungers for meaning—but this generation is demanding it from their leaders. They're done with empty mission statements and power-hungry bosses. They're done with toxic work cultures dressed up in perks and hashtags. They want real. They want relational. They want leaders who are willing to get off the pedestal and get into the trenches. Servant leadership isn't optional in this climate—it's oxygen. And the research agrees: cultures rooted in trust, humility, and shared purpose outperform the rest in engagement, innovation, and longevity (Van Dierendonck & Patterson, 2015).

Servant leadership is no longer an abstract ideal—it's a strategic, moral, and spiritual imperative. Greenleaf's vision, echoed in biblical principles like *"The greatest among you will be your servant"* (Matthew 23:11, NIV), is

CHAPTER 1: What Is Servant Leadership—Really?

being reborn in boardrooms and classrooms across the globe. Grand Canyon University underscores this in its leadership approach, where character-driven, service-minded professionals are the goal—not just polished resumes (Colangelo, 2022). The world doesn't need more influencers. It needs leaders with impact. And that's what servant leadership delivers—then, now, and forever.

The Business World Started Listening

You know something's real when billion-dollar companies start listening. In the years following Greenleaf's writings, organizations like **Southwest Airlines, Starbucks, The Container Store,** and **TDIndustries** began adopting his principles. They built **people-first** companies—and they didn't just succeed, they **dominated.** Low turnover. High engagement. Skyrocketing performance. Greenleaf never promised instant gratification—but he delivered **long-term transformation** wherever his words were lived out (Spears, 1995).

These companies didn't just change their org charts—they changed their soul. They shifted the definition of success from stock prices to human capital. And guess what? The results followed. Southwest Airlines was repeatedly ranked as one of the best places to work, not because of fancy perks, but because of servant leadership at every level (Autry, 2001). Starbucks thrived because it saw baristas as partners, not pawns. And TDIndustries was nationally recognized for decades because they made "servant leadership" part of their DNA, not just their marketing (Keith, 2008). These aren't outliers. They're blueprints.

The Legacy Lives On—Through You

Robert Greenleaf started a fire, but it's up to *us* to keep it burning. You're not reading this book by accident. You're here because you know leadership has to mean more. You're tired of titles without trust, systems without soul, and companies without character. Greenleaf handed us the blueprint. Jesus modeled it. And now **it's your turn to live it.** Not just with passion—but with purpose. Not just with heart—but with *heat*. Let this be the generation that doesn't just talk about servant leadership—but *embodies* it.

Robert Greenleaf didn't just offer an alternative leadership model—he offered a rebuke to everything broken about the old one. His challenge was clear: "A new moral principle is emerging that the only authority deserving one's allegiance is that which is freely and knowingly granted by the led to the leader in response to the servant stature of the leader" (Greenleaf, 1977, p. 10). That's not fluff. That's revolution. And it demands courage. Because it's easy to bark orders and hide behind policies. It takes guts to serve when no one's watching, to sacrifice when no one's clapping, and to stay grounded when the spotlight finds you.

CHAPTER 1: What Is Servant Leadership—Really?

The fire Greenleaf lit wasn't meant to stay in academic journals or boardroom seminars. It was meant to reshape homes, schools, companies, and churches. His words echo louder today because the need is louder. As Kouzes and Posner (2017) affirmed, "Leadership is not about personality; it's about behavior—an observable set of skills and abilities." Servant leadership isn't a feeling—it's a flame. A decision. A daily choice to lift instead of crush, to coach instead of control, and to build something so much bigger than yourself. The legacy isn't some distant dream. It's in your next conversation, your next hire, your next meeting.

Jesus: The Ultimate Servant Leader

"For even the Son of Man did not come to be served, but to serve, and to give his life as a ransom for many."
— *Mark 10:45 (NIV)*

Greenleaf Had the Vision—Jesus Had the Blueprint

Robert Greenleaf may have coined the term, but **Jesus Christ embodied the truth.** Greenleaf observed the failures of power-hungry leadership and proposed a radical new idea—*what if leaders served first?* But Jesus didn't propose it—**He lived it.** Before the world had language for it, Jesus was on His knees, washing feet, lifting the broken, healing the outcast, and leading a revolution of love. Greenleaf had the vision. But **Jesus was the blueprint.** Everything that makes servant leadership powerful today flows directly from how Christ led 2,000 years ago.

Jesus didn't build a movement by flexing authority—He did it by embodying humility. In an empire obsessed with status and dominance, He flipped the script. He chose the lowest seat at the table. He led by walking with the wounded, not commanding from a throne. When the disciples argued over who was the greatest, He shattered their egos with a basin of water and a towel (John 13:3–5). He taught that true leadership isn't about being recognized—it's about being responsible. And in that moment, He redefined leadership for every generation to come.

This wasn't a performance. It wasn't PR. It was purpose. Jesus didn't just serve to teach a lesson—He served to **set a standard**. One the world still hasn't fully caught up to. Where Greenleaf theorized about empowering others, Jesus made Himself nothing—taking on the very nature of a servant (Philippians 2:7). That wasn't weakness. It was divine strength under total control. His legacy wasn't built through coercion or command—it was built through compassion, courage, and sacrificial love. And if we want to lead like Him, it starts by laying down the title and picking up the towel.

The Towel Over the Title

Let's paint the picture: the Son of God—perfect, holy, all-powerful—**wrapped a towel around His waist and knelt to wash His disciples' dirty feet.** This wasn't symbolic. It

CHAPTER 1: What Is Servant Leadership—Really?

was stunning. Unheard of. He had every right to demand worship. Instead, He modeled worth. While leaders today fight to prove their value, **Jesus lowered Himself to reveal ours.** That moment in the upper room wasn't just hospitality—it was a leadership masterclass. *"Now that I, your Lord and Teacher, have washed your feet, you also should wash one another's feet"* (John 13:14, NIV). That's not a suggestion. It's a **call to live different.**

Let's paint the picture again—but this time, let it hit different. The Son of God—flawless, divine, the Alpha and Omega—didn't sit back and wait for honor. He got up. He took off His outer robe, wrapped a servant's towel around His waist, and knelt down to wash the dirt-caked feet of flawed, doubting men. This wasn't a symbolic gesture. This was the King of kings doing the work of the lowest servant in the house. He didn't just tell them about love—He touched them with it. And in that moment, Jesus didn't lose authority—He redefined it.

He wasn't threatened by humility. He was powered by it. That upper room wasn't a boardroom—it was a battlefield where pride was defeated by love. Jesus didn't cling to His divine rights—He laid them down, one foot at a time. And then, after drying off His hands, He looked up and dropped the ultimate leadership charge:

> **"Now that I, your Lord and Teacher, have washed your feet, you also should wash one another's feet" (John 13:14, NIV).**

That wasn't a sweet suggestion—it was a divine command. A call to leadership that flips the world's system upside down. He didn't reach for a scepter. He reached for a towel. And He dared us to do the same. So if you're still clutching your title tighter than your towel, you might be leading the wrong way.

He Led From Among, Not Above

Jesus never distanced Himself from the people He led. He **walked with them.** Ate with them. Cried with them. He wasn't unreachable—He was **unshakable in compassion.** While earthly leaders build walls of separation, Jesus tore them down. His leadership wasn't built on fear or formality. It was built on proximity and love. And that kind of closeness? That kind of *presence*? That's what gives servant leadership its unmatched power.

Jesus never led from a throne of distance—He led from the dirt of shared experience. He didn't hide behind titles or robes; He stepped into the tension, the noise, the pain. He walked through storms with His followers, not around them. He touched lepers when others ran. He ate with sinners when others judged. He wasn't afraid of the mess. He met people in it—and that's why they followed Him with everything they had.

While modern leadership often hides behind polished speeches and corner offices, Jesus broke through the barriers. He didn't pull rank—He pulled people close. And

CHAPTER 1: What Is Servant Leadership—Really?

the result? Loyalty forged in love, not fear. He didn't build hierarchies—He built heart connections. He wasn't untouchable—He was unforgettable. He proved that real leaders don't elevate themselves above others—they get low enough to lift them.

That's why His leadership still transforms lives 2,000 years later. Because He didn't just talk about love—He lived it. He didn't just send help—He *was* the help. He didn't direct from a distance—He moved in step with the ones He led. And every time He reached out, healed, forgave, or restored, He modeled a new kind of authority—one rooted in humility, not hierarchy.

When the world teaches leaders to command respect, Jesus taught us to *earn* it through compassion. When others built their platforms, He carried a cross. When others sought applause, He sought hearts. Servant leadership isn't soft—it's fierce with love. Fierce enough to show up when it's uncomfortable. Fierce enough to sacrifice convenience for connection. And that fierce, faithful presence? That's what breaks chains and rebuilds trust.

Jesus led from within the story, not from the sidelines. He wasn't waiting for perfection—He was walking with people in their brokenness. That's the power of proximity. That's the power of presence. That's the power of a King who didn't just sit above the people—but stepped into their shoes. That's why His name still holds weight—not because He demanded it, but because He earned it with every act of selfless love.

And that's the kind of leader this world is starving for today. Not someone shouting from the top, but someone kneeling beside them in the trenches. Not someone hiding behind policies—but someone willing to live out the purpose. That's the blueprint. That's the fire.

And if that wasn't enough—**He gave everything. Not for applause. But for people.**

He Gave Everything—Not for Applause, But for People

Most leaders only serve when it's convenient, when it's strategic, or when it helps their image. Not Jesus. He served when it was messy. When it was hard. When it cost Him everything. *"Who, being in very nature God... made Himself nothing... being made in human likeness... He humbled Himself by becoming obedient to death— even death on a cross!"* (Philippians 2:6–8, NIV). That's not just leadership. That's **divine sacrifice**. He didn't lead from luxury—He led from love. And He didn't just serve His friends—**He served His enemies.**

He didn't give to be thanked. He gave because love *demands* action. Jesus redefined leadership by enduring betrayal, rejection, mockery, and death—just so others could rise. While the world teaches leaders to protect their crown, Jesus laid His down. And in doing so, He

CHAPTER 1: What Is Servant Leadership—Really?

showed us that the truest measure of leadership isn't how many follow you—it's how much you're willing to give for those you lead. This wasn't a PR stunt. It was the revolution of redemption.

His Model Wasn't Temporary—It Was Transformational

The leadership style Jesus used wasn't designed for one generation. It was designed to **outlast every trend.** That's why we're still talking about it today. That's why it works in churches and classrooms, Fortune 500 companies and family dinner tables. His model wasn't based on culture. It was based on the *Kingdom*. Jesus proved that servant leadership isn't just holy—it's **universal.** If it worked with twelve unqualified fishermen and tax collectors, it'll work with your team, your staff, and your school. Every time.

The Cross Was the Ultimate Act of Servant Leadership

Make no mistake: **the cross was not a loss.** It was the **greatest victory of all time**—and it was won through service. Jesus carried our sin, our shame, our guilt, and our burden—not because He had to, but because **He chose to.** That's the heart of a servant leader: taking responsibility for things that aren't your fault to free the people who can't fix them. It doesn't get more real than that. *"For even the Son of Man did not come to be served, but to serve..."* (Mark 10:45, NIV). That's servant leadership—and **that's our King.**

His Legacy Was Multiplication, Not Control

Jesus didn't leave behind a political party. He didn't build an army. He didn't write a book. He left **people**—transformed by love, trained in truth, and fueled by service. He multiplied servant leaders who would change the world. That's the goal. That's the standard. Jesus didn't cling to power—He gave it away. And the movement that started in small towns and broken places became **the greatest movement in history.** That's what servant leadership *does*.

The Crown Will Always Follow the Towel

The world teaches us to chase the crown. Jesus teaches us to **pick up the towel.** And here's the mystery of the Kingdom—when you serve with the towel, **God places the crown.** *"Therefore God exalted Him to the highest place and gave Him the name that is above every name..."* (Philippians 2:9, NIV). Jesus went low, so the Father lifted Him high. That's the rhythm of true leadership. And if you want your leadership to echo into eternity—**lead like the King who served.**

CHAPTER 1: What Is Servant Leadership—Really?

Call to Action: Chapter 1 — Rise and Serve

Let's stop playing games.

You've seen it now. You've read the truth. You've tasted what servant leadership really is—not some soft alternative to strong leadership, but the **strongest form of leadership** the world has ever seen. The kind of leadership that doesn't shout orders from a pedestal but **kneels down and changes the game from the ground up.** You've seen its power. You've seen its purpose. And you've seen its **unchallengeable potential** to transform lives, businesses, and communities.

Now it's your turn.

This isn't a feel-good theory. This is **a calling.** A mandate. A model passed down from Christ Himself and proven in boardrooms, classrooms, locker rooms, and living rooms across the world. The time for passive leadership is dead. The time for status-chasing, ladder-climbing, self-serving bosses is over. If you've ever said, *"Things can be better than this,"* then know this: **YOU are the one who's supposed to make it better.**

So here's the charge:
Decide. Right now. Who will you be?
Will you lead like the world—or will you lead like the One who washed feet, fed thousands, restored the broken,

and called it greatness?

You don't need a new position.
You need a new posture.

Start today.
Serve first.
Lead boldly.
And never, ever settle for leadership that doesn't start with love.

7-DAY SERVANT LEADERSHIP CHALLENGE

Theme: From Pedestals to Purpose

Each day is designed to strip away ego, deepen your posture of service, and activate trust-building leadership.

DAY 1: Flip the Script

Action:
Write a new personal leadership mantra. Replace "climb higher" with "lift others."

Challenge:
Reflect on any behaviors where you sought recognition over restoration—and commit to reversing them this week.

DAY 2: Serve Before You Speak

CHAPTER 1: What Is Servant Leadership—Really?

Action:
Begin your day with this question: "Who can I build today?" Write down the name and one practical way to serve them.

Challenge:
Do something anonymously that helps a teammate or colleague without taking any credit.

DAY 3: Choose Posture Over Position

Action:
Reframe your mindset—your title is not your identity. Write down 3 ways to lead without authority.

Challenge:
Lead a conversation, meeting, or moment without asserting rank—only asking questions and listening well.

DAY 4: Own a Mistake

Action:
Think of one mistake you've made as a leader. Say it out loud. Then write down what you learned.

Challenge:
Model humility. In your next group setting, admit a leadership misstep and what it taught you.

DAY 5: Champion Someone's Growth

Action:
Identify someone who's been overlooked or

underestimated. Send a message that affirms their potential.

Challenge:
Create an opportunity for them to step up this week—delegate a task, ask for input, or give them the floor.

DAY 6: Replace Control With Courage

Action:
List 3 ways you've micromanaged or withheld trust. Choose one area to release control.

Challenge:
Empower someone else to lead in that area—and make space for their creativity to rise.

DAY 7: Build, Don't Break

Action:
Ask your team this: "What's one thing I could do to better support you?" Just listen—don't defend.

Challenge:
Follow up with a change. Show them their voice matters by taking action within 48 hours.

Optional Bonus: Day 8 Rally

Post-Challenge Reflection:
Write a half-page reflection titled: *"What's Changed In Me?"*

Then choose one action you'll continue for the next 30

CHAPTER 1: What Is Servant Leadership—Really?

days—and invite a colleague to take the challenge with you.

The Greatest Among You

CHAPTER 2: The Business Case for Servant Leadership

Stop the Eye Roll—Start the Awakening

Let's get something straight right now: servant leadership is **not** soft. It's not for the fragile. It's not for those who want to hold hands and sing kumbaya in the breakroom. It's for leaders who want to **build empires that last.** Still think it sounds too "touchy-feely"? Then let's talk results. Because the data is in, and the verdict is clear—**servant leadership outperforms traditional leadership in every category that matters.** Let that sink in before you brush this off.

The truth is, servant leadership doesn't just "feel good"—it works. In a world where employee disengagement is draining billions from the economy, servant leaders stand out because they lead with empathy, clarity, and purpose. These aren't buzzwords—they're proven performance drivers. Companies led by servant-minded executives experience lower turnover, stronger innovation, and significantly better team morale. It's not a coincidence. It's the consequence of leadership that puts people first and profits second—knowing full well that when people flourish, so does the bottom line (Liden et al., 2014).

So if you're still rolling your eyes, thinking this is all emotion and no execution, here's your wake-up call: you can't afford not to lead this way. In today's market, culture isn't a luxury—it's a competitive advantage. And the leaders who are winning aren't the ones with iron fists—they're the ones with open hands and open hearts. Servant leadership doesn't lower the bar—it raises it. And it raises people with it. Want proof? Let's look at the numbers.

Higher Engagement = Higher Profits

Gallup has been telling us for years that employee engagement drives profit. You want high-performing teams? **You better start serving them.** Servant leaders create environments where people feel seen, heard, valued, and trusted—and guess what happens when they do? Productivity spikes. Creativity explodes. Customer satisfaction goes through the roof. Companies in the top quartile of employee engagement are **21% more profitable** and experience **59% less turnover** (Gallup, 2020). That's not theory. That's **ROI on fire.**

Gallup has been telling us for years that employee engagement drives profit. You want high-performing teams? You better start serving them. Servant leaders create environments where people feel seen, heard, valued, and trusted—and guess what happens when they do? Productivity spikes. Creativity explodes. Customer satisfaction goes through the roof. Companies in the top quartile of employee engagement are 21% more profitable and experience 59% less turnover (Gallup, 2020). That's not theory. That's ROI on fire.

And it's not just Gallup shouting this from the mountaintops. A meta-analysis by Harter, Schmidt, and Hayes (2002) covering over 7,900 business units found that organizations with engaged employees had higher customer loyalty, lower absenteeism, and better profitability. When people are cared for, they care more. When they feel safe, they risk big ideas. When they feel trusted, they take ownership. That's the servant leadership effect—and it transforms your organization from the inside out. You're not just building a stronger team. You're building a performance culture that becomes unstoppable.

SIDEBAR: The Engagement Equation

When employees feel:

- **Seen** → They show up.

- **Heard** → They speak up.

- **Valued** → They give more.

- **Trusted** → They take ownership.

Servant leadership isn't a "perk." It's the most profitable leadership system ever created.

"Engagement doesn't cost you—it multiplies your return."

Low Turnover Isn't Luck—It's Leadership

Servant leadership doesn't just attract talent—it **keeps it.** Toxic leaders cause good people to flee. But servant leaders create cultures where people stay, grow, and thrive. Turnover costs businesses thousands—sometimes millions—in hiring, training, lost knowledge, and damaged morale. Want to slash those costs? Start serving your people. **People don't quit jobs—they quit bosses.** But they'll stay loyal to leaders who **fight for them, build them, and believe in them** (Liden, Wayne, Zhao, & Henderson, 2008).

Servant leadership doesn't just attract talent—it keeps it. Toxic leaders cause good people to flee. But servant leaders create cultures where people stay, grow, and thrive. Turnover costs businesses thousands—sometimes millions—in hiring, training, lost knowledge, and damaged morale. Want to slash those costs? Start serving your people. People don't quit jobs—they quit bosses. But they'll stay loyal to leaders who fight for them, build them, and believe in them (Liden, Wayne, Zhao, & Henderson, 2008).

Let's be real: free snacks and ping-pong tables won't fix a toxic culture. People don't stay because of perks—they stay because of purpose and people. When leaders choose to serve, trust takes root. And when trust takes root, employees commit at a deeper level. You don't have to beg them to stay—they'll turn down higher-paying offers just to keep following someone who actually gives a damn. That's not luck. That's leadership. And the more your people believe in your heart, the harder they'll fight for your mission.

SIDEBAR: Loyalty is Earned, Not Bought

You can't outpay poor leadership.
But you can *outlead* your competitors through compassion, consistency, and character.

> **"When leaders care deeply, employees commit fiercely."**

Innovation Thrives in Safety

Servant leaders don't just demand innovation—they make it **safe to innovate.** Google's famous Project Aristotle showed that the number one factor in high-performing teams is **psychological safety**—and servant leaders create it by design (Duhigg, 2016). They don't punish risk. They **reward initiative.** They don't shoot down ideas—they **ask better questions.** Innovation can't thrive under fear. But it **flourishes under trust.** That's why servant-led organizations lead the pack—not follow it.

Servant leaders don't just demand innovation—they

make it *safe* to innovate. Google's famous Project Aristotle showed that the number one factor in high-performing teams is psychological safety—and servant leaders create it by design (Duhigg, 2016). They don't punish risk. They reward initiative. They don't shoot down ideas—they ask better questions. Innovation can't thrive under fear. But it flourishes under trust. That's why servant-led organizations lead the pack—not follow it.

Psychological safety isn't some soft leadership buzzword—it's the *foundation* for innovation. Harvard's Amy Edmondson, the global authority on team dynamics, proved that people take creative risks when they feel safe to fail and supported to grow (Edmondson, 1999). Servant leaders normalize failure as a stepping stone, not a death sentence. They let people dream big, test fast, and recover strong. If innovation is the engine—servant leadership is the ignition. It lights the fire where breakthrough happens.

SIDEBAR: Innovation Is a Trust Exercise

Fear says, "Don't mess this up."
Servant leadership says, "Try boldly—I've got your back."

> **"If you want people to think differently, lead them differently."**

CHAPTER 2: The Business Case for Servant Leadership

Customer Satisfaction Starts With Employee Loyalty

Want to know the real secret to customer service excellence? **It's how you treat your team.** When employees feel served, they turn around and serve others. When they feel inspired, they inspire. When they feel valued, they bring **value.** Southwest Airlines, Chick-fil-A, Ritz-Carlton—these companies lead the world in customer satisfaction because they lead their people **with purpose and humility.** Happy employees make loyal customers. It's that simple.

Want to know the real secret to customer service excellence? It's how you treat your team. When employees feel served, they turn around and serve others. When they feel inspired, they inspire. When they feel valued, they bring value. Southwest Airlines, Chick-fil-A, Ritz-Carlton—these companies lead the world in customer satisfaction because they lead their people with purpose and humility. Happy employees make loyal customers. It's that simple.

According to Heskett, Jones, Loveman, Sasser, and Schlesinger (1994), employee satisfaction is directly tied to customer satisfaction, and both drive profitability. This is known as the *Service-Profit Chain*—and servant leadership is the human engine behind it. When employees feel psychologically safe, respected, and empowered, they treat customers not like transactions but like relationships (Liden et al., 2008). It doesn't start at the cash register—it starts at the team meeting. It starts with a leader who says, "How can I serve you, so you can serve them?"

SIDEBAR: The Ripple Effect of Service

You can't expect employees to pour joy, patience, or purpose into customers if their own cup is empty. Servant leaders fill the team's cup first.

> **"Customer loyalty is earned in the break room before it ever shows up in the boardroom."**

Servant Leaders Multiply Leadership

Servant leadership isn't just good for performance—**it's a leadership factory.** Because servant leaders don't build followers. They build **more leaders.** They mentor. They invest. They develop. And those leaders go on to do the same. What happens next is exponential—**your impact multiplies.** You don't just grow a team. You grow a legacy. Traditional leaders hoard influence. Servant leaders **unleash it.** And organizations that do that don't just win—they **transform.**

Servant leadership isn't just good for performance—it's a leadership factory. Because servant leaders don't build followers. They build more leaders. They mentor. They

CHAPTER 2: The Business Case for Servant Leadership

invest. They develop. And those leaders go on to do the same. What happens next is exponential—your impact multiplies. You don't just grow a team. You grow a legacy. Traditional leaders hoard influence. Servant leaders unleash it. And organizations that do that don't just win—they transform.

This multiplier effect has been validated in research across industries. Liden, Panaccio, Meuser, Hu, and Wayne (2014) found that servant leadership significantly predicts the development of leadership capacity in others—what they call "follower performance elevation." It's not theory—it's blueprint. When leaders make it their mission to reproduce other leaders, the organization becomes anti-fragile. You aren't relying on one charismatic figure at the top. You're growing a forest of impact, rooted deep and rising strong. This isn't a leadership model—it's a legacy machine.

SIDEBAR: Legacy Over Limelight

The greatest measure of your leadership is not how many follow you—
but how many lead because of you.

> **"Servant leaders don't guard the throne—they give away the crown."**

Servant Leadership Future-Proofs Your Culture

Times change. Markets shift. Technologies evolve. But people will always need **purpose, respect, trust, and dignity.** Servant leadership gives you a framework that's timeless. It adapts. It scales. It doesn't break when pressure hits. You can build systems on it. You can raise leaders on it. You can anchor your culture to it. **The world is moving too fast to be led by fragile egos.** The future belongs to leaders who serve.

Times change. Markets shift. Technologies evolve. But people will always need purpose, respect, trust, and dignity. Servant leadership gives you a framework that's timeless. It adapts. It scales. It doesn't break when pressure hits. You can build systems on it. You can raise leaders on it. You can anchor your culture to it. The world is moving too fast to be led by fragile egos. The future belongs to leaders who serve.

The research is clear: organizations grounded in servant leadership are more agile, more innovative, and more sustainable over time (Eva et al., 2019). Why? Because servant leadership bakes resilience into the cultural DNA. It creates psychological safety, strengthens relational capital, and fuels long-term commitment. When crisis hits, servant-led cultures bend—they don't break. They don't fall apart—they rise together. And in a world that's constantly evolving, the ability to endure and

CHAPTER 2: The Business Case for Servant Leadership

elevate isn't just valuable—it's vital.

SIDEBAR: Built to Last

Most leadership strategies adjust to trends.
Servant leadership withstands storms.

> "Trends fade. Titles shift. But cultures built on service endure forever."

Stop Managing. Start Building.

You can keep managing people if you want—checking boxes, driving quotas, grinding your team until they either comply or collapse. Or you can **start building something that matters.** Servant leadership is not about lowering the bar. It's about **raising people to clear it.** It doesn't ignore performance. It **fuels it with purpose.** The best leaders serve. The best teams thrive. And the best cultures rise together. This isn't hype. This is the new standard. **And it starts with you.**

You can keep managing people if you want—checking boxes, driving quotas, grinding your team until they either comply or collapse. Or you can start building something that matters. Servant leadership is not about lowering the bar. It's about raising people to clear it. It doesn't ignore performance. It fuels it with purpose. The best leaders serve. The best teams thrive. And the best cultures rise together. This isn't hype. This is the new standard. And it starts with you.

Management may organize the work, but servant leadership unleashes the worker. When you lead with purpose, accountability becomes ownership. People no longer need to be micromanaged because they feel trusted, valued, and equipped. Studies show that servant leadership not only improves performance—it amplifies intrinsic motivation, the deepest form of drive (van Dierendonck, 2011). That means people don't just *do* the work—they *believe* in it. And belief? That's what builds movements, not just metrics.

When leaders stop obsessing over control and start obsessing over contribution, everything changes. The team becomes more than employees—they become builders, partners, and legacy creators. You stop managing tasks and start multiplying transformation. And that, my friend, is how revolutions are born—not in corner offices, but in the hands of servant leaders who choose impact over ego and people over power.

SIDEBAR: From Compliance to Commitment

Managing is about checklists.
Building is about connection.

> **"Stop managing tasks. Start building people."**

That's the **business case for servant leadership.**
Not fluff. Not fiction. Just **facts backed by fire**.

CHAPTER 2: The Business Case for Servant Leadership

The Numbers Don't Lie—They Roar

In a world driven by bottom lines and benchmarks, you better believe people want proof. Well, here it is: **research overwhelmingly shows that servant leadership boosts performance, strengthens culture, and crushes turnover.** This isn't wishful thinking—it's data from Harvard, Gallup, Google, and top organizational journals. Want to win in business? Serve first. Companies that practice servant leadership outperform their competitors across key metrics—and they do it with teams that are energized, loyal, and thriving.

This isn't just good business—it's **the best business**. The proof is pounding on the boardroom table, demanding attention. Servant-led organizations experience higher employee engagement, stronger customer retention, and exponential innovation—because they've tapped into the one thing that drives all of it: *human potential*. That's the real edge. It's not just about what your people do—it's about who they become under your leadership. And when they're led by someone who sees them, serves them, and believes in them? They move mountains.

Let the skeptics cling to outdated models built on fear and control. The world is shifting—and the smartest companies know it. According to a study published in *The Leadership Quarterly*, servant leadership is directly tied to enhanced job performance, organizational citizenship behaviors, and employee satisfaction (Liden, Wayne,

Zhao, & Henderson, 2008). Translation? You don't lose power by serving—you *gain* unstoppable momentum.

SIDEBAR: Data with Soul

Servant leadership isn't soft. It's *smart*. The data doesn't whisper—it *roars*:

- 21% higher profitability
- 59% less turnover
- 41% reduction in absenteeism
  (Gallup, 2020)

"It's not a feel-good strategy. It's a fireproof one."

Performance Gets Supercharged

Studies show that when people feel supported, trusted, and empowered, their **performance skyrockets.** A study published in *The Leadership Quarterly* found that servant leadership was directly linked to **higher employee productivity and job satisfaction** (Liden et al., 2008). Why? Because when people feel seen and valued, they don't just comply—they commit. Servant leaders don't micromanage—they **mobilize**. They turn employees into mission-driven warriors—and it shows in the results.

Let's be clear: performance doesn't thrive under pressure—it thrives under purpose. When people know their leader actually gives a damn—about their growth, their goals, their well-being—they go from clocking in to showing up. According to research in the *Journal of Applied Psychology*, servant leadership cultivates intrinsic motivation, leading to higher task performance and greater organizational commitment (Eva et al., 2019). This isn't about squeezing more out of your people. It's about pulling the best out of them.

Servant leaders don't just measure outputs—they ignite outcomes. They build environments where creativity flows, resilience rises, and mediocrity gets suffocated by mission. You don't need to yell to get results—you need to serve. Because when leadership is rooted in trust and love, the byproduct is excellence that can't be faked and can't be forced. It's earned—and it's exponential.

SIDEBAR: Results, Rewritten

The best performance strategy?
Care deeply. Serve boldly. Expect greatness.

> **"Servant leadership doesn't lower expectations—it raises people to exceed them."**

Culture Isn't Fluff—It's Firepower

Culture eats strategy for breakfast—and servant leadership builds culture like nothing else. Research from Greenleaf Center case studies and Gallup shows that servant-led environments are psychologically safer, emotionally healthier, and **culturally stronger.** Employees report **greater collaboration, stronger emotional intelligence, and a deeper sense of purpose.** Culture isn't about having a ping-pong table in the breakroom. It's about having a mission worth showing up for—and a leader who actually leads with it.

Let's kill the myth once and for all: culture is not soft—it's the strongest force in your organization. Strategy may set direction, but culture determines speed, resilience, and unity. And servant leadership? It's the engine behind elite culture. When leaders serve, trust rises. When trust rises, walls fall. According to Gallup, psychologically safe teams outperform others by 27% and innovate more frequently (Gallup, 2020). Servant leadership doesn't just support culture—it *builds it from the inside out.*

This isn't about perks. It's about purpose. The best cultures don't need slogans on the wall because values are already alive in the hall. Servant leaders embed mission into moments—how they correct, how they collaborate, how they care. They don't just preach values—they personify them. And that creates cultures where people don't just survive the workweek—they come alive in it. It's not fluff. It's firepower—and it's how you scale excellence at every level.

SIDEBAR: Culture Is the Catalyst

Culture doesn't come from policies—it flows from people.
And it starts with how you lead.

CHAPTER 2: The Business Case for Servant Leadership

> "Servant leadership doesn't decorate culture—it detonates it."

Retention Skyrockets with Servant Leadership

Here's the gut-punch stat: companies with disengaged employees have **59% more turnover** Gallup (2017). But when servant leadership is in place, that flips. Employees stay longer, grow faster, and **care deeper.** A servant-led team doesn't feel like a contract—it feels like a calling. They don't just work there. They *believe* there. You don't have to bribe people to stay when your leadership style makes them feel like family and purpose is woven into every task.

Let's call it what it is: the employee turnover epidemic is a leadership problem—not a generational one. Gallup's 2017 research found that disengaged employees lead to 59% more turnover, costing U.S. companies an estimated $1 trillion annually in lost productivity, rehiring, and retraining. But here's the flip side: when leaders lead with *service instead of status*, the game changes completely. Servant leadership transforms "jobs" into journeys and "bosses" into builders. People don't just clock in—they commit.

Why? Because humans aren't wired for transactions—they're wired for transformation. When employees feel valued, heard, and developed, they don't chase the next paycheck—they plant roots. Studies show that servant leaders increase employee commitment, foster stronger emotional bonds with teams, and create cultures of meaningful belonging (Liden et al., 2008). That's not just leadership—it's legacy. The result? Loyalty that money can't buy, turnover that drops like a rock, and teams that *refuse to leave because they finally feel like they matter.*

SIDEBAR: Loyalty Is Earned

You don't retain talent with perks—you retain it with purpose.
When people feel trusted, developed, and empowered, they stay.

> **"Great leaders don't fight turnover. They fight for people."**

The Greenleaf Effect in Action

The Greenleaf Center's ongoing research has found that servant leadership significantly increases **trust, organizational commitment, and team effectiveness**. One study showed that teams led by servant leaders consistently outperform traditional hierarchies in innovation, initiative, and cross-department collaboration. Why? Because people don't build walls when their leaders are building them up. Servant leadership creates **buy-in at every level.** You don't need to coerce when people feel called.

Robert Greenleaf didn't just coin a term—he sparked a global shift in how we measure greatness. Today, his

CHAPTER 2: The Business Case for Servant Leadership

blueprint is backed by rigorous data and enterprise-wide results. The Greenleaf Center's ongoing research confirms what visionaries already know: **servant leadership isn't a soft ideal—it's a strategic edge.** Studies consistently show that servant-led teams outperform those led by traditional hierarchies across trust metrics, employee commitment, initiative, and cross-functional collaboration (Greenleaf Center for Servant Leadership, 2023).

Why? Because servant leadership removes the walls that fear and ego build. When people are lifted, not leveraged, they stop protecting turf and start sharing ideas. Servant-led environments don't rely on positional power—they thrive on *relational trust*. This is how movements are built. When people feel supported by leadership, they don't just comply—they co-create. They don't ask, "What do I need to do?"—they ask, *"What can I build with you?"* That shift in energy? That's what scales organizations with purpose and velocity.

SIDEBAR: The Greenleaf Multiplier

Servant leadership doesn't subtract control—it multiplies momentum.
It doesn't dilute structure—it fuels collaboration.

> **"You don't need to coerce when people feel called."**

Psychological Safety = Innovation and Risk-Taking

Google's Project Aristotle turned the corporate world upside down with one core discovery: **psychological safety is the #1 factor in high-performing teams** *Duhigg, C. (2016).* And guess what kind of leader creates that environment? Servant leaders. They don't just "allow" risk—they **welcome** it. They don't punish failure—they *learn* from it. That kind of safety produces boldness. Boldness births innovation. Innovation changes everything.

Google's *Project Aristotle* didn't just produce a good insight—it dropped a bombshell on outdated leadership models. After studying 180 teams across their organization, Google found that **psychological safety**—not raw talent, not experience, not education—was the **#1 predictor** of high performance (Duhigg, 2016). Think about that. The smartest people in the world realized that innovation doesn't grow in control—it grows in trust.

And trust? That's the currency of servant leadership.

Servant leaders create spaces where people don't whisper ideas—they **declare them**. They don't fear being wrong—they hunger to get better. Failure becomes feedback, not a firing squad. This shift creates a greenhouse for risk-taking, ideation, and problem-solving. When the environment is safe, people bring their

CHAPTER 2: The Business Case for Servant Leadership

full selves to the table. That's not just a cultural advantage—it's an innovation engine. In servant-led organizations, you'll find more than performance. You'll find *breakthroughs*.

SIDEBAR: The Courage to Risk

Fear kills innovation before it's born.
Servant leaders build trust so strong, it becomes a launchpad.

> **"In cultures led by servants, risk isn't reckless—it's revered."**

Servant Leadership Boosts Emotional Intelligence and Purpose

Servant leaders don't just manage tasks—they grow people. And research shows that when leaders demonstrate empathy, listening, and empowerment, it **raises emotional intelligence across the organization.** People become better communicators. They deal with conflict in healthier ways. And they're more connected to *why* their work matters. Purpose is the most potent motivator on the planet—and servant leadership is its delivery system.

Servant leaders don't just manage tasks—they **grow people**. They cultivate self-awareness, empathy, and resilience not through workshops, but through daily example. Studies show that when leaders prioritize active listening, vulnerability, and empowerment, emotional intelligence skyrockets across teams (Barbuto & Wheeler, 2006). Conflict becomes constructive. Feedback becomes fruitful. People stop guarding themselves and start growing. Why? Because they're being led by someone who sees them as human first—and talent second.

And when emotional intelligence rises, **so does purpose.** Servant leaders don't just hand out tasks—they connect people to *why* their work matters. Purpose isn't a line on a corporate banner—it's the pulse of a healthy culture. And in servant-led spaces, that pulse beats strong. Work stops being transactional and starts becoming transformational. People rise. Teams gel. Mission takes root. This isn't leadership theory—it's leadership **truth** that touches both heart and performance (Hunter et al., 2013).

SIDEBAR: You can train skills. But emotional intelligence? That's modeled.
Servant leaders teach it through every interaction.

> **"People don't grow in silence. They grow in safe, seen, servant-led cultures."**

CHAPTER 2: The Business Case for Servant Leadership

When the Data Matches the Spirit, You've Got a Revolution

Servant leadership isn't just spiritually powerful—it's **strategically brilliant.** The world has been looking for a way to blend profitability with purpose, excellence with empathy, growth with grit. This is it. **This is the model that delivers.** You don't have to sacrifice performance for people—or people for performance. With servant leadership, you get **both.** The research proves it. The stories echo it. The future demands it.

Servant leadership isn't just spiritually powerful—it's **strategically unstoppable**. For decades, business leaders believed they had to choose between compassion and competitiveness, mission and margin, soul and scale. But servant leadership proves that **you don't have to choose**—you can win with both. Organizations led by servant leaders don't just feel better to work in—they **outperform** their competitors across key metrics like retention, innovation, engagement, and profitability (Liden et al., 2008; Spears, 1995). When heart and data align, that's not soft—it's seismic.

This is the revolution the marketplace has been begging for. The most progressive institutions, from universities like Grand Canyon to corporate titans like Starbucks and TDIndustries, have been quietly proving it for years: **put people first, and performance follows** (Colangelo, 2022). Servant leadership gives you a blueprint for building cultures where character drives commerce, and trust fuels transformation. When the spreadsheets start echoing the scriptures? You're not just running a business. **You're leading a movement.**

SIDEBAR: The Data Isn't Just In—It's Demanding Action

When the world's best research points to servant leadership, we're not dealing with a trend.
We're witnessing a turning point.

> "Servant leadership isn't the alternative. It's the awakening."

The Lie of the Bottom Line

For too long, we've been fed a lie: that putting people first is a "nice to have," a bonus, a perk you sprinkle in when the profits are already strong. **Wrong.** Putting people first isn't a luxury—it's the *most powerful, profit-driving force* your organization can unlock. Companies obsessed with numbers but blind to people always hit ceilings. They burn out talent, exhaust their teams, and wake up wondering why innovation died and turnover is through the roof. But servant leaders? They see people as **the source** of profit—not a cost to be minimized.

For too long, we've been fed a lie: that putting people first is a "nice to have," a bonus, a perk you sprinkle in when the profits are already strong. **Wrong.** Putting people first isn't a luxury—it's the most powerful, profit-driving force

CHAPTER 2: The Business Case for Servant Leadership

your organization can unlock. Companies obsessed with numbers but blind to people always hit ceilings. They burn out talent, exhaust their teams, and wake up wondering why innovation died and turnover exploded. But servant leaders? They see people as the **source** of profit—not a cost to be minimized.

This myth—the one that says servant leadership is too "soft" for high performance—has been completely debunked by modern research. Studies from Harvard Business Review and The Leadership Quarterly show that organizations led by values-based, service-oriented leadership outperform their competitors in every vital category: from productivity to retention to ROI (Heskett et al., 1994; Liden et al., 2008). The bottom line isn't the enemy—it's just not the starting line. Because when you build from the foundation of **people-first leadership**, the profits don't shrink—they **scale**. It's not magic. It's math with meaning.

SIDEBAR: What Gets Ignored, Decays

Leaders who chase numbers and ignore people may hit their short-term targets—
But they'll miss their long-term legacy.

> **"Servant leaders don't ignore the bottom line. They build it from the bottom up."**

When You Prioritize People, You Multiply Performance

Want more output? More efficiency? More drive? **Then put your people first.** Studies by Gallup and Harvard Business Review prove that when employees feel valued, empowered, and supported, **productivity jumps by 17-21%** *Gallup (2017).* Why? Because nobody goes all-in for a boss who treats them like a number. But they will go to war for a leader who believes in them. That's not theory. That's a battlefield-tested fact. **People rise when they're served with vision and respect.**

Performance doesn't rise from pressure—it rises from purpose. And purpose is ignited when people feel genuinely seen, heard, and valued. Gallup's landmark research confirms what servant leaders have known all along: when employees feel supported and empowered, productivity doesn't just improve—it explodes by 17–21% (Gallup, 2017). This isn't just good management. This is transformational leadership. You don't need louder quotas—you need deeper connection. Because people won't bleed for metrics, but they will rise for meaning.

You want innovation? Ownership? Results that reverberate across every department? Then serve your people. When employees believe their leader believes in them, they bring more than effort—they bring excellence. Harvard Business Review research shows that high-trust cultures outperform low-trust ones by 286% in total

CHAPTER 2: The Business Case for Servant Leadership

return to shareholders (Zak, 2017). The math is simple: when you prioritize people, they multiply your mission. The return isn't just financial—it's cultural, emotional, and exponential.

SIDEBAR: Companies with high employee engagement outperform competitors in profitability, productivity, and retention (Gallup, 2017; Zak, 2017).
Because people don't perform for fear—they rise for purpose.

> **"Treat people like your greatest asset—and they'll perform like it."**

Loyalty You Can Bank On

Customer loyalty starts with employee loyalty. When you put your people first, they stay longer, perform better, and represent your brand with pride. Turnover is expensive—training costs, lost knowledge, and cultural breakdowns destroy momentum. But servant leadership builds a culture of belonging. People don't walk away from places where they feel **seen, heard, and loved.** That's not kumbaya—that's retention math. Lower turnover means **higher margins.** Period.

Loyalty isn't bought with perks—it's built with presence. Servant leaders create cultures where people don't just clock in—they commit. Why? Because they're seen. Heard. Invested in. That's why companies with strong servant leadership models enjoy higher retention, longer tenure, and deeper employee advocacy (Liden et al., 2008). This is more than feel-good fluff. It's structural fortitude. A loyal team is an unshakable asset. When disruption hits, it's not your software that saves you—it's your people.

This kind of loyalty can't be mandated—it's earned. It shows up in after-hours effort, in the extra call made, in the teammate who stays late because the mission matters. That's the unspoken power of servant leadership: it creates a tribe, not just a workforce. Loyalty becomes more than a metric—it becomes your movement. And movements don't die when markets shift—they get louder, bolder, and more resilient. This is leadership that lasts. Organizations with servant leadership at the helm experience up to 50% higher employee retention and engagement scores (Liden et al., 2008; Gallup, 2017).
Because people don't leave when they feel led—they leave when they feel used.

> "Serve them right—and they'll stay through the storm."

Servant Leadership Turns Employees Into Advocates

Servant-led cultures do something special—they **turn team members into missionaries.** These aren't just workers—they're believers. They go home and talk about their job with joy. They invite others to apply. They protect

CHAPTER 2: The Business Case for Servant Leadership

the culture like it's sacred. They don't just guard the company's reputation—they **elevate** it. That kind of energy doesn't come from a pay raise. It comes from **purpose.** And when purpose lives at the core of a company, your brand becomes magnetic.

Servant leadership creates more than productive teams—it creates passionate believers. In this kind of culture, people don't just clock in—they buy in. They speak about their work with pride, invite their friends to apply, and defend the mission like it's their own. Why? Because they feel seen. They feel trusted. And when someone feels valued at work, they carry that energy into every conversation outside of it. They become advocates, recruiters, brand ambassadors, and culture carriers—without ever being asked.

This is the invisible engine behind great companies. Research shows that organizations with engaged employees outperform those without by up to 202% (Gallup, 2017). But you can't fake engagement. It only grows in soil rich with trust, care, and meaning. Servant leadership plants the seeds—and the harvest is explosive. When purpose becomes the heartbeat of the culture, loyalty becomes contagious, and advocacy becomes automatic. That's how movements are built from the inside out.

People talk about work that matters.
They share stories about leaders who care.
And they become the proof that your culture is real.

"Servant leaders don't recruit with incentives—they recruit with impact."

Healthier Teams = Healthier Bottom Line

The ROI of putting people first doesn't stop at profits—it touches **mental, emotional, and physical health.** Servant-led environments have **less stress, fewer sick days, and stronger resilience** under pressure. Why? Because people aren't walking on eggshells. They aren't running from power-hungry egos. They're showing up whole. **Healthy teams innovate. Burned-out teams break.** You want your company to scale? Start by healing the culture from the inside out.

The ROI of servant leadership goes far beyond spreadsheets—it reaches deep into the human soul. Companies that lead with service don't just see better results—they see better people. The research is undeniable: psychologically safe workplaces reduce burnout, absenteeism, and turnover (Duhigg, 2016; Liden et al., 2008). In servant-led environments, employees experience lower stress, improved mental health, and deeper connection to their mission. And when people feel safe and supported, they don't just survive—they soar.

You want your organization to be resilient? Then stop squeezing output from exhausted teams and start fueling their health. Servant leaders protect energy instead of

CHAPTER 2: The Business Case for Servant Leadership

draining it. They normalize balance instead of glorifying burnout. They build systems of care that pay dividends in productivity, creativity, and loyalty. A burned-out employee costs far more than a supported one. And a healed team? That's your competitive edge in a world that's burning out fast.

SIDEBAR: Servant leadership boosts morale, trust, and emotional bandwidth.
It turns mental exhaustion into mental agility.

> "Burnout doesn't come from doing too much. It comes from doing too much without meaning."

Innovation Explodes Where People Are Empowered

Let's be blunt: people don't share ideas when they're scared. They stay quiet. They shrink back. They hoard creativity because bad leaders hoard power. But servant leaders **invite creativity.** They reward contribution. They give credit. They **clear the way for new thinking—and then celebrate it.** Want to know why companies like Apple and Netflix win? Because they empower teams to **fail forward and create boldly.** And they root that power in trust.

Let's be blunt: people don't share ideas when they're scared. They stay quiet. They shrink back. They hoard creativity because bad leaders hoard power. But servant leaders invite creativity. They reward contribution. They give credit. They clear the way for new thinking—and then celebrate it. Want to know why companies like Apple and Netflix win? Because they empower teams to fail forward and create boldly. And they root that power in trust.

Empowerment is not a perk. It's a performance strategy backed by data and built on trust. Research from *The Leadership Quarterly* reveals that empowered employees demonstrate greater innovation, stronger collaboration, and a higher commitment to organizational goals (Amundsen & Martinsen, 2014). Servant leaders don't just tolerate innovation—they engineer it by creating psychological freedom and decision-making autonomy. That's how you build cultures that don't just adapt to change—they drive it.

Empowered people think differently. They act courageously. They stop asking for permission and start producing solutions. When you remove fear and inject ownership, you release the full force of human potential. That's the multiplier effect of servant leadership. It doesn't just extract performance—it unleashes genius. Want to ignite creativity, drive breakthroughs, and disrupt your industry? Start by empowering the people you lead.

"Fear paralyzes potential. Trust awakens it."

Every System Gets Better When People Come First

Want better meetings? Start with better leaders. Want

CHAPTER 2: The Business Case for Servant Leadership

better marketing? Start with **more inspired employees.** Want better client retention? Start with **culture alignment.** The health of your people shows up **in every corner of the company.** Servant leadership isn't just a "style." It's the root system that nourishes every branch. And when the roots are healthy, **growth is inevitable.** Every department improves when leadership flows from humility, service, and strength.

The brilliance of servant leadership is that it's not siloed—it's systemic. The effects ripple through every meeting agenda, customer interaction, marketing decision, and policy update. When people are prioritized, communication flows more clearly, feedback loops are tighter, and execution gets sharper. Teams stop playing politics and start playing for each other. As Greenleaf taught, "The work exists for the person as much as the person exists for the work" (Greenleaf, 1970). That shift in thinking? It's what turns stagnant systems into high-performance ecosystems.

And let's get one thing clear: healthy systems aren't an accident—they're architected by leaders who serve. When empathy is engineered into how you hire, onboard, coach, and reward, the whole machine moves faster and smoother. Productivity isn't forced—it's unlocked. Culture alignment becomes second nature. From the break room to the boardroom, everything improves when leaders decide the people *are* the strategy. And servant leadership isn't just the heart behind it—it's the framework that holds it together.

Want more ideas? Serve more people.
Want faster pivots? Empower your team.

> "The brain lights up when the heart feels safe. That's where breakthroughs happen."

You Can't Afford Not to Lead This Way

Here's the truth: **you're already investing in something.** Maybe it's control. Maybe it's ego. Maybe it's fear. But what if you invested in your **people** instead? What if you led like Jesus—stooping to serve, empowering the broken, building the overlooked? The ROI wouldn't just show up on balance sheets. It would echo in the hallways, radiate through your brand, and multiply into legacy. **Put people first—and you'll never lead second-rate again.**

There's no sugarcoating it: the business world is starving for purpose. People are desperate for leaders who aren't chasing titles but **carrying crosses.** And whether you're in a boardroom, a break room, or a locker room, there's one leadership model that never fails—**God's.**
It's not built on pride. It's not about dominance. It's built on **sacrifice, service, humility, and love.**

Let's look at what the Bible says about **what leadership really means:**

CHAPTER 2: The Business Case for Servant Leadership

> **"Do nothing out of selfish ambition or vain conceit. Rather, in humility value others above yourselves... In your relationships with one another, have the same mindset as Christ Jesus."**
> — *Philippians 2:3–5, NIV*

That's the mission statement of **servant leadership.**
Jesus didn't come to flaunt power—He came to **redeem, restore, and release others into their calling.**
He touched lepers, washed the feet of fishermen, and defended the woman caught in sin.
And just before He endured the cross, He knelt down, took up a towel, and **served.**
That wasn't weakness. That was **Kingdom authority** in action.

Want more?

> **"Whoever wants to become great among you must be your servant, and whoever wants to be first must be your slave—just as the Son of Man did not come to be served, but to serve, and to give his life..."**
> — *Matthew 20:26–28, NIV*

That's Jesus laying down the **greatest leadership principle in history.**
Greatness isn't measured by how many people answer to you—it's measured by how many people you **lift up.**

In the Kingdom of God, *service isn't weakness—it's warfare.*
And when leaders finally wake up to that reality, they don't just change companies—they change *legacies*.
They become more than influencers. They become **builders of movements** that glorify God and heal the world.

So what's the bottom line?

If your leadership doesn't look like Jesus, it's not leadership at all.
Serve first. Lead strong.
And never forget: the King wore a crown of thorns, not gold.

Call to Action: Chapter 2 — Step into the Revolution

Let's cut the fluff:
You've seen the evidence.
You've read the research.
You've witnessed the rise of servant-led giants like Chick-fil-A and Southwest.
You've stared into the sacred blueprint of biblical leadership—and now you stand at the crossroads.

No more pretending this is just a "nice idea."
This is a revolution.
A seismic shift in how leadership should be done.

CHAPTER 2: The Business Case for Servant Leadership

And the best part? **It's not reserved for the elite.**
It's for every single person who's bold enough to say, *"There's a better way—and I will lead it."*

Do you want to build a team that lasts?
A business that breathes life?
A culture that crushes mediocrity and multiplies purpose?
Then you must become a **servant first.**
Not tomorrow. **Today.**

Here's your next step:

- Meet with your team. Ask one question: *"What do you need from me to do your best work?"* Then shut up and **listen.**

- Walk your floor. Get to know names, stories, dreams. **Look people in the eyes** and let them know they matter.

- Pick one act of service today—**unexpected, unprompted, and unconditional.** Start changing your culture from the inside out.

Leadership isn't a title.
It's a towel.

So grab it.
Step up. Bend low. And watch what God can do when a

leader finally gets out of the way.

7-Day Servant Leadership Action Challenge

Chapter 2: The Business Case for Servant Leadership
Theme: *People First = Performance That Lasts*

DAY 1 – LISTEN LIKE A LEADER
Ask your team (or a few direct reports):

"What's one thing I can do to help you thrive here?"
Then *listen*—don't interrupt, don't defend, don't fix. Just hear them.
Why it matters: Listening is the gateway to psychological safety (Edmondson, 1999).

DAY 2 – SPOTLIGHT THE UNSPOTLIGHTED
Write a personal thank-you message (email or handwritten) to someone on your team who rarely gets recognition. Be specific.
Why it matters: Recognition activates trust and belonging—core drivers of retention (Gallup, 2020).

DAY 3 – SERVE SOMEONE SECRETLY
Do one invisible act of service: clean a break room, refill supplies, bring in coffee for no reason—without announcing it.
Why it matters: Servant leaders model humility, not for applause but for alignment (Greenleaf, 1977).

DAY 4 – GET ON THE GROUND FLOOR
Spend 30 minutes engaging with frontline employees. Learn their roles. Ask what's working and what's not.
Why it matters: Leaders who walk the floor build cultures that trust the mission (Liden et al., 2008).

DAY 5 – EMPOWER, DON'T ESCALATE
Delegate one meaningful decision to someone lower in the chain than usual—and *trust their judgment*.
Why it matters: Empowerment fuels innovation and ownership (Amundsen & Martinsen, 2014).

DAY 6 – OPEN THE MIC
Hold a 15-minute team huddle and ask:

"What's one idea you've had that we haven't heard yet?" Celebrate *every* contribution.
Why it matters: Innovation thrives in environments where it's safe to speak (Duhigg, 2016).

DAY 7 – CONNECT TO THE "WHY"
In your next meeting or memo, tie a task, goal, or metric to the greater mission. Remind your people:

"Here's why this work matters."
Why it matters: Purpose is the deepest motivator and most sustainable fuel (Hunter et al., 2013).

Challenge Wrap-Up:

You don't need a committee to change culture.
You don't need a new system to build trust.
You need **courageous, consistent acts of servant leadership.**

Start small.
Stay faithful.
Watch the performance multiply.

"Serve first. Lead always. Repeat daily."

CHAPTER 3: Servant Leadership in Action

Where Purpose Puts on Work Boots

> *"This is where mission leaves the whiteboard, rolls up its sleeves, and walks into the real world—mud, mess, and all."*

The Stage Is Set—Now Let's Walk It Out

Everything we've covered so far has been leading to this moment. You've learned what servant leadership is, why it works, and how it transforms everything it touches. But now it's time to strip off the theory and roll up the sleeves. **This is where real leaders step forward—not with titles, but with towels.** This chapter is about living it, breathing it, bleeding for it when necessary—because **servant leadership isn't a philosophy; it's a lifestyle.**

Because let's be clear: this isn't about hype. It's not about reading one more book, posting one more quote, or hosting one more meeting where nothing changes. It's about dying to ego, putting others first, and choosing the long, hard road of humility and transformation. It's about facing every obstacle with a servant's heart and a warrior's will. At Grand Canyon University, servant leadership is more than a theory—it's the first pillar of its business college because they know the world doesn't need more bosses; it needs more builders (Colangelo, 2022).

Jesus said, *"I have set you an example that you should do as I have done for you"* (John 13:15, NIV). That wasn't a metaphor. It was a mandate. Leadership that doesn't resemble Christ is counterfeit. His life wasn't just a lesson in compassion—it was a masterclass in leadership that flipped the world upside down. This next chapter isn't about adding more ideas to your brain; it's about unleashing the movement inside your heart. You've got the roadmap. Now let's walk the narrow path—and lead like Jesus.

SIDEBAR: The Stage Is Set—Now Let's Walk It Out

- **Reminder:** You've studied the principles—now live the proof.
- **Action:** Trade your title for a towel. Today, serve someone with no expectation of recognition.
- **Scripture:** *"Whoever wants to become great among you must be your servant."* — Matthew 20:26 (NIV)
- **Challenge:** Identify one place in your leadership where you've clung to control—and surrender it this week in favor of empowering someone else.

CHAPTER 3: Servant Leadership in Action

Leadership That Looks Like Jesus

The greatest leader who ever lived didn't wear a crown—He wore humility. He didn't demand service—**He washed feet.** If you're going to lead with eternal impact, your leadership has to look like **Christ's leadership.** That means embracing humility, justice, mercy, and courage—day in and day out. As *Micah 6:8 (NIV)* declares, *"What does the Lord require of you? To act justly and to love mercy and to walk humbly with your God."* That's not just a memory verse. **That's a mandate.**

Jesus modeled the type of leadership this broken world is desperate for—one that confronts injustice, uplifts the marginalized, and holds nothing back for the sake of others. His power wasn't in political force or persuasive titles—it was in submission to God and sacrifice for people. Grand Canyon University teaches that servant leadership reflects "the character of Christ" and forms the foundation for transformative business practice (Grand Canyon University, n.d.). Your leadership doesn't need to echo the boardroom—it needs to echo the Upper Room, where Jesus knelt down and scrubbed the dust off of failure and pride.

This is the call: when others climb the ladder, you carry the cross. When others hoard power, you share it. And when others chase influence, you create impact through love, truth, and relentless service. That's where real legacy is built—in homes, in huddles, in staff meetings, in unseen moments of radical faithfulness. It's not flashy, but it's unstoppable. And it's time for a generation of leaders to rise up and lead not by position, but by posture—on their knees, with their hearts set on eternity.

SIDEBAR: The Battlefield Is Boardrooms and Break Rooms

- **Truth Bomb:** You don't need a pulpit to preach—your posture preaches louder than your words.
- **Real-World Reminder:** Leadership isn't proven on a stage. It's proven in how you treat the janitor, the intern, the customer, and the critic.
- **Scripture Charge:** *"In your relationships with one another, have the same mindset as Christ Jesus..."* (Philippians 2:5, NIV)
- **From the Source:** "Servant leaders do not simply manage—they minister. They care deeply and lead humbly, modeling Jesus in every domain" (Colangelo, 2022).

The Battlefield Is Boardrooms and Break Rooms

Don't wait for some big, glamorous moment to prove you're a servant leader. **This battle is fought in the trenches of daily life.** It happens in team meetings, hallway conversations, crisis calls, and cafeteria tables. The real victories aren't always celebrated with applause—they're earned in how you show up for your people when no one's watching. **Servant leadership**

CHAPTER 3: Servant Leadership in Action

shows up in the small things and wins big over time.

Because that's where culture lives—in the moments no one else deems important. It's in how you respond when a team member drops the ball. It's in the patience you show when stress is high and resources are low. Servant leaders set the tone in every atmosphere they enter, not through domination but through presence. As Robert Greenleaf taught, the test of a servant leader is whether those around them grow—*"do they, while being served, become healthier, wiser, freer, more autonomous?"* (Greenleaf, 1977).

At Grand Canyon University, the business curriculum emphasizes integrating faith and action in the workplace, teaching that "our ethics must match our execution" (Grand Canyon University, n.d.). That means we don't compartmentalize Christ—we carry Him into every boardroom, break room, and decision we make. Your mission field might not be overseas. It might be behind a desk, leading a team, or managing a shift. Every space becomes sacred when you show up as a servant.

SIDEBAR: Where Legacy Is Written

- **Reminder:** You don't become a servant leader on stage—you prove it at 7:03 AM when no one's watching and someone needs you.
- **Actionable Insight:** Ask yourself each day, *"Who can I serve before I speak? Who can I elevate before I execute?"*

- **Scripture Fuel:** *"Whatever you do, work at it with all your heart, as working for the Lord, not for human masters."* — Colossians 3:23 (NIV)
- **Legacy Principle:** Culture is shaped more in five-minute interactions than five-year plans.

Leading with Both Courage and Compassion

Some people mistake servant leadership for being soft. They think serving others means avoiding hard conversations or being passive. **Wrong.** It takes **more courage** to lead from humility than it does to dominate from fear. It takes strength to admit when you're wrong, wisdom to empower others, and bravery to step back and let others rise. *1 Peter 5:2–3 (NIV)* nails it: *"Be shepherds of God's flock… not lording it over those entrusted to you, but being examples to the flock."* That's courage wrapped in compassion. That's servant leadership.

True servant leaders bleed both steel and grace. They confront injustice, correct what's broken, and protect their people—but they do it without pride, ego, or applause. It takes deep inner security to speak truth without crushing people and to correct without condemning. Grand Canyon University teaches that servant leadership is a "bold yet humble" calling, one where truth and love operate side by side (Colangelo, 2022). In other words: real leadership doesn't bark orders—it builds people.

CHAPTER 3: Servant Leadership in Action

Jesus flipped the entire leadership model on its head by leading through crucifixion, not coercion. His authority wasn't diminished by His humility—it was magnified by it. When you lead like Jesus, you carry both the sword of courage and the towel of service. One hand fights for justice; the other washes feet. That balance is the heartbeat of servant leadership—and it's the kind of leadership the world is starving for. And when it's lived out with integrity and fire, people notice. They remember. And they follow.

SIDEBAR: Strength Wrapped in Compassion

- **Misconception Alert:** Serving others doesn't mean weakness—it means knowing exactly who you are in Christ and leading from that strength.
- **Leadership Check-In:** When was the last time you corrected someone in love, not just with facts? When was the last time you led through listening?
- **Scripture Backbone:** *"Speak the truth in love, growing in every way more and more like Christ..."* — Ephesians 4:15 (NIV)
- **Scholar's Insight:** "The most effective leaders are those who unite courage with compassion, conviction with empathy. That's the essence of servant leadership" (Grand Canyon University, n.d.).

The Stories That Prove It Works

We're not building this movement on emotion—we're building it on **evidence.** In this chapter, you're going to hear from real leaders—faith-driven CEOs, community builders, educators, coaches—who didn't just talk about servant leadership, they **lived it in the fire.** And when they led from a place of love and service, they watched their teams, cultures, and profits explode. These aren't fairy tales. **These are case studies in Kingdom-driven leadership.**

Servant leadership isn't some lofty ideal; it's a high-performance engine built on trust, purpose, and people. Research continues to validate what the Word of God and real-world experience have already confirmed: when leaders prioritize service, the results follow. According to Grand Canyon University, businesses grounded in servant leadership experience "enhanced morale, engagement, and long-term growth because they place people above process and mission over metrics" (Grand Canyon University, n.d.). We're not here to guess. We're here to build—on principles that *work*.

And we've got the receipts. From locker rooms to boardrooms, you'll hear stories of turnarounds that never should've happened, but did—because a leader dared to lead like Jesus. You'll read about failing schools that became thriving campuses, struggling teams that became champions, and broken companies that became beacons of culture and impact. These are the stories that

CHAPTER 3: Servant Leadership in Action

defy logic, but they don't defy truth. When you lead with service at the center, you don't just spark change—you spark movements.

SIDEBAR: Tested in Fire. Proven in Results.

- **Leadership Myth Busted:** "Kindness kills productivity." Lie. Servant leadership multiplies it.
- **Thought Leader Insight:** "The modern business world is catching up to what Christ taught 2,000 years ago—service isn't a weakness. It's a weapon." — Colangelo, 2022
- **Kingdom Clarity:** *"By their fruit you will recognize them."* — Matthew 7:16 (NIV)
- **Data Drop:** Teams led by servant leaders show 18–40% higher levels of trust, engagement, and retention (Liden et al., 2008). That's not fluff. That's fact.

You'll Face Resistance—Lead Anyway

Let's be real: the world doesn't always reward servant leadership at first. Some people will scoff. Others will resist. You might even feel like you're swimming upstream in a river of toxic egos. But here's the truth—**those who endure as servant leaders change the tide.** They win trust slowly, earn loyalty deeply, and build cultures that last long after the storms. The easy path doesn't change the world. **The servant's path does.**

The resistance isn't a sign you're failing—it's confirmation you're fighting for something eternal. The enemy doesn't waste ammo on people who aren't a threat. So when the pressure comes, when critics whisper, and when you feel unseen, misunderstood, or out of place, *stay planted*. The harvest is coming. Galatians 6:9 (NIV) reminds us: *"Let us not become weary in doing good, for at the proper time we will reap a harvest if we do not give up."* Real leaders keep serving when applause turns to silence.

At Grand Canyon University, leadership students are taught that perseverance is a pillar of faith-driven business—because Kingdom impact isn't built on convenience; it's built on conviction (Colangelo, 2022). Servant leaders don't serve to be seen. They serve to shake things up, to flip tables when needed, and to wash feet when no one else will. You won't always get the credit—but you'll always get the fruit. And what you build will stand the test of fire.

SIDEBAR: Armor Up. Stay Low. Lead Through the Fire.

- **Spiritual Warfare Truth:** If you're not facing resistance, you're probably not disrupting darkness.
- **Leadership Grit:** Don't adjust your calling to match people's comfort zones.
- **Scripture for the Storm:** *"Consider him who endured such opposition from sinners, so that you will not grow weary and lose heart."* — Hebrews 12:3 (NIV)

CHAPTER 3: Servant Leadership in Action

- **Faith + Business Insight:** "Servant leaders endure storms not just with resilience, but with purpose. Resistance is part of the refinement." — Grand Canyon University, n.d.

The Fruit That Follows Obedience

When you lead with service, the fruit doesn't just show up in numbers—it shows up in people. In marriages healed, potential unlocked, students inspired, families fed, and employees who find purpose instead of just paychecks. That kind of leadership doesn't just change organizations—it **rebuilds broken hearts** and breathes life into every room it enters. The world is groaning for this kind of leadership, and God is calling **you** to deliver it.

This is the evidence of obedience: not just metrics on a spreadsheet, but movements in people's souls. Servant leadership unlocks what transactional leadership never touches—the inner dignity of human beings made in the image of God. As Jesus said in John 15:5 (NIV), *"If you remain in me and I in you, you will bear much fruit; apart from me you can do nothing."* When we abide in Him and lead with His heart, the results multiply in ways we can't manufacture—revived culture, exponential trust, generational impact.

At Grand Canyon University, future leaders are reminded that obedience to God's design for leadership brings "missional alignment and measurable outcomes" (Grand Canyon University, n.d.). It's not either/or. It's both. When you serve with integrity, humility, and bold obedience, *the fruit shows up in both the boardroom and the baptismal.* The team gets stronger. The people grow deeper. The mission goes further. And in a world dominated by noise, your obedience becomes a signal that awakens something holy in the hearts of those you lead.

SIDEBAR: This Is What Obedience Builds

- **Spiritual Insight:** The fruit of servant leadership is always bigger than what can be measured. It shows up in *transformed lives.*
- **Kingdom ROI:** Organizations led by servant leaders report higher morale, retention, innovation—and most importantly, purpose.
- **Scripture Confirmation:** *"If you are willing and obedient, you will eat the good things of the land."* — Isaiah 1:19 (NIV)
- **Academic Reinforcement:** "Obedience to God's model for leadership is the foundation for sustainable, ethical growth—internally and externally." — Grand Canyon University, n.d.

The Towel Is Waiting—Pick It Up

As you step into this chapter, remember this: servant leadership won't be handed to you in a title or policy manual. It's handed to you **every time you choose to bend lower, lift others higher, and lead with courage soaked in love.** Real leaders don't wait for permission—they respond to purpose. So pick up the towel. Lean into

CHAPTER 3: Servant Leadership in Action

the challenge. And get ready to lead **like the King of Kings led—by serving first and leading strong.**

This is your moment. You don't need more credentials—you need more conviction. The towel isn't glamorous. It doesn't go viral. But it transforms lives. Jesus didn't grab a crown when He had the chance—He grabbed a towel, knelt down, and changed the definition of greatness forever (John 13:12–17, NIV). That wasn't weakness. That was power under control. That was the Son of God teaching the future leaders of the Church what leadership truly looks like.

At Grand Canyon University, students are challenged to live out their calling by leading with "intentional service and Spirit-led discipline" (Colangelo, 2022). That's not just for the classroom—that's for every corner of culture. The world doesn't need louder leaders. It needs *lower* leaders—those willing to stoop so others can rise. The towel is more than a symbol. It's your strategy. Your signal. Your starting line. And your legacy begins the moment you pick it up.

SIDEBAR: It's Not Just a Towel—It's a Torch

- **Symbol of Surrender. Weapon of Revival.** The towel isn't just for cleaning feet. It's for building kingdoms.
- **Scripture Fuel:** *"Now that I, your Lord and Teacher, have washed your feet, you also should wash one another's feet."* — John 13:14 (NIV)

- **Legacy Leadership Insight:** "Greatness begins when leadership becomes service. The towel is the tool that changes the world." — Grand Canyon University, n.d.
- **Your Rally Cry:** Pick up the towel. Burn the excuses. Serve with fire.

Leading with Humility and Courage

"It takes a lion's heart to kneel like a servant. True leaders don't flex power—they carry it quietly, and unleash it when people need it most."

The Two Pillars of Real Leadership

The world loves to separate humility and courage—as if you have to choose between being kind or being bold. But servant leadership **doesn't divide those values—it marries them.** True greatness stands on **two legs: humility and courage.** Humility keeps you grounded. Courage keeps you moving. Together, they form the spine of every servant leader who refuses to bow to fear or bow up with pride.

Humility without courage becomes passivity. Courage without humility becomes arrogance. But together, these two pillars create a leadership posture that is both rooted and resolute. According to Grand Canyon University's Colangelo College of Business, "Servant leaders lead

CHAPTER 3: Servant Leadership in Action

from a position of strength—strength grounded in humility and exercised through bold, values-driven action" (Colangelo, 2022). These are not opposites; they are interdependent virtues that unlock influence in both the spiritual and professional realms.

Scripture is just as clear. In Joshua 1:9 (NIV), God commands, *"Be strong and courageous. Do not be afraid... for the Lord your God will be with you wherever you go."* And yet, Jesus models in Matthew 11:29 (NIV), *"I am gentle and humble in heart."* The servant leader integrates both realities—leading with fire in the soul and grace in the step. This synthesis is what separates servant leaders from power-hungry managers. One rules from above. The other leads from among. And only one builds a legacy that lasts.

SIDEBAR: The Strength of the Spine

- **Two Pillars. One Spine.**
  The strongest leaders aren't loud—they're anchored. Humility keeps you stable. Courage pushes you forward.
- **Spiritual Blueprint:**
  "God opposes the proud but shows favor to the humble...Humble yourselves, therefore, under God's mighty hand, that he may lift you up in due time." — 1 Peter 5:5–6 (NIV)
- **Academic Insight:**
  "Without courage, leadership is simply consensus. Without humility, it's tyranny. Servant

leadership requires both in constant tension." — (Greenleaf, 1977; Grand Canyon University, n.d.)
- **Leadership Challenge:**
Write down one way to practice boldness this week—and one way to practice humility. Then *do both.*

Humility Isn't Weakness—It's Unstoppable Strength

Let's get this straight: **humility is not weakness.** It's not self-doubt, and it's definitely not shrinking back. Humility is the decision to **put others first even when you could have taken the spotlight.** It's choosing to serve when you could dominate. Jesus, the Lion of Judah, knelt down with a towel and washed the feet of men who would betray Him. Tell me that's weakness. **That's fearless leadership.**

> *"Do nothing out of selfish ambition or vain conceit. Rather, in humility value others above yourselves."* — Philippians 2:3 (NIV)

Humility Builds Unshakable Trust

You want people to follow you? To believe in your mission? Then **drop the mask and lead with humility.** Humble leaders create space for others to grow. They don't hoard credit—they give it away. And in doing so, they build **cultures of trust** where people speak up, step

CHAPTER 3: Servant Leadership in Action

up, and show up. Arrogance builds fear. But **humility breeds loyalty.** Every time.

Trust isn't built through charisma—it's built through consistency and humility. As Patrick Lencioni explains in *The Five Dysfunctions of a Team*, trust is foundational to team success and only flourishes in environments where leaders are vulnerable and authentic (Lencioni, 2002). When leaders admit mistakes, ask for help, and celebrate others, they become relatable—not unreachable. Grand Canyon University teaches that "humility invites collaboration and fuels sustainable success," positioning servant leadership as the key to long-term influence (Grand Canyon University, n.d.).

Jesus embodied this perfectly. In John 13, the Son of God knelt down and washed His disciples' feet—not to be seen, but to serve. That moment wasn't just radical—it was revolutionary. It broke down fear and built up trust. If the Savior could lead from His knees, so can we. And when we do, we create a culture where people don't just follow the mission—they *own it*.

SIDEBAR: Trust Is the Currency. Humility Is the Bank.

- **Leadership Reminder:** People don't follow titles. They follow leaders who show up human.
- **Scripture for Strategy:**
  "Whoever exalts himself will be humbled, and whoever humbles himself will be exalted." — Matthew 23:12 (NIV)

- **Scholarly Insight:**
"Trust flourishes when leaders exhibit humility, admit limitations, and lead from authenticity." — (Lencioni, 2002; Grand Canyon University, n.d.)
- **Action Step:**
Ask your team: *What's one way I can serve you better?* Then listen—and act.

Courage Isn't Loud—It's Loyal

Courage is often misunderstood. It's not about being the loudest voice in the room or charging into every situation like a wrecking ball. **Courage is doing what's right even when it's terrifying.** It's standing for your values when the crowd wants compromise. It's protecting your people when they're under fire and having the tough conversations when everyone else runs. Courage isn't flash—it's **faithfulness in the fire.**

Loyal courage shows up when it's inconvenient, unglamorous, and often unnoticed. It shows up when a coach defends a struggling player, when a CEO refuses to cut corners, or when a teacher refuses to give up on the kid everyone else wrote off. Grand Canyon University defines this kind of courage as "leadership integrity"— the alignment between belief and behavior, even when it costs you (Colangelo, 2022). And Robert Greenleaf reminded us that the servant-leader must first choose to lead, and then choose again every day in small, faithful decisions—even under pressure (Greenleaf, 1977).

CHAPTER 3: Servant Leadership in Action

This isn't Hollywood courage. This is Kingdom courage. Joshua didn't shout his way into the Promised Land—he walked faithfully around Jericho until God moved. Jesus didn't storm Rome—He endured the cross. *This is the kind of courage that rewrites culture.* Quiet. Loyal. Unshakable. The kind of courage that builds a team, earns respect, and transforms a generation not with noise—but with unwavering conviction.

SIDEBAR: Courage Is What You Do When It Hurts

- **True Grit Check:**
  If courage only shows up when it's easy, it's not courage—it's convenience.
- **Scripture Fuel:**
  "Be strong and courageous. Do not be afraid… for the Lord your God will be with you wherever you go." — Joshua 1:9 (NIV)
- **Scholar's Voice:**
  "Leadership courage is quiet loyalty to what's right, regardless of applause." — Grand Canyon University, n.d.
- **Challenge:**
  Identify one moment this week where fear tried to win. Next time, meet it with loyalty—*not volume*.

Courage and Humility Together Change Everything

On their own, humility and courage are powerful. **Together? They're world-shaking.** Humility keeps your ego in check, while courage keeps your mission alive. Humility listens. Courage acts. Humility serves in silence. Courage speaks when silence becomes sin. The leaders who blend both are the ones who **shift cultures, restore teams, and build legacies that echo for generations.**

This is the leadership formula that built the early Church, transformed nations, and still turns toxic workplaces into thriving communities. Jesus didn't just model humility or courage—He embodied both simultaneously. He washed feet and confronted corruption. He wept with friends and walked straight toward crucifixion. This is what servant leadership demands: the willingness to serve when it's hard and to stand when it's costly. As Robert Greenleaf emphasized, servant leaders are "sharpened by self-awareness and grounded by a deep desire to grow others" (Greenleaf, 1977). At Grand Canyon University, students are taught that *integrating humility and courage is what enables leaders to build both performance and purpose, truth and trust* (Colangelo, 2022).

In Philippians 2:3–4 (NIV), Paul calls us to "Do nothing out of selfish ambition… Rather, in humility value others above yourselves… not looking to your own interests but each of you to the interests of the others." But just two verses later, we're reminded that Jesus *didn't just feel humble—He acted on it.* That's the key: humility without courage is incomplete. But when you lead with both, people don't just follow you—they're changed by you.

SIDEBAR: This Combo Changes the Game

- **Leadership Chemistry:**
  Humility without courage is silence. Courage without humility is noise. Together? They're transformation.
- **Scripture Surge:**
  "Your attitude should be the same as that of Christ Jesus..." — Philippians 2:5 (NIV)
- **Scholarly Reinforcement:**
  "Servant leadership is sustained when leaders are humble enough to listen and bold enough to lead." — Grand Canyon University, n.d.
- **Challenge This Week:**
  Before you speak, ask: *Am I grounded in humility? Am I moving with courage?* If the answer is yes to both—*go all in.*

Leadership Is Not About Being Liked—It's About Being Real

Servant leadership isn't for the faint of heart. You will face resistance. You will disappoint people. You will be misunderstood. But your job is not to **please everyone**—it's to **serve them well.** And sometimes that means saying the hard things. Drawing the hard lines. Making the sacrificial call. Humility lets you admit when you're wrong. Courage helps you stay the course when you're right.

Chasing approval is the fastest way to lose authority. If your goal is to be liked, you'll compromise your values every time pressure shows up. But if your goal is to be real—to be honest, anchored, and mission-first—you'll earn something far deeper than applause: you'll earn trust. Paul said it plainly in Galatians 1:10 (NIV): *"Am I now trying to win the approval of human beings, or of God? ... If I were still trying to please people, I would not be a servant of Christ."* Robert Greenleaf called this clarity of motive the "moral authority" that distinguishes true servant-leaders from title-holders (Greenleaf, 1977).

At Grand Canyon University, leadership training focuses on *authenticity over acceptance*—because only when you lead with integrity, even when it costs you relational comfort, do you create a culture built on truth (Grand Canyon University, n.d.). Leadership isn't performance. It's presence. And your legacy won't be defined by how many people liked you—it will be defined by how many people grew because you led with bold, humble truth.

SIDEBAR: Stop Performing. Start Leading.

- **Reality Check:**
  If everyone likes you, you're probably not leading—you're performing.

CHAPTER 3: Servant Leadership in Action

- **Scripture Reminder:**
  "Woe to you when everyone speaks well of you..." — Luke 6:26 (NIV)
- **Academic Insight:**
  "Authenticity is the anchor of servant leadership. Without it, influence becomes manipulation." — Grand Canyon University, n.d.
- **Leadership Action:**
  Stand for truth. Say the hard thing. Lead like someone who answers to heaven, not headlines.

The Greatest Leaders Lead from Their Knees

Think about this: Jesus didn't command the room by flexing divine power. He **stooped. He washed. He wept.** And He still changed the world. He led from His knees—because the most powerful position a leader can take is that of **a servant.** Want to win your people? Start by loving them. Want to inspire your team? Start by **carrying their burdens.** That's not soft. That's **supernatural leadership.**

Our culture chases influence from platforms, but Jesus built legacy from the floor. He wasn't afraid to kneel—because He knew that Kingdom power flows through humility. Philippians 2:8–9 (NIV) says, *"He humbled himself by becoming obedient to death—even death on a cross! Therefore God exalted him to the highest place..."* Jesus didn't lose His power by kneeling—He activated it.

That's the heart of servant leadership: leading low so others can rise high. As Robert Greenleaf wrote, *"The servant-leader is servant first... It begins with the natural feeling that one wants to serve, to serve first"* (Greenleaf, 1977). And at Grand Canyon University, future leaders are taught to *begin with posture, not position*—because transformation starts at ground level (Grand Canyon University, n.d.).

Leading from your knees isn't about weakness. It's about strategic submission to a higher calling. It's choosing to lead in a way that confuses the world but awakens the soul. In doing so, you not only reflect the heart of Christ—you ignite a fire in others to do the same. The most transformational leaders don't shout commands. They carry crosses.

SIDEBAR: Lower Is the Way Up

- **Symbolism:** Jesus didn't grab a microphone—He grabbed a towel. He didn't posture—He *lowered* Himself.
- **Scripture Thunder:** *"Whoever wants to become great among you must be your servant..."* — **Matthew 20:26 (NIV)**
- **Academic Insight:** "Servant leadership reflects Christ's model: humility, love, and purposeful sacrifice in pursuit of lasting change." — Grand Canyon University, n.d.
- **Challenge:** Kneel before you lead today. In prayer. In posture. In presence. Watch how heaven

honors it.

The Call: Kneel Lower. Stand Taller.

So, here's your challenge: **Lead with both.** Don't settle for false dichotomies—"tough or tender," "strong or soft," "leader or servant." Be **all of it.** Be humble enough to serve. Be courageous enough to lead. Kneel lower than you've ever knelt—and stand taller than you've ever stood. That's the paradox of Kingdom leadership. And that's the path that **only the boldest are willing to walk.**

Real Stories from Faith-Based Leaders and CEOs

The Chicken Sandwich and the Calling

In a southern city packed with competition and fast food giants, a quiet revolution began in a corporate headquarters that closed its doors every Sunday. The leader wasn't loud or flashy—but his vision was bold: **put people first, honor God, and serve with excellence.** He didn't just preach servant leadership—**he practiced it at the drive-thru.** Whether it was cleaning a bathroom himself or hand-writing thank-you notes to staff, he created a culture where every employee felt seen, valued, and empowered. And it paid off: customer loyalty skyrocketed, employee retention surged, and a fast food company became **a national model for purpose-driven success.**

This wasn't just a business strategy—it was a Kingdom assignment. Truett Cathy didn't build Chick-fil-A on marketing gimmicks or cutthroat tactics. He built it on the back of *Matthew 23:11* (NIV): *"The greatest among you will be your servant."* And the results speak for themselves. Chick-fil-A consistently leads the industry in customer satisfaction, employee happiness, and profitability per location. Why? Because they understand what Wall Street often forgets: when you value people over profit, profit becomes a byproduct of purpose. As Grand Canyon University affirms, *"Organizations thrive when their leaders cultivate environments that reflect human dignity, ethical stewardship, and Christ-centered excellence"* (Colangelo, 2022).

In the world of conscious capitalism, Chick-fil-A stands as a blueprint for companies who want to be both *legendary* and *righteous*. This brand didn't rise on trend— it rose on truth. It shows what happens when a leader lays down ego and lifts up others. As Greenleaf taught, "Good leaders must first become good servants" (Greenleaf, 1977). Cathy didn't just create a better restaurant. He modeled what it looks like when business becomes ministry—and when servant leadership moves from the pulpit to the profit sheet. This is the movement we're building. And this is the proof that it works.

CHAPTER 3: Servant Leadership in Action

A Luxury Brand Built on Human Dignity

Now imagine a man leading one of the most elite hotel brands in the world—a place where luxury reigns and customer expectations are sky-high. You'd expect a hard-nosed, cutthroat executive at the top, right? **Wrong.**
The founder walked the halls not to inspect, but to **inspire.** He greeted staff by name, treated every housekeeper like royalty, and demanded excellence—**not through fear, but through belief in their potential.**
He built a brand known for legendary service, not because of marketing, but because he **loved his people—and his people loved the mission.**
This wasn't management. This was **ministry with marble floors.**

That leader was Horst Schulze, co-founder of The Ritz-Carlton, who famously declared, *"We are not servants. We are ladies and gentlemen serving ladies and gentlemen."* His philosophy wasn't just branding—it was servant leadership in luxury. Schulze believed that dignity wasn't reserved for the guest; it was required for every team member. Under his leadership, The Ritz-Carlton became synonymous with service, loyalty, and world-class performance—not through hierarchy, but through humility. As Robert Greenleaf emphasized, "The servant-leader shares power, puts the needs of others first and helps people develop and perform as highly as possible" (Greenleaf, 1977). And Grand Canyon University reinforces this idea, teaching that *"leaders who cultivate human dignity as part of workplace culture create environments where excellence becomes natural and trust becomes currency"* (Grand Canyon University, n.d.).

Schulze's leadership proves a profound truth: dignity scales. Whether you're managing a five-star resort or running a neighborhood school, people thrive where they are valued. His success didn't come from transactional efficiency—it came from transformational care. Servant leadership, when integrated into every detail—from how you greet a team member to how you respond to failure—doesn't just build a brand. It builds a movement. A legacy. A culture people want to belong to and fight for. This is the future of business. This is the theology of excellence.

A Car Dealer Who Led Like a Pastor

In the auto industry, competition is cutthroat and profit often trumps people. But not for one CEO who ran his dealership group like a church. He rejected the standard pressure-cooker culture and instead created an environment of **respect, generosity, and second chances.**

Employees received career coaching, financial literacy classes, and even sabbaticals. He refused to open on Sundays—not because of policy, but because of **conviction.**

And despite the odds, his company became one of the most successful regional auto groups in America. Why? Because **he knew that when you care for people,**

CHAPTER 3: Servant Leadership in Action

people care about your mission.

This wasn't soft leadership—it was sacred leadership. This CEO understood that creating a business grounded in dignity, purpose, and stewardship isn't just a faith decision—it's a strategic one. Colossians 3:23 (NIV) says, *"Whatever you do, work at it with all your heart, as working for the Lord, not for human masters."* That's what this leader modeled: building a workplace where people didn't just clock in—they came alive. Robert Greenleaf called this *"servant-first leadership"*, the kind that nurtures people into becoming "healthier, wiser, freer, and more autonomous" (Greenleaf, 1977). Grand Canyon University reinforces this framework in its business curriculum, asserting that *"Christ-centered business practices lead to both human flourishing and institutional excellence"* (Grand Canyon University, n.d.).

By putting ministry before margins, this leader didn't just retain talent—he transformed lives. He redefined success in an industry known for burnout, and in doing so, proved that servant leadership isn't limited by sector—it's powered by soul. The dealership became more than a place to buy cars. It became a place to rebuild lives. That's what happens when you lead like a pastor and manage like a Kingdom builder.

Giving It All Back

Then there's the business owner who gave most of his wealth away before retirement—not as a PR stunt, but as

a **response to a divine calling.**
He believed his company didn't belong to him; it belonged to God. So he lived modestly, capped his salary, and reinvested his success into **global missions, community development, and employee well-being.** He turned his financial stewardship into a **faithful testimony**—not just of business done right, but of business done **righteously.**
He didn't need a stage to preach—**his company was his pulpit.**

This kind of radical generosity is what Robert Greenleaf described as the ultimate outflow of servant leadership: *"The servant-leader always puts others' highest priority needs first. The best test... is: do those served grow as persons?"* (Greenleaf, 1977). This leader's legacy wasn't built on quarterly earnings—it was built on eternal investments. His profits didn't terminate on himself—they multiplied through global impact. As Grand Canyon University teaches, *"Kingdom-minded business owners see their wealth as a resource for transformation, not accumulation"* (Colangelo, 2022). Proverbs 11:25 (NIV) reinforces this truth: *"A generous person will prosper; whoever refreshes others will be refreshed."*

He showed us that business can be a vessel of worship. That you can write paychecks and still preach the gospel. That it's possible to lead in such a way that boardrooms become mission fields and spreadsheets become stories of redemption. Giving back wasn't the end of his journey—it was the evidence that he had led with God at

CHAPTER 3: Servant Leadership in Action

the center the entire time. His obedience spoke louder than any keynote ever could.

When Profit Meets Purpose

These stories all share a common thread: servant leadership isn't just morally right—it's **strategically brilliant.**
These leaders didn't sacrifice results for relationships— they **amplified results by valuing relationships.** Their courage to lead with faith, compassion, and humility didn't weaken performance—it fueled it. Revenue grew. Culture deepened. Impact exploded. **Because when you put people first, everything else follows.**

Decades of research affirm what scripture and experience have shown all along: when purpose drives profit, the result is sustainable, values-aligned growth. Jim Collins, in *Good to Great*, emphasized that organizations led by Level 5 leaders—those marked by deep humility and fierce resolve—consistently outperformed their peers (Collins, 2001). Robert Greenleaf argued that servant-leaders develop "the capacity to create institutions that serve," embedding human dignity into the very DNA of a business (Greenleaf, 1977). Grand Canyon University extends this framework by teaching that *"faith-informed leadership is not just a theological approach—it's a catalyst for lasting excellence and resilient organizations"* (Grand Canyon University, n.d.).

Servant-led companies do more than compete—they transform. Studies have shown that companies built on trust, empathy, and empowerment outperform others in innovation, employee engagement, and long-term profitability (Liden et al., 2008). This is the model conscious capitalism advances: stakeholder value over shareholder dominance, long-term purpose over short-term wins. When leaders connect their bottom line to their higher calling, what emerges is not just organizational performance—but cultural renewal. This is where Kingdom values and business brilliance collide—and the results speak for themselves.

My Story in the Trenches

I've been in the workforce since I was fifteen. I've had bosses who thought their title made them divine—**who screamed, belittled, and crushed creativity like it was a threat to their ego.**
It made work feel like war. It drained people of their purpose. **Burnout was the currency of that culture.** But I've also seen what happens when a leader steps in—not with arrogance, but with heart. When a leader picks up the towel instead of the megaphone, **hope starts to grow.** That's the kind of leader I want to be. That's the kind of leader this world desperately needs.

CHAPTER 3: Servant Leadership in Action

Servant Leadership Is Already Winning

These aren't theories from a seminary classroom or fluffy ideas from a self-help book. These are **battle-tested principles** being lived out in real companies, with real pressure, and real bottom lines.
These men and women **built empires without sacrificing their souls.**
They didn't silence their faith—they led through it.
They didn't climb ladders over people—they lifted others **as they climbed.**
And in doing so, they proved that **servant leadership isn't just a good idea—it's the only leadership worth following.**

The data supports what these stories declare: servant leadership creates high-performance environments built on trust, purpose, and resilience. According to Liden et al. (2008), organizations that adopt servant leadership experience higher employee satisfaction, stronger team collaboration, and improved financial outcomes. That's not conjecture—it's empirical truth. Robert Greenleaf's vision is no longer fringe theory; it's boardroom strategy. At Grand Canyon University, students are trained to understand that *servant leadership is not simply a moral choice—it's a market advantage fueled by Kingdom character* (Grand Canyon University, n.d.). These leaders don't conform to a secular mold of success—they redefine it by leading from within, driven by mission and guided by moral conviction.

This leadership model is already shaping the future. From Wall Street to warehouses, classrooms to clinics, faith-driven and purpose-centered leaders are reshaping what success looks like. And they're not just surviving—they're *thriving*. Culture is shifting. The old models are cracking. The world is waking up to what Jesus taught all along: *"Whoever wants to become great among you must be your servant"* (Matthew 20:26, NIV). This isn't a trend. It's a takeover. And it's happening now.

This Is YOUR Moment

So what's holding you back? If God can use a fast food chain, a luxury hotel, a car dealership, and a crane company to transform lives—**He can use you.**
You don't have to be famous. You don't have to be perfect.
You just have to be **willing.**
Because when faith and leadership collide with service and courage, **a movement is born.** And right now—*this* is your invitation to lead like that.

You've read the evidence. You've heard the stories. Now it's your turn to pick up the towel, plant your flag, and go make impact. As 2 Timothy 1:7 (NIV) reminds us, *"For the Spirit God gave us does not make us timid, but gives us power, love and self-discipline."* Grand Canyon University echoes this by stating that *"faith-informed leaders are not passive—they are bold, wise, and deeply others-centered"* (Colangelo, 2022). You are called to lead with your sleeves rolled up, your heart on fire, and your feet

CHAPTER 3: Servant Leadership in Action

firmly planted in purpose. The movement doesn't start when you get the title—it starts when you *decide to lead anyway*.

This is your moment—not someday. Not after your next promotion. Not when you feel "ready." Now. The world is watching, heaven is cheering, and your legacy is on the line. Lead like Jesus. Serve with boldness. And go build something that lasts.

Challenges Faced and Victories Won

> "The fiercest battles shape the strongest leaders—and the scars you carry become the stories that set others free."

The Cross Before the Crown. Every servant leader will face resistance—**that's not a possibility, it's a promise.** When you lead with humility in a pride-driven world, you will be misunderstood.
You'll be told you're not strong enough, bold enough, or cutthroat enough to succeed. **But you don't serve to be understood—you serve because it's right.**
Jesus faced resistance every time He chose compassion over condemnation, service over self-promotion. If He carried a cross before wearing a crown, **so will we.**

Resistance is the proving ground of servant leadership. According to Greenleaf (1977), true servant leaders are *"initiated by challenge and sustained through sacrifice,"* because they lead not for applause, but for impact. This is not weakness—it is resilient strength formed in the fire of rejection, setbacks, and scrutiny. Research from Grand Canyon University emphasizes that *"resistance to servant leadership often emerges in environments where hierarchy, ego, and fear dominate—but those who persist build cultures of lasting trust, growth, and performance"* (Colangelo, 2022). Servant leaders may not rise fastest, but they rise with the most loyalty behind them— because they've been refined by adversity, not shaped by approval.

And isn't that the pattern of the Kingdom? *"If anyone would come after me, he must deny himself, take up his cross daily and follow me"* (Luke 9:23, NIV). This isn't just spiritual metaphor—it's a leadership roadmap. The crown may be your calling, but the cross is your curriculum. Every betrayal, every sacrifice, every misunderstood decision becomes a chapter in your leadership story. And the ones who stay faithful in the pain are the ones trusted with the platform. Because when you lead from the cross, you don't just gain influence—you model the very essence of Christ.

Servant Leaders Get Hit Hard—But They Don't Break

One CEO told his board he was cutting executive bonuses to invest more in his entry-level employees. The

CHAPTER 3: Servant Leadership in Action

backlash was instant. Investors threatened to pull out. Industry peers mocked him.

But he stood his ground, believing that investing in people would return greater dividends than padding the C-suite. Five years later? Retention was up. Productivity was at record highs. Profits surged. **Vision proved victorious.**

Servant leaders absorb impact others avoid. They get hit hard because they dare to challenge the status quo. But what separates them isn't protection—it's perseverance. Research affirms that leaders who remain consistent in their values—even under pressure—earn deeper trust and build stronger organizational cultures over time (Liden et al., 2008). Robert Greenleaf wrote that *"the ultimate test of a servant-leader is whether the people served grow as persons"* (Greenleaf, 1977). That growth often comes with pushback. Grand Canyon University teaches that *"leaders must be prepared to navigate resistance with moral clarity and emotional resilience—because servant leadership demands both conviction and compassion in conflict"* (Colangelo, 2022).

When others fold to fear, servant leaders rise in faith. Their decisions may cost them in the short-term, but the long-term dividends are undeniable. They're the ones who walk through criticism and come out refined. The ones who carry the weight, take the hits, and still keep loving their people. Like Nehemiah rebuilding a wall with one hand and defending with the other, they refuse to stop serving—even while under fire. Because they know: *God doesn't waste a battle that's fought with integrity.*

The Cost of Courage

Servant leaders often pay a high price for choosing integrity over shortcuts. One leader refused to bend during a compliance issue that could have saved millions by staying silent.

He lost key clients. His company faced public scrutiny. His board nearly replaced him.

But he stayed true. And because he refused to compromise, **his credibility grew**, new partnerships emerged, and his company became **a model of ethical excellence.**

Sometimes standing for something means you stand alone—**but in time, the crowd follows character.**

The cost of courage is real—and often immediate. But so is the reward. Research on ethical leadership confirms that companies led by morally courageous leaders develop stronger reputations, deeper internal trust, and more sustainable long-term performance (Brown & Treviño, 2006). Greenleaf argued that servant leaders must be *"firm in their values, even when the cost is personal"* (Greenleaf, 1977). Grand Canyon University prepares students to lead in this exact tension, teaching that *"biblically rooted leadership prioritizes integrity over popularity, conviction over convenience"* (Colangelo, 2022). These moments of costly decision-making become crucibles—refining the leader and elevating the organization.

As Proverbs 10:9 (NIV) reminds us, *"Whoever walks in*

CHAPTER 3: Servant Leadership in Action

integrity walks securely, but whoever takes crooked paths will be found out." Servant leaders may lose deals, clients, or favor in the moment—but they gain something money can't buy: unshakable credibility. And in the long arc of leadership, it's integrity that draws the right partners, inspires loyalty, and earns the respect that flash and power never could. That's the price—and the prize—of courageous leadership.

Turning Betrayal into Breakthrough

One story tells of a school leader who poured into her staff—mentoring, developing, and empowering them—only to have one of her protégés undercut her for a promotion.
The pain was deep. But instead of retaliating, she coached that person through the role—even when it meant sacrificing recognition.
Her influence only deepened. Her team watched and learned: *this is what greatness looks like.*
Years later, that former rival became her biggest ally—and said, *"You changed the way I lead because you didn't fight me. You served me."*
Victory doesn't always come in applause—it comes in legacy.

Betrayal is one of the most emotionally volatile leadership challenges, yet servant leaders see it not as a curse—but as a classroom. Leadership expert Patrick Lencioni emphasizes that *vulnerability and trust are the glue of effective teams,* but they only hold when a leader chooses grace over vengeance (Lencioni, 2002). Robert Greenleaf called this *"healing leadership,"* noting that true servant leaders respond to betrayal not by escalating conflict, but by modeling reconciliation and inner strength (Greenleaf, 1977). Grand Canyon University affirms this principle, teaching that *"Kingdom-minded leaders treat betrayal as an invitation to elevate character, not diminish it"* (Colangelo, 2022). These leaders aren't passive—they're principled. And by refusing to mirror broken behavior, they elevate the standard for everyone watching.

When Jesus was betrayed by Judas, He didn't curse him—He called him "friend" (Matthew 26:50, NIV). That wasn't weakness. That was unstoppable authority—choosing grace under pressure. Servant leaders today are invited into that same response: to lead in the wounds, to serve those who slander, and to transform betrayal into breakthrough. Because when legacy is the goal, the battle isn't for control—it's for character.

The Battle of Burnout

Let's be real—serving others can be exhausting. When you carry your team's burdens, their pain can wear on your soul.
Servant leaders sometimes feel **invisible, underappreciated, or alone** in the fight. But those who endure find strength in the deeper calling.
Because this isn't about ego—it's about impact. The burnout that comes from **serving purpose** is still real,

CHAPTER 3: Servant Leadership in Action

but it's redeemed.

As Scripture says, *"Let us not grow weary in doing good, for at the proper time we will reap a harvest if we do not give up."* (Galatians 6:9 NIV).

Burnout is not a sign of failure—it's a signal that your capacity needs to be realigned with your calling. Academic research shows that while servant leaders often experience emotional labor, they also report higher levels of meaning, motivation, and long-term resilience than authoritarian counterparts (Eva et al., 2019). Robert Greenleaf understood this when he wrote that the servant-leader must *"withdraw and renew,"* recognizing that periods of solitude, reflection, and spiritual re-centering are vital for sustained influence (Greenleaf, 1977). At Grand Canyon University, students are taught to lead from overflow—not depletion—by anchoring their identity in Christ, practicing rhythms of rest, and embracing the biblical principle of Sabbath as both leadership wisdom and personal necessity (Colangelo, 2022).

You may feel weary, but you're not weak. The weight you're carrying is proof of what you're building. And when you lead with eternity in mind, even the fatigue becomes holy ground. Because in God's economy, nothing poured out in service is ever wasted. The battle of burnout isn't won by pushing harder—it's won by *refueling smarter* and remembering who you're really serving.

The Vindication of Vision

Many servant leaders are mocked in the early years. They're told their teams are "too soft" or "too idealistic." But time has a way of revealing the truth. One nonprofit leader was ridiculed for prioritizing values over rapid growth. She turned down funding from toxic partners and stayed small when everyone told her to scale.
But in five years, she had more impact, more loyal donors, and a stronger foundation than those who chased growth at the cost of their soul.
Her victory wasn't loud—but it was lasting.

Vision grounded in values is rarely rewarded immediately—but it is always vindicated over time. Business research confirms that organizations led by ethical, people-first principles enjoy stronger stakeholder trust, longer employee retention, and deeper brand loyalty (Sisodia et al., 2014). Robert Greenleaf saw this in action, writing that *"the servant-leader's vision must be one that endures—not one that dazzles temporarily and fades under scrutiny"* (Greenleaf, 1977). Grand Canyon University frames this as "Christ-centered strategy"—a model that sacrifices speed for sustainability, and volume for virtue (Colangelo, 2022). The world often applauds what's fast and flashy—but history honors what's faithful. And in God's timing, a vision that was once mocked becomes the new standard others strive to emulate.

"Though it linger, wait for it; it will certainly come and will

CHAPTER 3: Servant Leadership in Action

not delay." (Habakkuk 2:3, NIV). That's what vindication looks like—not a viral moment, but a generational movement. The leaders who hold the line through mockery, setbacks, and loneliness are the ones who leave legacies built not on applause, but on alignment—with truth, with purpose, and with God.

The Rewards You Can't Quantify

The victories of servant leadership can't always be measured in spreadsheets. They show up in stories: a single mom promoted to manager because someone believed in her.
A high school student who stayed out of trouble because their coach listened. A team that gave their all because their leader didn't just see them as workers—but as **people with purpose.**
These victories may not make headlines. But they **echo through lives**, and ripple across generations.
Servant leadership creates more than results—it creates resurrection.

Robert Greenleaf reminded us that *"the secret of servant leadership is in the intangible... the growth, the healing, and the wholeness of the people served"* (Greenleaf, 1977). These wins may never boost a quarterly report, but they transform families, communities, and legacies. Grand Canyon University defines this as *Kingdom impact*—where success is not only measured in revenue, but in redemption (Colangelo, 2022). Scholarly studies affirm this: organizations that prioritize empathy, development, and relational leadership generate higher long-term engagement and cultural stability (Liden et al., 2008). What begins as unseen influence often becomes the anchor of lasting transformation.

The best leaders won't be remembered by the number of deals closed or titles earned—but by the lives they restored and the hope they sparked. *"Well done, good and faithful servant"* (Matthew 25:21, NIV) is the only applause that truly matters. Servant leadership leaves a legacy no ledger can hold—a legacy written in people, not profit.

The Fire Refines the Faithful

So yes, servant leadership is hard. It will test your patience, shake your resolve, and stretch your soul. But it will also **forge your legacy in fire.** The very challenges meant to break you will become the proving ground of your calling.
Because on the other side of every challenge is a deeper level of trust, influence, and impact that can only be earned—not taken.
The world needs leaders who have **walked through the fire and came out shining—**not because they demanded power, but because they stayed faithful to purpose.
And that leader, my friend? **Is you.**

This isn't comfort-zone leadership—it's crucible leadership. The fire is God's workshop, where He shapes

CHAPTER 3: Servant Leadership in Action

grit into grace and trials into testimony. Scripture says, *"When you pass through the waters, I will be with you... when you walk through the fire, you will not be burned; the flames will not set you ablaze"* (Isaiah 43:2, NIV). Robert Greenleaf understood this refinement well, writing that the servant-leader *"must experience trial as the initiator of growth, becoming a model of perseverance for the ones they lead"* (Greenleaf, 1977). Grand Canyon University reinforces this in its leadership model: *"Faithful leaders become fire-tested agents of transformation, grounded not in ease, but in endurance"* (Colangelo, 2022).

Research confirms that resilient leadership—especially servant leadership forged under pressure—results in higher team loyalty, long-term performance, and transformational culture (Hunter et al., 2013). But beyond the data lies destiny. The fire you're in isn't there to consume you—it's there to *commission* you. It's carving the kind of leader the world can't manufacture: one forged in truth, anchored in love, and unshakable in purpose. This is the kind of leadership heaven backs. And it's your time to rise from the furnace—not bitter, but blazing.

The Divine Blueprint for Leadership

Micah 6:8 is not a suggestion—it's a **summons**. "He has shown you, O mortal, what is good. And what does the Lord require of you? To act justly and to love mercy and to walk humbly with your God."

The Greatest Among You

That is **God's three-fold leadership model**—Justice. Mercy. Humility.
Not ambition. Not dominance. Not manipulation.
The world may chase charisma and image, but God demands **character and compassion.** If you want to lead in His name, this is your roadmap.

These aren't abstract values—they're action codes. To *act justly* means to align decisions with righteousness, truth, and the moral courage to stand even when it costs you. To *love mercy* means to lead with empathy, grace, and forgiveness—not because it's easy, but because it's Christlike. And to *walk humbly with your God* means to stay anchored in purpose, submitted in prayer, and free from ego. Robert Greenleaf's framework echoes this divine sequence: servant leadership begins with character, advances through care, and culminates in wisdom-guided influence (Greenleaf, 1977). Grand Canyon University reinforces this mandate, teaching that *"authentic leadership starts not with charisma, but with a Christ-modeled inner life that shapes how we lead outwardly"* (Colangelo, 2022).

This verse isn't just personal—it's organizational. Build a business, a team, or a school on these three values, and you'll create a culture heaven can bless. The divine blueprint isn't outdated—it's unmatched. And it's not about perfection—it's about posture. When justice, mercy, and humility govern your leadership, you don't just build systems—you build *sacred influence*.

Act Justly: Leading With Righteous Conviction

To "act justly" means to **lead with courage and moral clarity**—to stand up for what's right even when it costs you.
Justice isn't just about systems—it's about **every daily decision.** It's how you treat your team when no one is watching. It's how you allocate resources.
It's refusing to sacrifice people for profit. Servant leaders act justly not to earn favor, but because they know they are **stewards of the King's authority**, not owners of it.

Justice in leadership means building environments where truth is honored, equity is pursued, and power is used to uplift, not to oppress. In Proverbs 21:3 (NIV), we're reminded: *"To do what is right and just is more acceptable to the Lord than sacrifice."* Robert Greenleaf framed this pursuit as the call to use influence to *"serve the highest needs of others,"* particularly the marginalized and voiceless (Greenleaf, 1977). Grand Canyon University teaches that *acting justly requires alignment between spiritual identity and strategic execution,* where biblical ethics guide every budget, hiring choice, and policy (Colangelo, 2022). Justice is not a political stance—it's a Kingdom principle. It is a reflection of the heart of God and a non-negotiable for those who lead in His name.

When leaders act justly, they create organizations that

carry a moral spine and a sacred mission. They reject favoritism, root out toxicity, and make hard calls—not because it's popular, but because it's right. That's righteous conviction. That's how leaders become builders of cultures that don't just work—but worship.

Love Mercy: Lead With Grace, Not Guilt

The second command—"love mercy"—is a thunderclap of compassion in a leadership world gone cold. We've all seen leaders who punish mistakes, crush innovation, and see empathy as weakness. But God says, **"love mercy."** Not tolerate it—**love it.**
Real servant leaders are quick to forgive, quick to restore, and relentless in lifting others up.
Grace doesn't make teams lazy. It makes them loyal. When your people know you love mercy, they'll **walk through fire for you.**

Mercy-centered leadership is not about being soft—it's about being spiritually secure. In James 2:13 (NIV), we're told, *"Mercy triumphs over judgment."* This isn't just theology—it's strategy. Robert Greenleaf emphasized the leader's role as a healer: *"There is something subtle communicated to one who is being served and led if, implicit in the compact between servant-leader and led, is the understanding that the search for wholeness is something they share."* (Greenleaf, 1977). Grand Canyon University builds on this truth, teaching that *grace-driven cultures produce emotionally intelligent, highly resilient teams rooted in mutual respect and restoration* (Colangelo, 2022). When a leader chooses mercy, it doesn't erase accountability—it elevates humanity.

Mercy rewrites culture. It gives space for growth. It sets a new tone where people don't fear failure—they find freedom to rise again. The greatest leaders lead from a place of redeemed experience, not unreachable perfection. And when you lead with mercy in your mouth and grace in your hands, you don't just develop employees—you awaken purpose.

Walk Humbly With Your God: The Posture of True Greatness

And then comes the core—"walk humbly with your God." Not sprint ahead. Not stand over. Not drag behind. **Walk humbly**—step by step, in rhythm with the Spirit.
This is where **ego dies and purpose lives.**
Servant leadership isn't about being the loudest—it's about being the most **aligned** with the One who called you.
Humility isn't weakness—it's a **weapon** that disarms pride, elevates others, and makes space for divine power to move through you.

In Philippians 2:5–7 (NIV), Paul writes, *"In your relationships with one another, have the same mindset as Christ Jesus... who made himself nothing by taking the very nature of a servant."* This is the heartbeat of servant leadership: divine authority expressed through radical humility. Greenleaf taught that servant leaders "strive to be servants first," and it is in that posture—knees down, hands open—that their greatest strength emerges (Greenleaf, 1977). Grand Canyon University calls this "kingdom-calibrated leadership," where daily decisions are shaped not by self-interest, but by spiritual obedience (Colangelo, 2022). Walking humbly means your leadership isn't driven by outcomes—it's guided by presence. It's not about keeping control; it's about keeping in step with Christ.

When you walk humbly with God, you stop performing and start transforming. You make room for wisdom, discernment, and supernatural impact that human strategy can't replicate. The posture of humility is the launchpad for Kingdom authority. And the leaders who bend low enough to follow God? They're the ones God trusts to lead others high.

Shepherd the Flock—Not Dominate the People

Now let's go to 1 Peter 5:2–3: "Be shepherds of God's flock that is under your care, watching over them—not because you must, but because you are willing... not lording it over those entrusted to you, but being examples to the flock."
This verse is a **divine smackdown on toxic leadership.**

CHAPTER 3: Servant Leadership in Action

It doesn't say *dominate* the flock. It says *shepherd* them. Lead by **willingness, not obligation. By example, not by force.**
Servant leaders don't just manage tasks—they **guide souls.**

This isn't a leadership suggestion—it's a sacred commission. True servant leadership flows from a heart posture of care, not control. Greenleaf warned that domination breaks trust and produces fear, while servant leadership invites growth and builds legacy (Greenleaf, 1977). Grand Canyon University echoes this truth: *"Biblical leadership rejects coercion and instead embraces discipleship—forming people through relational guidance, not positional power"* (Colangelo, 2022). To shepherd is to feed, to protect, to pursue, and to stay present—even when it's inconvenient. It's not about titles or performance—it's about spiritual stewardship. Leaders who shepherd well don't just run organizations—they build people into who God created them to be.

Willing Hearts Win the War

Notice Peter says, "not because you must, but because you are willing."
The Kingdom doesn't need reluctant rulers. It needs **radical servants.**
Your title means nothing if your heart isn't in it. The greatest influence doesn't come from being placed in authority—it comes from **choosing to lead with love.**

Willing leaders change the world because they choose to care **when it's hard, thankless, and inconvenient.** That's servant leadership.

Willingness is the difference between obligation and obedience. It's what transforms leadership from duty into destiny. Jesus said in John 10:18 (NIV), *"No one takes it from me, but I lay it down of my own accord."* That's not passive submission—it's *voluntary surrender with unstoppable authority.* Greenleaf saw this willingness as the essence of servant leadership: *"The servant-leader is servant first... it begins with the natural feeling that one wants to serve, to serve first"* (Greenleaf, 1977). Grand Canyon University frames this as *"calling-informed leadership,"* where internal motivation driven by love, faith, and purpose outweighs any external pressure to perform (Colangelo, 2022). The war is not won by those who are told to lead—but by those who *choose* to. Every time you choose to love, forgive, show up, or sacrifice—especially when you don't have to—you declare spiritual war against pride, indifference, and control.

Willing leaders don't wait to be crowned—they go to battle. Not for glory. Not for gain. But because they *can't not care*. And in the Kingdom, *that* is where the real power flows.

Leadership Without Lording

Peter also says, "not lording it over those entrusted to you."

CHAPTER 3: Servant Leadership in Action

That hits HARD in today's power-hungry culture.
Too many bosses operate like tyrants in suits, treating people like pawns instead of souls. But God's Word rebukes that model and raises the standard: **don't lord—lead.**
Don't intimidate—**inspire.**
If Jesus, the Lord of Heaven, knelt down to serve… what excuse does any of us have to be prideful? True leaders **kneel before they lead.**

Jesus Himself said in Matthew 20:25–28 (NIV), *"The rulers of the Gentiles lord it over them… Not so with you. Instead, whoever wants to become great among you must be your servant."* That's not a metaphor—it's a manifesto. Robert Greenleaf echoed it when he wrote that *"authority should flow from moral stature, not positional status"* (Greenleaf, 1977). Grand Canyon University teaches that *"spiritual leadership does not dominate; it disciples—elevating others through influence anchored in humility, not hierarchy"* (Colangelo, 2022). This means leaders must confront the temptation to lead through fear, ego, or control. Power without purpose corrodes the soul. But when leadership flows from submission to Christ, it becomes a tool for transformation—not tyranny.

To those entrusted with influence: your people don't need a boss—they need a shepherd. They don't need your ego—they need your example. And when you stop lording and start leading, your team won't just comply—they'll *commit*.

Set the Example, Ignite the Movement

Peter ends by saying, "being examples to the flock." That's your call. Not to coerce, but to **embody.**
Servant leadership isn't taught first—it's **caught** through consistent example.
Your people are watching. Your family is watching. Your community is watching.
And when they see a leader who acts justly, loves mercy, walks humbly, leads willingly, shepherds gently, and lives what they preach?
They'll follow—not because they have to, but because **they believe.**

Paul told Timothy, *"Set an example for the believers in speech, in conduct, in love, in faith and in purity"* (1 Timothy 4:12, NIV). This is how movements begin—not with microphones, but with models. Greenleaf wrote that *"the servant-leader must be the example of what they wish to cultivate in others. Without that, leadership becomes hypocrisy."* (Greenleaf, 1977). Grand Canyon University affirms this in its servant leadership framework: *"Leadership impact is maximized when values are visibly lived—not just declared"* (Colangelo, 2022). Your leadership is either building trust or eroding it, every single day. But when people see a leader who doesn't need a spotlight because they're lit from within— *they follow, they grow, and they multiply.*

CHAPTER 3: Servant Leadership in Action

Legacy doesn't start when you retire—it starts the moment your example becomes someone else's inspiration. Be the leader who doesn't just deliver results—be the leader who births *revival*.

> *"He has shown you... act justly, love mercy, walk humbly."* — Micah 6:8
> *"Be shepherds... not lording it over... but being examples to the flock."* — 1 Peter 5:2–3 (NIV)

7-DAY SERVANT LEADERSHIP ACTION CHALLENGE

Theme: *Lead With the Towel, Not the Title.*

Each day includes:

- **Core Principle**
- **Scripture Fuel**
- **Challenge Task**
- **Reflection Prompt**

Day 1: The Towel Test

The Greatest Among You

Core Principle: Leadership starts with service.
Scripture Fuel: *"Now that I, your Lord and Teacher, have washed your feet, you also should wash one another's feet."* — John 13:14 (NIV)
Challenge Task: Do something today that's "beneath" your title—something inconvenient, unglamorous, or unnoticed. Clean, carry, help—whatever it is, serve someone without being asked.
Reflection Prompt: How did it feel to lead without credit? Who benefited from your presence?

Day 2: Power Down, Purpose Up

Core Principle: Influence doesn't come from control—it comes from presence.
Scripture Fuel: *"Not lording it over... but being examples to the flock."* — 1 Peter 5:3 (NIV)
Challenge Task: Identify one area where you've used authority to control. Release it. Empower someone else to lead.
Reflection Prompt: What happened when you chose influence over instruction? How did your team respond?

Day 3: Start Lower

Core Principle: Legacy begins on your knees.

CHAPTER 3: Servant Leadership in Action

Scripture Fuel: *"Whoever wants to become great among you must be your servant."* — Matthew 20:26 (NIV)
Challenge Task: Begin your day in prayer for your team. Then write a handwritten note or send a personal message to encourage someone who needs it.
Reflection Prompt: What shifted when you lowered yourself for someone else's sake?

Day 4: Lead the Way (By Living It)

Core Principle: What you live is louder than what you say.
Scripture Fuel: *"Set an example for the believers in speech, in conduct, in love..."* — 1 Timothy 4:12 (NIV)
Challenge Task: Model the values you preach. Identify one area where your actions haven't matched your message—and align them.
Reflection Prompt: Where was the gap between your values and your actions—and how did bridging that gap inspire those around you?

Day 5: Courage in the Quiet

Core Principle: You don't need a stage to lead.
Scripture Fuel: *"Be strong and courageous... the Lord your God will be with you."* — Joshua 1:9 (NIV)

Challenge Task: Have a hard conversation you've been avoiding—speak truth in love.
Reflection Prompt: How did your courage open doors for restoration, respect, or change?

Day 6: Mercy Over Metrics

Core Principle: Grace creates growth.
Scripture Fuel: *"Mercy triumphs over judgment."* — James 2:13 (NIV)
Challenge Task: Identify someone who failed or fell short—and show them grace instead of judgment. Encourage their growth.
Reflection Prompt: How did showing mercy build deeper trust? What fruit could come from that moment?

Day 7: The Tipping Point

Core Principle: Revival starts with your example.
Scripture Fuel: *"Whatever you do, work at it with all your heart..."* — Colossians 3:23 (NIV)
Challenge Task: Ask this to someone you lead: *"How can I serve you better?"* Then act on their answer.
Reflection Prompt: What did you learn from listening? What would your team say if someone asked, "What kind of leader are they?"

CHAPTER 3: Servant Leadership in Action

Final Call to Action:

Burn the script. Pick up the towel. Lead with fire and humility. The movement starts with you.

The Greatest Among You

CHAPTER 4: Servant Leadership and Organizational Culture

"Culture eats strategy for breakfast." —Peter Drucker

Culture Isn't a Perk—It's the Pulse

You don't have to hang motivational posters on the wall to have a culture.
You already have one. The only question is—**is it healthy or is it toxic?**
Culture is the invisible current that shapes every meeting, every decision, every conversation. It's not what leaders say—it's what leaders **tolerate**, what they **celebrate**, and what they **repeat**.
Servant leadership recognizes that culture isn't formed by accident—it's **crafted with intention.** And when that intention is rooted in love, humility, and purpose? **Everything changes.**

Culture doesn't wait for your permission—it flows from your presence. Every eye roll left unchallenged, every toxic behavior excused for performance, every policy that contradicts your values silently broadcasts your real priorities. As Harvard Business School has long emphasized, culture eats strategy for breakfast—not because strategy doesn't matter, but because culture determines how strategy lives or dies in the hands of your people. Servant leadership shifts the cultural center of gravity from self-preservation to shared purpose. It aligns authority with authenticity, power with presence, and success with service. This isn't optional—it's operational. You can't compartmentalize Christlike leadership and expect a unified culture. If culture is the pulse, then the leader is either its pacemaker or its pathology.

In elite organizations, culture isn't an afterthought—it's architecture. It's the intentional scaffolding of norms, narratives, and non-negotiables that direct behavior long after the meeting ends. Servant leaders engineer culture by designing rituals that reinforce values, hiring and firing based on fit over flash, and publicly celebrating the unseen actions that reflect the mission. According to Greenleaf's foundational work, culture is sustained not by declarations, but by *devotion*—daily, deliberate choices to prioritize people over politics, and mission over metrics. Grand Canyon University reinforces this by teaching that "faith-informed culture formation requires alignment between spiritual identity and structural clarity" (Colangelo, 2022). Great cultures don't happen by chance. They are forged by leaders who understand that the pulse of their team is the prophecy of their future.

CHAPTER 4: Servant Leadership and Organizational Culture

Leaders Are the Thermostat, Not the Thermometer

Most leaders simply reflect the culture around them—they adapt, compromise, or conform to keep the peace. But servant leaders don't reflect—they **set the temperature.**
They're thermostats, not thermometers.
They determine the emotional climate by how they respond to pressure, how they treat people when it's inconvenient, and how they correct course when things go sideways.
They know that **whatever is allowed becomes the culture**, and whatever is repeated becomes the norm. So they step up, speak out, and set the tone for love, truth, and excellence.

Thermostatic leadership is the act of cultural calibration—intentionally shaping the atmosphere with values that don't fluctuate under pressure. Research in organizational behavior supports this: leaders set "normative climates" that influence everything from ethical decision-making to emotional resilience (Schneider, Ehrhart, & Macey, 2013). In other words, the tone a leader sets becomes the tone the team sustains. Servant leaders create climates where humility is modeled, courage is rewarded, and empathy is practiced daily. They're not passive observers—they are active architects, building culture not by force, but by faithfulness to principle. Whether it's a boardroom in crisis or a team in transition, servant leaders anchor the environment in trust, not turbulence.

This is why consistency matters more than charisma. The greatest culture shifts aren't ignited by slogans—they're ignited by a leader's steady hand when the heat rises. According to Spears (1995), servant leadership turns leaders into moral compasses, especially in uncertain environments. That means your attitude under pressure doesn't just affect you—it recalibrates the entire team. Servant leaders don't chase applause. They chase alignment. They adjust the internal temperature until the atmosphere is ready for purpose, performance, and breakthrough. When you serve with vision and walk with integrity, you don't just shift behavior—you shift belief. And when belief shifts? The culture transforms from the inside out.

Culture Begins in the Soul of the Leader

Before you can lead others, you must first lead yourself. You cannot build a servant-led organization if you are ruled by ego, pride, fear, or insecurity.
The servant leader says: "It starts with me." They **model honor, embody humility**, and **walk the mission** daily. Because what you build externally will only be as strong as what you embody internally.
If you want to build a culture of excellence, empathy, and empowerment—you better be ready to **live it when no one's watching.**

CHAPTER 4: Servant Leadership and Organizational Culture

Culture is not engineered from the outside-in—it is cultivated from the inside-out. Research on authentic leadership confirms that values-driven leaders create stronger trust, higher engagement, and deeper cultural alignment across organizations (Walumbwa et al., 2008). But authenticity isn't a style—it's a soul condition. Servant leaders don't perform character—they become it. They win the private battles that no one sees so they can lead the public battles that everyone feels. This is why spiritual and emotional maturity must precede sustainable influence. Leaders must confront their own shadows, surrender their egos, and embody the very transformation they want to see in others. You can't export a culture you haven't first cultivated within.

This is the divine paradox: your inner world determines your outer impact. As Proverbs 4:23 (NIV) teaches, "Above all else, guard your heart, for everything you do flows from it." Culture doesn't flow from policies—it flows from the purity and purpose of the leader's heart. That's why the most dangerous leader isn't the one with bad strategies—it's the one with unchecked insecurity. Servant leadership demands daily surrender, soul-level honesty, and radical alignment with eternal values. Because when the leader's soul is right, the culture breathes life. When the leader's spirit is off, the culture suffocates. Your team will rise—or rot—based on what flows from your core.

Your Values Mean Nothing Without Action

A value that isn't practiced is just a **pretty lie.** Servant leadership doesn't slap values on the website and call it culture. It asks: *What do our values look like when we're tired? When we're angry? When we're under pressure?*

Do we still show mercy when the deadline's looming? Do we still speak truth when it's uncomfortable? Do we still act with integrity when no one else is?

That's where culture lives—not in what you say, but in **what you prove with your choices.**

Servant leadership turns vision statements into cultural rhythms. According to Schein (2010), culture is shaped not by what's posted on the walls, but by the behaviors consistently modeled, rewarded, and repeated. This means your vision has to show up in how meetings are run, how conflicts are resolved, how new hires are welcomed, and how setbacks are handled. Servant leaders operationalize values—they don't just verbalize them. They anchor culture in the mundane moments of organizational life: how we respond to mistakes, how we recognize effort, how we invest in others. That's where the real vibe is set—not in branding, but in behavior. And when that behavior is rooted in empathy, humility, and courage, the culture becomes contagious.

Scripture underscores this principle with surgical clarity:

CHAPTER 4: Servant Leadership and Organizational Culture

"Let us not love with words or speech but with actions and in truth" (1 John 3:18, NIV). Culture dies in silence and hypocrisy—but it thrives in truth-filled, action-driven leadership. Servant leaders embody vision through vibe. They show up with presence, lead with love, and serve with consistency. And because culture is always downstream of leadership, the leader who lives the mission becomes the thermostat for transformation. The result? Organizations where values aren't just slogans—they're seen, felt, and multiplied at every level.

From Vision to Vibe: How Servant Leadership Shapes Every Corner

Servant leadership is not just a boardroom buzzword—it shapes **every hallway, every policy, every paycheck.** It turns meetings into mission moments. It turns evaluations into encouragement. It turns watercooler chatter into genuine connection.
When servant leadership becomes your DNA, it doesn't just affect top-level executives—it cascades through every department, every frontline worker, every new hire. Culture is not a department—it's **discipleship in motion.**

When servant leadership becomes more than a strategy and transforms into a lifestyle, every corner of your organization pulses with purpose. As Fry and Slocum (2008) emphasize, organizations grounded in spiritual leadership frameworks experience holistic cultural alignment—where values are not just communicated, but experienced in day-to-day operations. From hiring decisions to disciplinary processes, servant leadership reorients power away from control and toward collaboration. It shifts HR from gatekeeping to growth, meetings from micromanagement to mission alignment, and workplace culture from political maneuvering to purpose-driven unity. This is how culture becomes embodied—not top-down, but inside-out.

This cultural embodiment echoes the teachings of Christ, who not only preached truth but lived it "full of grace and truth" (John 1:14, NIV). Servant leadership breathes life into teams when it stops being a program and starts being a presence. Research confirms that when leaders live their mission visibly, it influences team identity, job satisfaction, and organizational citizenship behaviors (Liden, Wayne, Zhao, & Henderson, 2008). Servant leaders carry culture on their shoulders until it flows through everyone's hands. And when it does? Vibe becomes vision realized—people know who they are, why they're here, and how to carry the mission forward. That's not accidental culture. That's Kingdom-shaped culture.

SIDEBAR: Vision Cascades—Culture Multiplies

Vision without embodiment is confusion.
Culture without leadership is chaos.
But when servant leaders live the mission…

- **Hiring reflects values.**

- **Systems reflect trust.**

- **People reflect purpose.**

"When your vibe echoes your values—culture stops being forced. It starts being felt."

Culture isn't built by HR. It's built by how leaders show up.

Culture as Your Greatest Asset—or Your Greatest Liability

Companies spend millions on strategy and ignore culture until it breaks them. But the most effective servant leaders know: **Culture IS strategy.**

Want to improve retention? Start with culture. Want to increase innovation? Start with culture. Want to unleash purpose, passion, and performance? You guessed it—start with culture.

A toxic culture will eat your mission alive. But a servant-led culture will **multiply your mission, ignite loyalty, and fuel unstoppable momentum.**

> "The best organizations are not driven by rules, but by values—deeply embedded, consistently practiced values." —John C. Maxwell

Culture doesn't just influence performance—it *determines* it. According to Cameron and Quinn (2011), an organization's cultural framework is the single most reliable predictor of long-term effectiveness. When culture aligns with servant leadership principles—trust, humility, empowerment, and shared mission—it becomes a force multiplier. People don't just work for a paycheck—they work with passion, conviction, and identity. That's why elite organizations don't treat culture like background music—they treat it like the backbone. Because in times of stress, people don't fall back on policies—they fall back on culture. And servant leadership ensures that what they fall back on will carry them, not crush them.

The consequences of neglecting culture are dire. Toxic environments create fear, stifle innovation, and lead to emotional exhaustion and high turnover (Edmondson, 1999; Liden et al., 2008). But servant-led cultures cultivate psychological safety, foster resilience, and produce what Sinek (2014) calls "circles of safety"—ecosystems where people feel protected, known, and driven by a shared 'why.' Culture is not a slogan—it's the collective soul of your organization. And that soul can either rot from neglect or rise with intentional care. When leaders embrace their role as cultural architects, they don't just change metrics—they change the emotional and spiritual climate of their teams.

SIDEBAR: The Culture Equation

Culture = What You Tolerate + What You Celebrate + What You Model

CHAPTER 4: Servant Leadership and Organizational Culture

- Celebrate dignity
- Model empathy
- Tolerate nothing less than truth and honor

"If culture is the soil, then servant leadership is the seed. What you plant determines what you'll harvest."

God Cares About Your Culture

Don't think for a second that the Bible is silent on organizational life. God cares how we treat people—**in the workplace, in the classroom, in the trenches of leadership.**

Romans 12:10 says, *"Be devoted to one another in love. Honor one another above yourselves."*

That's not just personal advice—it's **cultural instruction.** Galatians 5:13 says, *"Serve one another humbly in love."* What would your workplace look like if **that** became your employee handbook?

Servant leadership is not just good leadership—it's **God-honoring leadership.**

Organizational culture is not a secular concept—it's a sacred opportunity. Scripture speaks directly to how we conduct ourselves in every realm of life, including leadership and organizational behavior. Ephesians 4:2–3 commands, *"Be completely humble and gentle; be patient, bearing with one another in love. Make every effort to keep the unity of the Spirit through the bond of peace."* That's not abstract spirituality—that's the bedrock of healthy organizational culture. These verses form the blueprint for a workplace where conflict becomes collaboration, power is exercised through service, and vision is carried out in unity. Research supports this divine model: organizations rooted in servant leadership display stronger collaboration, more trust, and a deeper sense of community across all levels (Liden et al., 2014).

The marketplace may reward short-term success, but the Kingdom measures sustainability through faithfulness, justice, and love. Proverbs 11:14 says, *"Where there is no guidance, a people falls, but in an abundance of counselors there is safety."* God not only affirms leadership—He defines it as collective, humble, and righteous. Servant-led cultures thrive because they echo heaven's values: dignity, mercy, and truth. In the world of business, this is more than a competitive advantage—it's spiritual stewardship. When you lead with a Kingdom mindset, culture becomes a ministry tool, people become sacred trust, and leadership becomes worship through work. This is not theory. This is theology applied to the boardroom, and it changes everything.

SIDEBAR: Heaven Has a Culture Code

- *Romans 12:10* — *"Honor one another above yourselves."*
- *Galatians 5:13* — *"Serve one another humbly in love."*
- *Ephesians 4:2* — *"Be completely humble and*

gentle..."

These aren't suggestions. They're Kingdom culture codes.

> "Culture isn't just built by leaders—it's judged by God. Build it like He's watching. Because He is."

The Movement Starts With You

You're not just reading a book—you're stepping into a **movement.**
You have the power to shift the culture of your organization, your team, your church, or your business. Not by shouting louder—but by **serving deeper.**
If you dare to believe that honor matters, that people matter, and that values lived out in love can change the world—**then you're exactly the kind of leader this world is desperate for.**
This chapter isn't just a guide—it's your **playbook for transformation.** Let's build a culture that doesn't just perform—it **multiplies purpose.**

But here's the raw truth: transformation never starts with an org chart—it starts in the mirror. Every cultural revolution begins when one leader dares to go first. According to Cameron and Quinn's *Competing Values Framework* (2011), cultural change succeeds only when the leader models consistent values and behaviors that ripple throughout the organization. You can't demand excellence if you don't live it. You can't preach purpose if you don't bleed it. Your influence doesn't come from your position—it comes from your posture. And servant leadership demands a posture of humility, love, and relentless faithfulness to the mission—even when it's hard, even when it costs you.

This movement isn't powered by charisma—it's powered by conviction. By one leader choosing to embody the kind of culture others want to belong to. In the words of Ephesians 4:1, we are urged "to live a life worthy of the calling you have received." That means stepping boldly into your influence—not for ego, but for impact. This is not theory—it's spiritual infrastructure for real leadership. When you lead with integrity, when you elevate others, when you serve with intention, you don't just build culture—you birth movements. And in a world fractured by fear, what it needs most is a leader bold enough to serve with love and fierce enough to stay faithful.

How Values Become Behaviors

Culture Is Not What You Say—It's What You Do. Walk into any breakroom in America, and you'll see the same thing—core values framed in cursive on the wall: *Integrity. Teamwork. Excellence. Respect.*
But too often, those values are **decoration, not direction.** The real values of an organization aren't what's printed—they're what's **practiced.**
If your stated values don't align with your leadership behaviors, your culture becomes confused, cynical, and

CHAPTER 4: Servant Leadership and Organizational Culture

fractured.

Servant leadership is the bridge that connects what you **say you value** with how you **actually behave**—especially when the pressure's on.

Values only gain traction when they're modeled consistently by leadership. In the absence of alignment between stated values and daily decisions, culture collapses into performative management. As Edgar Schein (2010), one of the foremost experts in organizational culture, argued: "The only thing of real importance that leaders do is to create and manage culture." That begins by living the values out loud—demonstrating grace under pressure, integrity in private, and compassion in conflict. Servant leadership brings those values to life by refusing to separate character from execution. Your people don't follow posters—they follow patterns. And if your actions don't match your mission, your culture will reflect the gap.

In Scripture, Jesus warned the Pharisees about honoring God with their lips while their hearts were far from Him (Matthew 15:8). The same indictment applies to organizations whose core values become hollow slogans. Servant leaders close that gap—not by demanding virtue from others, but by embodying it themselves. They don't need a campaign to enforce values because their presence becomes the standard. That's how trust is built. That's how cultures are transformed. When values are practiced at every level—from the C-suite to the frontlines—those behaviors embed into the organizational DNA and multiply. The result? A culture that no longer performs values for appearances—but breathes them as identity.

SIDEBAR: The Alignment Equation
Stated Values + Modeled Behavior = Trusted Culture

- Talk without action breeds cynicism.
- Behavior without values creates chaos.
- But values lived consistently? That's how movements start.

"Culture isn't changed by mission statements. It's changed by leaders who live them."

Values Require Consistent Modeling

Values don't take root because you announced them in a meeting—they take root because leaders **live them in the margins.**
That means showing patience when things go wrong, extending grace when people fall short, and staying humble when praise is poured out.
Values become behaviors when employees see their leaders choosing the harder right over the easier wrong—**consistently, authentically, and unapologetically.**
Jesus didn't just teach love, grace, and humility—**He embodied them** in every interaction, even when He was tired, interrupted, betrayed, and beaten.
If our King could model values on the road to the cross, we can model them in the boardroom, classroom, or

CHAPTER 4: Servant Leadership and Organizational Culture

breakroom.

Organizational psychologist Dr. Brené Brown (2018) emphasizes that *"clear is kind"*—but clarity means nothing without consistency. Consistent modeling from leadership transforms values from abstract ideals into operational reality. According to Kouzes and Posner (2017), credibility is the foundation of leadership—and credibility is built when people witness repeated alignment between what leaders claim and how they act. Servant leaders understand this: one act of grace, one moment of integrity, one hard truth told with humility—it all accumulates. It's not about perfection. It's about persistence. Culture isn't shaped by a single keynote—it's shaped by the everyday grit of consistent example.

This principle echoes throughout Scripture. Paul instructs believers in Philippians 4:9 (NIV), "Whatever you have learned or received or heard from me, or seen in me—put it into practice." That is discipleship through demonstration. In the same way, servant leaders disciple their teams through what they embody—not just what they explain. Leadership behaviors that align with values—especially under pressure—build psychological safety, trust equity, and long-term cultural sustainability (Edmondson, 1999). It's not the applause moments that define leadership. It's the quiet, faithful modeling when no one's watching. That's what drives belief. That's what creates follow-through. That's how real servant leadership multiplies.

SIDEBAR: Lead When It's Hardest

Your team watches you most:

- When things fall apart
- When someone messes up
- When no one says thank you
- When you're under fire

That's when values become culture—or just words on a wall.

"Repetition under pressure is the birthplace of trust."

From Beliefs to Habits

The greatest leaders know that transformation doesn't happen at the level of belief—it happens at the level of **habit.**

Beliefs inspire, but habits **solidify.** When values are embedded into daily systems—staff meetings, onboarding, conflict resolution—they stop being ideals and start being **instincts.**

You don't rise to your level of goals—you fall to your level of systems (Clear, 2018).

Servant leaders know this, and they engineer their environments to **reward behaviors** that reflect the mission, not just the metrics.

James Clear's (2018) insight—*"You don't rise to the level of your goals, you fall to the level of your systems"*—is more than a productivity mantra; it's a leadership

CHAPTER 4: Servant Leadership and Organizational Culture

mandate. Servant leaders who wish to drive transformation must build habits that align with deeply held beliefs. The real genius of transformational leadership lies not in inspiration but in integration. As Collins and Porras (1994) found in *Built to Last*, enduring companies embed core values into rituals, processes, and rhythms. Whether it's how meetings begin, how promotions are determined, or how conflict is resolved—these "habitual behaviors" signal what truly matters. In servant-led cultures, values aren't laminated—they're lived, and they're lived repeatedly.

Scripture reinforces this principle with divine precision. In Hebrews 5:14 (NIV), it says, *"But solid food is for the mature, who by constant use have trained themselves to distinguish good from evil."* Constant use—habits—develop discernment and discipline. A leader's spiritual maturity and cultural effectiveness don't grow from belief alone, but from *practiced obedience*. Servant leaders embed these beliefs into systems that normalize humility, reward collaboration, and elevate mission over ego. Culture then becomes less about charisma and more about consistency. It's not the extraordinary act that changes an organization—it's the repeated, value-aligned behavior that redefines what's expected and acceptable. That's how beliefs become backbone.

SIDEBAR: Systems Shape Soulwork
What you normalize, you multiply.
What you schedule, you sanctify.
What you repeat, you reinforce.

Want a stronger culture? Build systems where values become habits.

> "Consistency creates credibility. Systems sustain servant leadership."

Small Decisions Shape Deep Culture

Culture isn't shaped by big speeches—it's shaped by **small decisions.**
How you handle lateness. How you welcome a new hire. How you speak when you're frustrated.
Every little decision is either reinforcing your values or eroding them.
Servant leaders obsess over the little things, not because they're controlling—but because they understand the **ripple effect of everyday leadership.**
As Jesus said, *"Whoever can be trusted with very little can also be trusted with much"* (Luke 16:10, NIV). That's Kingdom-level leadership.

Culture isn't crafted in conference rooms—it's formed in a thousand quiet moments that no one tweets about. Research in organizational psychology shows that micro-behaviors—like how a leader responds to stress, handles dissent, or gives feedback—are key drivers of cultural clarity or confusion (Weick, 1995). These small decisions create what Schein (2010) calls the "cultural DNA" of an organization. Leaders may intend to shape culture through big initiatives, but it's the minute, repeated behaviors that build—or break—trust. In a servant-led environment, these micro-decisions are acts of stewardship. They whisper, "This is who we are," long before a mission statement ever does.

Jesus framed it with divine simplicity: "Whoever can be trusted with very little can also be trusted with much" (Luke 16:10, NIV). That's not just a spiritual truth—it's a leadership principle. The best servant leaders treat every moment like sacred soil. They know how you handle a late arrival says as much about your values as how you lead a board meeting. They realize that culture isn't set by slogans—it's formed in the trenches. As Drucker (2006) famously put it, *"Culture eats strategy for breakfast."* But servant leaders? They serve breakfast daily—one small, consistent, Kingdom-aligned decision at a time.

SIDEBAR: Micro-Decisions, Macro Impact
What feels small to you may feel monumental to them.
- How you correct.
- How you celebrate.
- How you listen.

These become the cultural compass.

> **"Every hallway moment is a culture-making moment."**

People Repeat What's Rewarded

You want your values to stick? Then **celebrate them.**

When a team member steps up to serve without recognition, call it out. When someone shows courage, honesty, or radical empathy—**make it visible.**

People replicate what gets rewarded. If results are all that matter, they'll chase numbers. If values matter most, they'll chase character.

Culture is not just top-down—it's **inside-out.** And servant leadership makes character the currency.

Behavioral science is clear: what gets rewarded gets repeated. B.F. Skinner's foundational work on operant conditioning shows that reinforcement—especially positive, public reinforcement—creates behavior patterns that stick (Skinner, 1953). In business environments, this means that when leaders acknowledge and celebrate behaviors rooted in the organization's core values, they're not just offering praise—they're architecting culture. Unfortunately, too many companies reward outcomes without examining the path taken to get there. But servant leadership flips that script. It rewards how results are achieved, not just what's achieved. That distinction turns character from a nice idea into a strategic imperative.

Jesus taught this principle long before modern psychology: "Where your treasure is, there your heart will be also" (Matthew 6:21, NIV). What you celebrate reveals what you value—and over time, it reshapes the very heart of your team. Servant leaders are intentional culture curators. They don't just wait for quarterly awards—they embed honor into everyday life. A quick thank you. A

CHAPTER 4: Servant Leadership and Organizational Culture

team-wide shoutout. A handwritten note for unseen service. These small acts shift the gravitational pull of the organization. Instead of chasing status or self-preservation, people begin to chase excellence with integrity—because that's what earns true celebration in a servant-led culture.

SIDEBAR: The Celebration Equation
Recognition × Repetition = Reinforced Values
Want more courage? Celebrate courage.
Want more service? Celebrate service.
Want more unity? Celebrate the unifiers.

> **"The applause you give today becomes the standard they aim for tomorrow."**

Accountability Is Not Optional

Values without accountability are just vague wishes. You can't build culture without courageous conversations. When people violate the values—**say something.**
Servant leaders confront with grace, correct with humility, and protect the culture without becoming tyrants.
This isn't about perfection—it's about alignment. When you protect your values with love and truth, you build a team that actually **trusts** the mission.

Accountability is not a leadership bonus—it's a culture-building non-negotiable. In Patrick Lencioni's *The Five*

Dysfunctions of a Team, he identifies lack of accountability as one of the greatest threats to cohesive, high-performing teams (Lencioni, 2002). Why? Because when violations go unchecked, culture decays. Servant leadership doesn't mean passive tolerance. It means courageous confrontation done with respect and purpose. Servant leaders address misalignment not to shame, but to shepherd. They understand that failing to confront is not kindness—it's compromise. And compromise slowly kills a culture's credibility.

Scripture affirms this tension: "Speak the truth in love" (Ephesians 4:15, NIV). Truth without love becomes harsh. Love without truth becomes hollow. But when you pair them, you get Kingdom-caliber accountability. Servant leaders don't dodge difficult conversations—they lean into them with empathy, clarity, and conviction. Because protecting the culture means guarding both the people and the purpose. And when team members see that accountability is applied consistently—not based on position or popularity—they begin to trust that the mission actually means something. That's when culture goes from words on a wall to a standard lived out in every hallway.

SIDEBAR: Love Holds the Line
Accountability isn't about catching failure.
It's about reinforcing purpose.
Grace says, "You're more than your mistake."
Truth says, "But we won't stay here."

> "Real servant leaders don't punish—they purify."

Build Rituals Around What You Believe

Want your values to last? Then ritualize them. Start every meeting with a moment of gratitude. Celebrate servant-hearted wins. Pray before big decisions (if it fits your context). Create hiring questions that test for humility. Add calendar checkpoints to review culture alignment. When your rhythms reflect your values, they become **a living culture**—not a dusty slogan.

Research shows that rituals are powerful tools for reinforcing identity and values. In high-trust, high-performing cultures, rituals aren't fluff—they're formational. According to organizational psychologist Adam Grant, repeated, value-aligned practices create what he calls "behavioral anchors," which reinforce cultural norms at scale (Grant, 2013). Servant leaders understand this: they don't wait for culture to "happen"—they design it. By intentionally embedding rhythms like weekly wins, service spotlights, or "gratitude rounds" into the structure of team life, they ensure that values don't fade with time—they deepen with repetition. Every ritual is a drumbeat that echoes your core beliefs.

This idea is profoundly biblical. The Old Testament is

filled with God-ordained rituals—feasts, offerings, Sabbaths—not because God needed routine, but because *we* need reminders. Deuteronomy 6:6–7 commands leaders to "impress [these values] on your children... talk about them when you sit at home, when you walk... when you lie down and get up." That's not just instruction—it's divine insight into how values stick. Servant leaders build rituals not as legalism, but as liturgy—sacred patterns that turn mission into movement and belief into muscle memory.

SIDEBAR: Culture Is Remembered in Rhythm
If it matters, ritualize it.
If it's sacred, schedule it.
"The repetition of what's right becomes the formation of who we are."

> **"Rituals turn values into habits—and habits into legacy."**

Values That Flow from the Throne

At the end of the day, the only values that endure are the ones that flow from **the King's character.**
Love. Grace. Truth. Mercy. Justice. Humility.
They aren't just good ideas—they are **God's identity.**
Romans 12:2 says, *"Do not conform to the pattern of this world, but be transformed by the renewing of your mind."*
That's what this is.
You're not just creating workplace culture. You're building a **Kingdom outpost**—where values shine like fire and

CHAPTER 4: Servant Leadership and Organizational Culture

behaviors echo eternity.

Servant leadership rooted in Kingdom values doesn't just change how people behave—it transforms who they become. When love isn't just a slogan, but a standard... when grace is more than policy—it's posture... when truth, justice, and humility become daily disciplines, not abstract ideals—something powerful happens: your culture becomes a *witness*. As theologian N.T. Wright notes, "Character is the pattern of life that anticipates God's future in the present." That's what your organization becomes—a living preview of heaven's values on earth.

You are not just forming a company—you're forming disciples through culture. And culture is the canvas where your leadership paints what you believe about God, people, and purpose. The values that flow from the throne room—agape love, radical grace, bold truth, and servant-hearted humility—don't just sustain organizations. They raise them from the ashes. So lead with values that carry eternal weight. Because when you build with what matters most, your impact won't just be measured in revenue—it'll be measured in resurrection.

SIDEBAR: From Kingdom to Culture
God's character isn't just personal—it's organizational. Culture rooted in heaven never rots on earth.

"Don't just build a company that works. Build a

culture that worships."

Servant Leadership as a System, not a Slogan

"Every system is perfectly designed to get the results it gets." — W. Edwards Deming

> "If you want to change the culture, you have to change the system. Vision inspires, but systems sustain."

If It's Not Built into the System, It Doesn't Exist

Too many organizations treat servant leadership like a bumper sticker—nice words, great optics, zero integration.
You don't need more slogans. You need a **system.**
A system is a **repeatable pattern of behavior**, driven by deeply held values, reinforced through structure, policy, training, and feedback.
Servant leadership becomes real when it's embedded into **how you hire, how you onboard, how you evaluate, how you reward, how you correct, and how you lead.**
It's not enough to believe in servant leadership—you have to **engineer it.**

If you want a servant-led culture, you must operationalize

CHAPTER 4: Servant Leadership and Organizational Culture

your convictions. That means translating values into visible, trackable actions—codified in handbooks, measured in evaluations, and embedded in onboarding, leadership development, and decision-making frameworks. Research from Liden et al. (2008) confirms that when servant leadership principles are woven into organizational systems, outcomes like employee engagement, retention, and innovation rise significantly. Why? Because systems create consistency—and consistency builds culture. A one-time training won't change your team. But a consistent, value-aligned system will.

The most transformative leaders aren't just inspiring—they're architects. They don't just cast vision—they build ecosystems that make that vision inevitable. Servant leadership becomes sustainable when it stops being personality-based and starts being process-driven. Leaders like Herb Kelleher at Southwest Airlines and Horst Schulze at Ritz-Carlton didn't leave their culture to chance—they hardwired service, empathy, and excellence into every system. That's the secret: if it's not in the system, it won't survive the storm. You want servant leadership to outlast the founder, the hype, and the crisis? Then it has to live in your systems.

Leadership Is a System of Influence

Leadership is not a title—it's a **mechanism of influence** that runs through every layer of your organization. And if that mechanism isn't built on the values of humility, service, truth, and love, it will default to **ego, fear, and control.**

Servant leadership doesn't just change the heart—it changes the **system of how power flows.**

It decentralizes arrogance and distributes ownership. It shifts from "command and control" to "coach and empower."

The system is the structure—and servant leadership becomes **the operating system.**

Leadership is not a title—it is a sustained system of influence, woven through the structures, symbols, and spoken words of your organization. At its core, leadership shapes what is celebrated, tolerated, and corrected. It is not confined to an org chart; it pulses through culture, cascades through communication, and ultimately defines the behaviors of a team. And make no mistake—*every* system will either elevate people or exploit them. The absence of intentional, value-driven leadership doesn't create neutrality—it creates a vacuum that gets filled with ego, fear, and control. Servant leadership reclaims that space with purpose, humility, and vision.

When servant leadership becomes the operating system, influence is no longer hoarded at the top—it is distributed throughout the body. This isn't about flattening hierarchy. It's about elevating humanity. It means empowering managers to mentor, not micromanage. It means reengineering your culture to reward character over charisma, contribution over control. Scholars like Robert Greenleaf (1970) and later Eva et al. (2019) proved that

CHAPTER 4: Servant Leadership and Organizational Culture

servant-led systems drive long-term effectiveness because they align power with purpose. And when purpose flows through structure, influence doesn't dominate—it liberates. Servant leadership becomes the invisible architecture that sustains trust, ignites innovation, and multiplies impact at scale.

Embedding the Mission in Every Layer

If you want servant leadership to last, it must exist beyond the corner office.
It has to **live in the policies, the playbooks, the procedures.**
That means rewriting job descriptions to prioritize empathy and collaboration. Rebuilding evaluation systems to reward team development, not just personal output.
Creating communication rhythms that promote listening instead of broadcasting.
When the structure itself supports service—**the culture will follow.**

If you want servant leadership to last, it must be architected into the bones of the organization. That means it cannot live only in vision statements or executive speeches—it must be embedded in every operational layer: hiring, training, performance evaluations, team rituals, disciplinary actions, and recognition systems. In short, the mission must not just *inspire*—it must *inform structure*. Servant leadership becomes self-sustaining only when it moves from abstract values to concrete systems. It becomes how the organization thinks, decides, and behaves, even when the founder or CEO is no longer in the room.

Organizations that endure don't just talk about servant leadership—they engineer it. That starts with rewriting the DNA of how success is defined. Job descriptions should prioritize emotional intelligence, team contribution, and ethical decision-making. Onboarding should do more than communicate rules—it should cast vision and cultivate belonging. Evaluations should measure how employees elevate others, not just how they advance themselves. Meeting structures should be designed to listen first, not lecture. According to Spears (1995) and Eva et al. (2019), organizations that institutionalize service-based values within systems experience increased loyalty, decreased internal conflict, and scalable impact. When your infrastructure is aligned with your identity, culture stops being fragile—and becomes forceful.

SIDEBAR: Structural Servanthood

- *Hiring*: Screen for humility, not just credentials.
- *Onboarding*: Start with the "why," not the rules.
- *Evaluations*: Reward coaching and collaboration, not just quotas.
- *Communication*: Build rhythms that prioritize listening.

CHAPTER 4: Servant Leadership and Organizational Culture

- *Correction*: Lead with grace, anchor with truth.

"If your mission lives only in the mouth of the leader, it dies when they leave. But if it's built into the systems—it lives forever."

Hiring and Firing by the Values

A system of servant leadership **starts at the gate.**
If you're hiring for skill alone and ignoring character, you're planting the seeds of cultural decay.
Servant-led organizations **hire slow and hire aligned.**
They look for humility, teachability, and a heart for mission—not just a fancy resume.
And when someone violates the core values persistently, servant leaders make the hard call: **they protect the team by parting ways.**
Because you can't build a Kingdom culture when you're protecting prideful behavior.

A servant-led organization understands this truth: every new hire is a cultural multiplier or a cultural threat. Talent without alignment is a ticking time bomb. According to Collins (2001), the most enduring companies place more weight on *who* is on the bus than where the bus is going. In servant leadership, the "who" must embody more than competence—they must reflect the mission. That means hiring becomes a sacred act of stewardship. You're not just filling a role—you're inviting someone into a movement. Leaders must craft hiring processes that test for humility, emotional intelligence, and value-alignment, not just technical mastery. A-values-first hiring system prevents culture erosion before it begins.

But hiring is only half the equation—courageous cultures also know when to let go. If someone repeatedly violates the values, no matter how skilled they are, they threaten the mission's integrity. Jesus didn't tolerate pride in the temple—and servant leaders can't afford to tolerate it in the boardroom. This isn't about being harsh. It's about being holy—set apart for something greater. According to Gino and Margolis (2011), unethical or misaligned individuals reduce team collaboration and increase organizational toxicity by up to 35%. Servant leadership requires the courage to part ways with destructive patterns—even when the cost is high—because the health of the whole is worth more than the talent of the few.

SIDEBAR: Hire on Mission, Fire on Values

- Don't just ask what they can do. Ask what they believe.
- Test for teachability, not just technique.
- If someone violates core values repeatedly, protect the culture—even if it hurts.

"The wrong hire can erode years of culture in months. Build with values—or watch your foundation crack."

CHAPTER 4: Servant Leadership and Organizational Culture

Training the Servant Way

Servant leadership isn't a poster on the wall—it's a **curriculum** in the classroom.
You train people to serve by giving them opportunities, language, mentorship, and consistent feedback.
Modeling is training. Storytelling is training. Reflecting and coaching after the mess is **also training.**
The best servant leaders use every moment—onboarding, staff meetings, retreats—as a chance to **reinstall the mission.**
You're not just managing tasks—you're **discipling people** into a new way of working.

If servant leadership is the culture you want, training is the soil that grows it. You cannot assume your people "just get it." As Kotter (1996) emphasized in his work on transformational change, vision without structured communication and training always collapses under the weight of ambiguity. That's why great servant-led organizations embed their values not just in the handbook—but in the habits, language, and rituals of their training systems. Orientation becomes formation. Staff meetings become recalibration. Feedback becomes discipleship. In other words, everything is training—especially the way leaders handle failure, feedback, and conflict.

Effective training in a servant-led system does more than transfer information—it shapes identity. It clarifies not just *what* we do, but *who* we are. This requires intentional scaffolding: onboarding that includes culture stories and core values, peer mentoring that prioritizes emotional intelligence and trust-building, and leadership development that focuses on moral courage and service under pressure. According to Kouzes and Posner (2017), exemplary leaders "model the way"—but that modeling must be systematic, visible, and measurable. In servant leadership, we're not just building better professionals—we're shaping people who lead with their soul. That requires more than process—it demands purpose.

SIDEBAR: Every Moment Trains Something

- Are your meetings training people to compete—or to collaborate?
- Is your onboarding forming disciples—or just explaining duties?
- Do your systems teach fear—or model faith and trust?

"Training is not an event—it's the ecosystem that forms the soul of your culture."

Accountability that Honors the Mission

Real systems have **guardrails.**
If servant leadership isn't supported by accountability, it will get diluted, distorted, or destroyed.

CHAPTER 4: Servant Leadership and Organizational Culture

That means building systems of **truth-telling**, where peer feedback and upward feedback are safe and expected. It means leaders invite correction, reward honesty, and stay open-handed with power.
When accountability is rooted in love and truth—it doesn't weaken servant leadership, it **strengthens it.**

In any enduring system, accountability is not a threat—it's a form of stewardship. Servant leadership does not sidestep hard conversations in the name of harmony; it embraces them in the name of alignment. As Collins (2001) asserts in *Good to Great*, the best organizations confront brutal facts, not because they are pessimistic, but because they are deeply committed to truth. Servant leaders create systems where accountability is normalized—not as punishment, but as protection. They do not shame; they sharpen. They do not dominate; they develop. This is accountability rooted not in ego, but in covenant—a mutual responsibility to uphold the mission with integrity.

Moreover, accountability becomes sacred when it flows both ways. It is not enough for team members to be held accountable to leadership—leaders must also be held accountable to the values they preach. That's why the most effective servant-led organizations build upward feedback systems, peer-to-peer evaluations, and mission reviews into their rhythms. According to Edmondson (1999), psychological safety—the bedrock of innovation and performance—only thrives when people feel empowered to speak up without fear. Servant leadership makes truth-telling a cultural expectation and confession a leadership virtue. Why? Because when correction is safe, trust grows. And when trust grows, culture thrives.

SIDEBAR: Truth Tells the Health of the House

- Accountability reveals whether your mission is real or just rhetoric.
- Systems that protect people but not the purpose will eventually fail both.
- You cannot be a servant leader and stay unchallenged.

"Grace without truth is cowardice. Truth without grace is cruelty. Servant leadership builds systems where both grow together."

Servant Systems Produce Scalable Impact

Here's the secret CEOs miss: when you build your organization around servant leadership, **you can scale without crumbling.**
You don't have to micromanage culture because the system does the work.
Servant leadership creates **self-correcting teams, mission-aligned hires,** and **values-driven decisions—** even when you're not in the room.
And because people feel seen, heard, and empowered— they stay longer, care more, and perform better.

CHAPTER 4: Servant Leadership and Organizational Culture

You want growth that lasts? Then **build it on a servant-led system.**

Scalability isn't just about adding—it's about aligning. In traditional models, growth often fractures culture because it stretches thin what was never strong. But servant leadership, when embedded into organizational systems, creates structural integrity that expands with force and fidelity. As Schein (2010) noted, "Culture is the residue of past leadership decisions." When those decisions are rooted in humility, service, and trust, they leave a legacy that scales. You're not just replicating outputs—you're reproducing ethos. And when that ethos is codified into hiring practices, leadership pipelines, meeting structures, and reward systems, culture becomes a multiplier, not a bottleneck.

What makes servant leadership uniquely scalable is its generative nature. It doesn't centralize success around a single charismatic leader—it decentralizes influence and multiplies ownership. You're not cloning one leader; you're cultivating dozens. That's why servant-led organizations exhibit what Heifetz (1994) called *adaptive capacity*—they remain agile under pressure because the values are carried by every team member, not just protected at the top. From startups to Fortune 500s, the businesses that scale with strength are the ones where mission isn't a slide deck—it's the system. And when the system honors people, people honor the mission.

SIDEBAR: Systems That Scale Are Systems That Serve

- You don't scale *ego*. You scale *ethos*.
- A servant system doesn't just transfer responsibility—it transfers belief.
- Culture that's hardwired into systems won't crumble under growth.

"If your system requires your constant presence to thrive, it's not a system—it's a dependency. Servant leadership builds cultures that stand even when you step away."

The Metrics That Actually Matter

Most organizations track what's easiest to measure—revenue, performance quotas, attendance logs, customer churn. These metrics fill dashboards and dominate meetings, but they don't tell the whole story. In fact, they often distract from what really builds sustainable success.

The servant leader knows: **what gets measured gets prioritized.** And when you measure the wrong things, you build the wrong culture. That's why Kingdom-minded leadership flips the script. We don't obsess over vanity metrics. We track vital signs of impact: trust, loyalty, creativity, alignment, emotional safety, spiritual health, and leadership reproduction.

The world measures output—**God measures overflow.** 1 Samuel 16:7 reminds us, *"People look at the outward*

CHAPTER 4: Servant Leadership and Organizational Culture

appearance, but the Lord looks at the heart." That's not just a spiritual truth—it's a leadership warning. High performance can mask a toxic team. Impressive numbers can camouflage burned-out souls. But servant leaders inspect what matters most—**what's happening below the surface.**

Want to know if your culture is healthy? Don't just check profits—check participation in hard conversations. Check how many team members feel safe speaking up. Check how many leaders you've raised, not just how many products you've launched. **Greatness is not just scale**—it's depth. It's multiplication. It's how many people are rising because of your leadership.

Business research backs this. Harvard Business Review and Gallup both report that psychological safety, team engagement, and trust are better indicators of long-term success than raw financials. In fact, high-trust companies outperform low-trust ones by 286% in total return to shareholders (Zak, 2017). **That's not soft. That's strategic.**

The servant leader's scoreboard looks different:

- Trust is the win.
- Growth is the pattern.
- Reproduction of leaders is the legacy.

So yes, keep tracking the numbers. But make sure you're

tracking the ones that move Heaven and earth.

SIDEBAR: The Servant Leader's Scoreboard
If you want to build a mission that outlives you, start measuring what God multiplies:

- Trust → Do your people feel safe, valued, and empowered?
- Loyalty → Would they follow you if the paycheck disappeared?
- Innovation → Are new ideas rewarded—or feared?
- Emotional Safety → Can your team fail without fear?
- Discipleship → Are you reproducing leaders—or guarding your position?

> **"Vanity metrics feed the ego. Kingdom metrics fuel the movement."**

Evaluation the Servant Way

Most evaluation systems are backwards. They're built to police behavior, not elevate potential. They focus on what's wrong instead of drawing out what's right. But servant leaders don't evaluate to catch mistakes—they evaluate to cultivate greatness.

Evaluation isn't a compliance tool—it's a discipleship opportunity.

In a servant-led culture, evaluation is no longer a one-

CHAPTER 4: Servant Leadership and Organizational Culture

way critique from boss to employee. It becomes a two-way covenant—a conversation rooted in truth, trust, and transformation. You're not just asking, "Did you meet the goal?" You're asking, "How can I help you grow? Where are you thriving? What's getting in the way of your best work? How can I better serve you?"

And yes—metrics still matter. But they're framed in the context of mission. Instead of asking, "Did you hit your numbers?" you ask:

- "Did you live our values?"
- "Did you lift others?"
- "Did you lead with humility, courage, and clarity?"

Because in the Kingdom, performance is never separated from purpose.

Jesus didn't evaluate Peter based on productivity—He called out his future even after failure (John 21:15–17). That's servant leadership in action. Restore. Refocus. Recommission.

The modern leader must redesign evaluation systems to reflect God's heart and your organization's values. Build feedback loops that include peer review, self-assessment, upward feedback, and spiritual reflection (when appropriate). And most importantly, evaluate leadership not by control—but by how much power was given away, how many leaders were multiplied, and how much character was modeled.

When evaluation becomes a tool for transformation instead of punishment, you don't just manage talent—you mobilize legacy.

SIDEBAR: Servant Leader Evaluation Questions
Ditch the checkbox. Ask questions that reveal the heart and fuel growth:

- "Where did you model our values the strongest?"
- "Where did you struggle to serve, and why?"
- "What do you need from leadership to rise?"
- "How did your work impact others this quarter?"
- "Whose growth did you invest in?"

> **"Don't just evaluate performance—evaluate impact. That's what builds movements."**

Designing Feedback Loops That Build, Not Break

Feedback isn't a luxury—**it's a leadership responsibility.** But in too many systems, feedback feels like a threat instead of a gift. It becomes a weapon of control instead of a tool for development.

Servant leadership flips that script. It creates feedback loops designed not to tear people down, but to build them up—with clarity, compassion, and courage.

CHAPTER 4: Servant Leadership and Organizational Culture

Great cultures don't avoid hard conversations—**they normalize healthy ones. They** create rhythms of reflection and truth-telling that are safe, expected, and consistent. Servant leaders model vulnerability first by inviting feedback from their teams. Because when a leader says, "How can I serve you better?" it builds trust faster than any title ever could.

Feedback loops in a servant-led system are:

- Frequent, not just annual.
- Multidirectional—top-down, bottom-up, and peer-to-peer.
- Formational, not just informational.
- Rooted in values, not just numbers.

In Kingdom leadership, correction is always tied to restoration, not condemnation. As Paul wrote in Ephesians 4:15, we are called to "speak the truth in love," so that the whole body may grow. The same is true in your organization: truth + love = transformation.

You want teams that grow fast, own their growth, and multiply results? Then build a culture where feedback flows freely, with grace and grit working together. That's not weakness—it's wisdom.

SIDEBAR: The Servant Leader's Feedback Formula

- Affirm identity (what's good, what's true)

- Address gaps (with clarity and humility)
- Align with mission (why this matters)
- Ask for their perspective (listen deeply)
- Activate growth (action step + support)

"Feedback should never be a surprise—it should be a sacred rhythm of mutual growth."

This Is the Infrastructure of Revival

Servant leadership is not just good for business—it's the **infrastructure of revival.**
It's the system that turns a toxic workplace into a sanctuary. That turns burned-out employees into mission-driven warriors.
That turns hierarchies of fear into **communities of purpose.**
If we're serious about changing our schools, our companies, our churches, our governments—**we must build better systems.**
And the best system ever designed? **It's the one Jesus built—where the greatest among you becomes the servant of all.** (Matthew 23:11, NIV)

Revival isn't sustained by emotion—it's sustained by infrastructure. And the most enduring infrastructure ever created is servant leadership. When embedded systemically, it doesn't just uplift individuals—it re-

CHAPTER 4: Servant Leadership and Organizational Culture

engineers the organizational ecosystem itself. Toxic cultures aren't healed through a one-time speech or a flashy rebrand. They're transformed through deeply-rooted systems that reflect the values of love, justice, humility, and truth in every policy, process, and protocol. Whether in a classroom, corporation, or congregation—when the structure is servant-led, revival becomes more than a spiritual moment. It becomes a cultural reformation.

Jesus didn't establish a leadership style—He architected a Kingdom framework. And that framework was built on downward mobility, sacrificial power, and radical inclusion. He washed feet. He fed the hungry. He empowered the overlooked. That wasn't symbolic—it was strategic. It was an operating system designed to overthrow pride, dismantle fear, and release people into purpose. If we want to see transformation that lasts—in education, in enterprise, in public service—we must build systems that carry the same DNA. Because true revival doesn't start with noise. It starts with structure that honors God and elevates people.

SIDEBAR: What Servant Leadership Builds

- Toxic systems oppress. Servant systems liberate.
- Emotion ignites revival. Structure sustains it.
- If you want the fire to last—build a frame that holds it.

**"Revival without structure fades. But servant

leadership is the infrastructure that carries the move of God into every office, classroom, boardroom, and street."

Building Psychological Safety and Mission Alignment

"People don't commit to jobs—they commit to environments where they're safe to speak, free to grow, and aligned with a mission that matters."

Safety Is the Soil Where Greatness Grows

If your team doesn't feel safe, they won't bring their full selves to the table. Period.
Psychological safety—the belief that you can speak up, make mistakes, and be human without fear of punishment—is **the #1 predictor of high-performing teams** (Google's Project Aristotle, 2015).
Without it, creativity dies, trust disappears, and initiative is suffocated.
Servant leaders **nurture safety**, not by coddling weakness, but by **inviting courage, rewarding honesty, and never weaponizing vulnerability.**
Because where there is no safety, there can be no sustained success.

Psychological safety is not about avoiding challenge—it's about building the **relational foundation** that allows challenge to lead to growth. In elite organizations, safety

CHAPTER 4: Servant Leadership and Organizational Culture

is not softness—it's **strategic infrastructure.** Harvard researcher Dr. Amy Edmondson showed that when leaders create spaces where people feel safe to speak up and take interpersonal risks, teams become more innovative, more agile, and far more resilient. Why? Because safety breeds ownership. And when employees feel they belong, they don't shrink from problems—they rise to solve them. That's not coddling—that's unleashing capability.

From a Kingdom lens, this is profoundly biblical. Jesus didn't create fear-based loyalty—He created **love-based transformation.** He called His disciples "friends" (John 15:15), not employees. He washed feet before issuing commands. And He welcomed the doubters, the deniers, and the broken into His circle without ever compromising truth. That's psychological safety in divine form. In your boardroom, classroom, or team huddle—when you lead like Jesus, walls fall, trust rises, and excellence is not just possible—it's **inevitable.**

Fear-Based Leadership Is a Silent Killer

We've all worked under fear-based leadership. You speak your mind? You're labeled a problem. You make a mistake? You're shamed.
This toxic culture doesn't just break morale—it **breaks people.**
Servant leadership flips the script: it creates a culture

where feedback is fuel, failure is a teacher, and authenticity is celebrated.

Instead of asking "Who messed up?" a servant leader asks, **"How can I help?"**

That one question changes the culture from judgment to **growth**.

Fear-based leadership might deliver short-term compliance, but it destroys long-term capacity. Research from the *Harvard Business Review* and Amy Edmondson's work on psychological safety confirms that environments ruled by fear stifle innovation, elevate stress, and lead to organizational decay. When people are afraid to speak, you lose the very insight that could save your systems. When fear drives performance, creativity becomes risk, and truth becomes a threat. That's not leadership—it's sabotage in a suit.

Servant leaders build trust by removing fear from the equation and replacing it with fierce clarity, consistent compassion, and courageous accountability. They know that excellence can't be demanded through intimidation—it must be cultivated through connection. As 1 John 4:18 reminds us, "There is no fear in love. But perfect love drives out fear." In the economy of God and in the best-run organizations, fear is not a management strategy—it's a mission failure. The future belongs to leaders who replace silence with safety, shame with service, and power with purpose.

CHAPTER 4: Servant Leadership and Organizational Culture

The Gospel Calls for Radical Safety

Jesus built the most psychologically safe community in history.
He washed the feet of the man who would betray Him. He welcomed doubters, misfits, and sinners—**and never withheld love or dignity.**
That's not weakness. That's **unshakable power under perfect control.**
Servant leaders embody that same posture. They don't demand trust—they **earn it** with humility, grace, and truth.
Galatians 6:2 (NIV) reminds us: *"Carry each other's burdens, and in this way you will fulfill the law of Christ."*

The life and ministry of Jesus Christ offer the most compelling blueprint for psychological safety ever recorded. He welcomed tax collectors (Luke 19:1–10), defended the dignity of the adulterous woman (John 8:1–11), and invited "doubting Thomas" to touch His wounds without rebuke (John 20:27). This wasn't passive tolerance—it was active, radical grace. Christ created an environment where people could bring their doubts, flaws, and failures into the light—and be met with love, not judgment. According to Spears (1995), one of the central tenets of servant leadership is "healing," which directly parallels the Gospel model: making space for brokenness to encounter restoration.

Psychological safety is not a soft idea—it's a sacred one. Galatians 6:2 reminds us that carrying one another's burdens is not optional—it is how we "fulfill the law of Christ." This call to radical empathy is echoed in modern leadership scholarship as well. Edmondson (1999) found that teams with high psychological safety exhibited greater collaboration, deeper innovation, and stronger emotional health. In other words, the Gospel doesn't just align with the science—it *surpasses* it. As a Kingdom leader, you are not merely managing performance—you are stewarding souls. And the safest cultures are led by those who reflect the character of Christ: firm in truth, lavish in grace, and relentless in love (Grand Canyon University, n.d.).

Safety Leads to Alignment

Here's the secret: when people feel safe, they stop hiding—and they start aligning.
Psychological safety is the **foundation of mission alignment** because people aren't distracted by fear. They stop playing defense and start playing offense—**for the mission.**
Alignment isn't about forcing everyone to say the same thing—it's about creating clarity, unity, and deep buy-in around your shared purpose.
And that alignment starts when people feel like they can be **seen, heard, and valued.**

When psychological safety is present, it unlocks mission alignment at every level of the organization. People no longer operate from a place of self-protection—they operate from shared conviction. According to Brown and

CHAPTER 4: Servant Leadership and Organizational Culture

Leigh (1996), psychological safety fosters "intrinsic motivation, job involvement, and emotional investment"—all of which are necessary precursors to true alignment. In cultures where fear is present, alignment is artificial—driven by compliance, not commitment. But when servant leaders prioritize safety, alignment flows naturally because people are invited to contribute, not coerced to conform.

In the biblical context, alignment always begins with safety in identity. Romans 12:4–5 reminds us that "each member belongs to all the others," and each has a unique role to play. True alignment doesn't flatten differences—it honors them under a unified mission. Servant leaders don't demand uniformity; they build unity through empathy, listening, and shared purpose. Gallup's research confirms that high-trust, psychologically safe teams show 64% higher engagement and 40% fewer quality defects (Gallup, 2020). When people feel safe, they stop hiding their gifts—and start aligning their gifts with the mission.

SIDEBAR: Alignment Grows Where Safety Is Sown

Fear stifles creativity. Safety activates ownership.

- Unsafe teams *comply*.
- Safe teams *commit*.
- Unsafe cultures chase metrics.

- Safe cultures chase mission.

Want clarity, buy-in, and bold execution? Create a culture where people feel safe to align—and empowered to act.

Alignment Is Clarity Plus Purpose

You can't have mission alignment without mission clarity. Servant leaders **paint the target so clearly** that everyone knows why they exist and how their role connects to the bigger picture.
But they don't just push the "what"—they constantly re-anchor people in the **why.**
When the mission is clear and the atmosphere is safe, people don't just comply—they **commit.**
Proverbs 29:18 (KJV) says, *"Where there is no vision, the people perish."* But when there IS vision—backed by safety—**the people flourish.**

Mission alignment without clarity is noise dressed as movement. Servant leaders eliminate that noise by translating values into vision, and vision into shared action. Kouzes and Posner (2017) argue that exemplary leaders "inspire a shared vision" by helping people see themselves in the story of the mission. In servant-led organizations, this isn't done through grandstanding—it's done through proximity, repetition, and conviction. Leaders don't just cast vision once—they embed it into onboarding, staff meetings, decision-making, and everyday language. That clarity gives people a compass, not just a calendar.

But clarity alone is not enough. It must be infused with purpose—anchored to the eternal, not just the quarterly. The Apostle Paul reminds us in 1 Corinthians 9:26 (NIV), "Therefore I do not run like someone running aimlessly." That is the call of a servant leader—to lead with direction, and to give others purpose in every step. When people understand both the mission and their meaningful role in it, they stop working for a paycheck—and start living out a calling. Clarity tells them where to go. Purpose gives them the reason to get there.

Safe Cultures Call Out the Best

In a servant-led environment, the team doesn't fear feedback—they **crave it.**
That's because feedback is no longer a threat—it's a sign that someone believes in you.
Servant leaders build this dynamic by offering correction wrapped in care and celebration saturated with sincerity. It's not about softening the truth—it's about **delivering truth in love** (Ephesians 4:15, NIV).
That kind of leadership creates champions—not just employees.

In a truly safe and servant-led environment, people don't fear exposure—they welcome elevation. Feedback becomes less about fixing flaws and more about **calling greatness forward**. When team members know correction comes from a place of love, not ego, they listen. When they see celebration is genuine and not political, they rise. This shift doesn't happen by accident—it's the fruit of leaders who have consistently modeled empathy, humility, and truth. Research shows that high-performing teams not only embrace feedback but actively seek it when the environment supports psychological safety (Edmondson, 1999; Duhigg, 2016). Feedback, then, becomes a **sacred trust**, not a scarlet letter.

The biblical framework reinforces this posture. Proverbs 27:17 declares, "As iron sharpens iron, so one person sharpens another." Sharpening isn't passive—it requires friction. But in safe cultures, that friction doesn't spark division—it ignites development. Servant leaders don't weaponize accountability; they **shepherd it with grace**, understanding that the goal is growth, not guilt. As Paul taught in 1 Thessalonians 5:11, "Encourage one another and build each other up." In these cultures, people don't just perform—they **transform**. They step into higher levels of maturity, ownership, and excellence because someone cared enough to call it out of them.

SIDEBAR: "Sharpen Without Shaming"

- Correction without love breeds resentment.
- Love without correction breeds mediocrity.
- Servant leaders do both—because **they care more about who you're becoming than how you're performing.**

Guardrails for Alignment: Systems That Call Us Back

Even the most purpose-driven organizations drift. It doesn't happen because people stop caring—it happens because clarity decays without reinforcement. That's why servant leadership doesn't just set vision—it builds **systems of recall**. Like spiritual disciplines anchor the believer, servant-led systems anchor the organization. They pull the team back to mission, values, and shared purpose—**not through control, but through consistency** (Colangelo, 2022). The goal isn't to micromanage; it's to **engineer rhythms that make alignment inevitable.**

These rhythms include **weekly mission check-ins, culture-based performance reviews**, and **team storytelling sessions** that reinforce real-life examples of the mission in motion. Great leaders understand what James Clear (2018) describes as "identity-based habits"—systems that reinforce who we are through what we do. In the same way, servant leadership becomes sticky when systems reflect identity: when hiring questions reveal humility, when onboarding models service, and when recognition is tied to values, not just metrics. Culture then becomes **auto-corrective**—because it's no longer dependent on charisma at the top.

Correction, in a servant-led culture, is not reactive—it's proactive and redemptive. Servant leaders establish **relational authority** that allows them to challenge drift without shame (Spears, 1995). They use pre-scheduled alignment reviews, 360-feedback cycles, and "mission pulse" surveys to monitor cultural health before cracks become canyons. And when drift does happen, they restore alignment through grace-filled conversations, clarity reboots, and collective re-centering around the "why." As Paul reminds us in 1 Corinthians 14:8, "If the trumpet does not sound a clear call, who will get ready for battle?" Servant systems make the call clear—again and again.

What separates average leadership from legacy leadership is **intentional design**. Systems are not bureaucratic barriers—they are **soul scaffolding**. They hold the weight of the vision when humans falter. That's why the best servant leaders don't just inspire action—they **architect alignment.** They turn culture into curriculum, values into workflows, and mission into policy. That's how you build a movement that survives fatigue, transitions, and storms. That's how you build something holy, resilient, and scalable. If your values are the heartbeat—then your systems are the veins that keep it circulating.

SIDEBAR: Rhythm Reinforces Mission

What to build:

- Mission-aligned 1-on-1 templates
- Values-based hiring rubrics
- Monthly "Culture Calibration" huddles
- Quarterly peer-to-peer feedback forums
- Annual clarity reset retreats

Remember:

Vision leaks. Alignment drifts. But systems pull the culture back to center.

"Systems don't suppress culture—they secure it."

Innovation and Risk-Taking

Innovation doesn't grow in the soil of fear—it blossoms in environments rich with trust, empathy, and psychological safety. Servant leadership creates the conditions where risk-taking is not just tolerated, but expected. Because when people know their worth isn't tied to perfection, they stop hiding their ideas. They start experimenting, iterating, and dreaming big. In a culture where the servant leader says, *"You can fail forward here,"* the boundaries of what's possible get shattered—and the future gets built.

Research consistently affirms this truth. Amy Edmondson, in her groundbreaking work on psychological safety, revealed that the highest-performing teams were not the ones with the fewest mistakes—but the ones most willing to **speak up about them** (Edmondson, 1999). Google's Project Aristotle backed it up, identifying psychological safety as the #1 predictor of team innovation and success (Duhigg, 2016). The Colangelo College of Business at Grand Canyon University (n.d.) echoes this in its values, recognizing that "conscious capitalism thrives when people are free to think boldly, fail safely, and grow purposefully." Servant leadership is the delivery system for that kind of freedom.

But innovation won't sustain itself without systems. Servant leaders design rituals, rhythms, and feedback loops that reward initiative over inertia. They normalize learning through failure, embed innovation into evaluations, and create platforms for collaborative ideation. When a team member tries something new and it flops—do you punish it or praise the courage? That decision becomes the culture. Servant leaders create "green zones" for experimentation—zones where the mission is sacred, but the method is flexible.

Jesus Himself modeled this. He empowered His disciples—young, unqualified, unpredictable people—to take bold action in His name. When Peter stepped out of the boat and sank, Jesus didn't scold him. He reached out and lifted him. That's the power of a servant-led system. It doesn't shrink people—it stretches them. Because when safety and mission alignment converge, people don't just innovate—they transform.

SIDEBAR: Breakthrough Requires Breathing Room
When people feel safe, they take smart risks.
When they take smart risks, they innovate.
And when they innovate under a servant leader—they multiply impact.

"Servant leadership builds the runway where bold ideas take flight."

3-Day Micro Challenge: Risk, Reward, and Rise

DAY 1 — CREATE THE GREEN ZONE
"Where can we try something bold without fear of failure?"

CHAPTER 4: Servant Leadership and Organizational Culture

- Schedule a 15-minute team huddle. Declare one area of your workflow, process, or project as your team's *"green zone"*—a space where experimentation is encouraged and failure is feedback.
- Ask your team: *"What's one crazy idea we've never tried but always wondered about?"*
- Commit to testing it—no judgment, just learning.

DAY 2 — CELEBRATE THE COURAGE
"What did someone try this week that took guts?"

- Highlight and celebrate an act of initiative, even if it didn't work.
- Make it visible—through an email shoutout, a Slack badge, or a team meeting story.
- Let your team hear you say: *"The courage to try matters more than the perfection of results."*

DAY 3 — INSTALL THE FEEDBACK LOOP
"What did we learn—and how do we build from it?"

- Gather input on what went well, what didn't, and what could be tried next.
- Capture the lessons learned and document them in a shared space.
- Build a recurring rhythm (monthly, quarterly)

where innovation debriefs become standard practice.

Tagline for the team to remember:
"Failure is the classroom. Innovation is the diploma. Servant leadership is the teacher."

Safety Multiplies Risk-Taking and Innovation

Want bold ideas? Want wild innovation? It doesn't happen in fear—it happens in **freedom.**
When people know they won't be mocked, micromanaged, or minimized, they'll dream bigger, try harder, and bounce back faster.
Psychological safety becomes your **creative multiplier.** And when servant leadership drives the culture, people don't just take risks—they take **mission-driven, aligned risks.**
That's where breakthroughs happen.

Fear stifles innovation before it ever begins. In environments where mistakes are punished and vulnerability is weaponized, creativity suffocates. But when psychological safety is woven into the fabric of the culture, people stop playing defense and start pioneering ideas. As Harvard's Amy Edmondson (1999) demonstrated in her foundational work on psychological safety, the most innovative teams aren't the ones with the smartest people—they're the ones where people feel

CHAPTER 4: Servant Leadership and Organizational Culture

safe enough to speak, stretch, and sometimes stumble.

In servant-led organizations, that safety isn't accidental—**it's intentional**. Leaders model humility, reward initiative, and normalize learning from failure. Instead of demanding perfection, they ask: ***"What did we learn?"*** This fosters an environment where people move from fear-based compliance to courageous contribution. Google's Project Aristotle (Duhigg, 2016) affirmed that psychological safety is the #1 predictor of high-performing, innovative teams. Servant leadership builds that safety not through passivity, but by creating a trust-filled culture where truth is spoken in love, and risk is celebrated as a path to growth (Ephesians 4:15, NIV).

Innovation doesn't thrive in the presence of ego—it thrives in the presence of trust. When teams know their leaders won't shame them for missteps, they bring their boldest ideas to the table. In conscious capitalism, this is seen as one of the defining features of stakeholder-focused leadership: creating value by empowering creativity at every level (Sisodia et al., 2007). And in a biblical worldview, this mirrors God's pattern of stewardship—where risk, investment, and responsibility are not only allowed but expected (Matthew 25:14–30).

Ultimately, servant leadership transforms innovation from a risky gamble into a righteous calling. It aligns creative risk-taking with the organization's greater mission, providing both the fuel of freedom and the guardrails of purpose. This is where the most disruptive innovation happens—not from pressure, but from alignment. Not from fear, but from trust. Not from dominance, but from service.

SIDEBAR: Innovation Requires Altitude, Not Anxiety

- Fear says: "Don't mess up."
- Servant leadership says: "Take the shot—I've got your back."
- Innovation isn't about recklessness—it's about courageous alignment.

"There is no fear in love. But perfect love drives out fear..." — 1 John 4:18 (NIV)

The Culture of the Kingdom

Ultimately, servant leadership creates a **culture that echoes Heaven**.
It is a space of grace, a system of dignity, a structure where truth and love **coexist without compromise.**
Psalm 133:1 says, *"How good and pleasant it is when God's people live together in unity!"* That unity comes when the soil is safe and the mission is shared.
It's not hype—it's Holy.
And it's exactly what your team, your school, your business, and your community have been waiting for.

Psalm 133:1 says, *"How good and pleasant it is when God's people live together in unity!"* That unity comes when the soil is safe and the mission is shared.

It's not hype—it's Holy.
And it's exactly what your team, your school, your business, and your community have been waiting for.

But make no mistake—this isn't about building comfortable teams. It's about building consecrated ones. A Kingdom culture doesn't just function well—it glorifies God. It doesn't just inspire performance—it releases purpose. When leaders serve with integrity, humility, and courage, they don't just lead organizations—they lead revivals.

Rally Cry:
This is your invitation. Not just to build a better team—but to build a holy one. A team that serves boldly, leads humbly, and transforms everything it touches.

Kingdom Culture Is Counterculture

In a world where leadership often means dominance, Scripture flips the script.
Romans 12:10 (NIV) says, *"Be devoted to one another in love. Honor one another above yourselves."*
This isn't a leadership tip—it's a **Kingdom command.**
The world says, "Climb over others to rise." Jesus says, "Lift others higher."
When servant leaders obey this, they don't just build teams—they build **family**, and that family creates a culture no bonus check can buy.

In modern organizational life, leadership is often

measured by authority, speed, and control. But in Kingdom culture, **leadership is measured by how well you lift, listen, and love**. As Grand Canyon University's Colangelo College of Business affirms, *"True leadership is servant-oriented and mission-aligned. It prioritizes people over power and legacy over ego"* (GCU, n.d.). That's what makes Kingdom culture so radical: it refuses to play by the rules of empire leadership and instead builds systems that reflect eternity.

Jesus didn't call leaders to climb ladders—He called them to carry crosses. Kingdom leaders don't rise by stepping over people. They rise by **raising people up**. That's why when you embed servant leadership into your systems—your hiring, your meetings, your decisions—you're not just building a better company or school. You're building a countercultural movement that reflects Heaven's design on Earth.

When leaders obey this, they don't just build efficient teams—they build spiritual families. They don't create followers—they cultivate disciples. And the culture that flows out of that posture? It's not shallow, hype-driven, or dependent on incentives. It's deep. It's joyful. It's resilient. It's a **culture no bonus check can buy—because it's built on love that the world can't manufacture.**

CHAPTER 4: Servant Leadership and Organizational Culture

SIDEBAR: The Two Cultures Compared

Empire Culture	Kingdom Culture
Dominate to rise	Serve to rise
Take credit	Give honor
Protect position	Elevate others
Demand results	Develop people
Fear-based compliance	Love-fueled alignment

"The last will be first, and the first will be last." – Matthew 20:16 (NIV)

That's not just a verse. That's your leadership philosophy.

Honor Over Ego

Let's not water this down—**honoring others above yourself** is a direct assault on ego-driven leadership. It means celebrating others' wins more than your own. It

means not needing the credit, not craving the spotlight. It means walking into the boardroom asking, **"Who can I bless today?"** instead of, "What can I get today?"
That's not soft. That's strength, restrained and redirected by mission.
And when leaders lead with that kind of honor, **trust explodes**—because people know they matter more than metrics.

Let's not water this down—honoring others above yourself is a **full-on assault against ego-driven leadership**. In a culture addicted to status and self-promotion, honoring others is downright rebellious. But it's also radically effective. Philippians 2:3–4 (NIV) commands, *"Do nothing out of selfish ambition or vain conceit. Rather, in humility value others above yourselves."* That's not theoretical. That's strategic. Because when you elevate others, you elevate everything.

Honor isn't passive—it's **active leadership discipline**. It's walking into the boardroom and thinking, *"Who can I bless today?"* instead of, *"What can I get today?"* It's celebrating others' wins with more joy than your own. It's relinquishing the spotlight to amplify someone else's voice. That kind of leadership isn't soft—it's **strength restrained by mission**. As Jim Collins wrote in *Good to Great*, the most transformational leaders are not ego-driven—they're servant-driven (Collins, 2001). The data confirms what the gospel already declared: honor multiplies results.

CHAPTER 4: Servant Leadership and Organizational Culture

At Grand Canyon University, the Colangelo College of Business instills this very principle, describing leadership as *"others-focused stewardship marked by moral clarity, emotional intelligence, and a devotion to service"* (GCU, n.d.). It's a direct rejection of empire-building leadership that hoards credit and manipulates perception. Servant leaders choose legacy over likes, and mission over me.

And here's the result: **trust explodes**. When a team sees their leader giving away honor instead of grabbing it, they stop posturing and start producing. They stop performing and start contributing. Because they know they are not tools to be used, they're people to be honored. And that kind of culture? It doesn't just perform—it multiplies.

Devotion Is the Fuel of Service

Paul writes, "Be devoted to one another in love"—not "be professional" or "be efficient."

Devotion is **relational fire.** It's the deep commitment to walk with people through storms, setbacks, and success. Servant leaders don't just tolerate their people—they are **devoted to them.**

This kind of devotion isn't a leadership trend—it's a reflection of Jesus, who said, *"As I have loved you, so you must love one another"* (John 13:34, NIV).

That's not weak leadership. That's **world-shaking commitment.**

Paul doesn't say, *"Be efficient with one another."* He says, *"Be devoted to one another in love"* (Romans 12:10, NIV).

That word—*devoted*—is dangerous to shallow leadership. It calls us past performance metrics into the **sacred realm of commitment.** Devotion means you show up even when it's inconvenient. You stand firm when others fall away. You don't lead people for what they produce, you lead them because they're worth it.

Servant leaders don't simply tolerate their people—they're **devoted to them** like family. In a corporate world obsessed with detachment and professional distance, devotion breaks the mold. And yet, the most resilient cultures aren't built by emotional detachment, they're built by leaders who are *relationally invested* and *spiritually grounded*. According to Greenleaf (1977), servant leaders operate out of a desire to serve first, not manage—because true leadership is born from love, not leverage.

Jesus gave us the blueprint. In John 13:34 (NIV), He said, *"As I have loved you, so you must love one another."* That wasn't a vague sentiment—it was a revolutionary standard. Jesus walked with His people in storms, through betrayals, across deserts. His love wasn't situational—it was sacrificial. That kind of devotion isn't a side note of leadership. It's the **engine that drives transformational service.**

Devotion fuels a culture of resilience, loyalty, and legacy. It transforms the tone of team meetings. It reshapes how we correct, how we celebrate, how we respond to failure. It says: *"I'm with you. I'm for you. I'm not going*

CHAPTER 4: Servant Leadership and Organizational Culture

anywhere." And in a world where people leave jobs because they feel unseen and uncared for, **devotion becomes your leadership superpower**.

SIDEBAR: Devotion Destroys Disengagement

"You can manage people with policies. But you transform them with presence."

Devotion isn't soft, it's **fireproof loyalty.** And in today's world, that's revolutionary.

Galatians 5:13 — Freedom That Serves

Galatians 5:13 (NIV) says, *"You, my brothers and sisters, were called to be free. But do not use your freedom to indulge the flesh; rather, serve one another humbly in love."*
That verse DESTROYS the myth that leadership is about entitlement.
True leadership says: **"My position gives me more responsibility, not more privilege."**
Servant leaders don't use power to indulge the flesh—they use it to **elevate others.**
Because real freedom in Christ means **laying your life down so others can rise up.**

Galatians 5:13 (NIV) delivers a direct blow to ego-driven leadership:

The Greatest Among You

> *"You, my brothers and sisters, were called to be free. But do not use your freedom to indulge the flesh; rather, serve one another humbly in love."*

That one verse **shatters** the myth that leadership equals privilege. It redefines freedom—not as autonomy for self—but as availability for others. In a culture where power is often hoarded and authority is leveraged for personal gain, this Scripture turns the system upside down. **Biblical leadership isn't a throne—it's a towel.** The higher you rise, the more responsibility you carry to serve.

> This mindset is echoed in the framework of **conscious capitalism**, which teaches that ethical business leadership isn't about maximizing self-interest, but maximizing stakeholder flourishing (Mackey & Sisodia, 2013). Freedom, in a Kingdom sense, isn't about doing whatever you want—it's about having the strength to choose what honors others and glorifies God.

Servant leaders understand this deeply: **true freedom produces radical responsibility.** Their leadership isn't fueled by control but by calling. They don't use their authority to indulge the flesh—they use it to *die to self* and *raise others up*. This is where Christ-centered leadership departs from the world's playbook. As Jesus said in Mark 10:43–45 (NIV), *"Whoever wants to become great among you must be your servant."*

CHAPTER 4: Servant Leadership and Organizational Culture

So if you've been given freedom in your role, don't waste it on ego, self-preservation, or applause. Use it to create opportunities, protect the vulnerable, and build systems of dignity. Because **leadership is not about how high you climb—it's about how many you lift while you're up there.**

SIDEBAR: Freedom Is for Foot Washing, Not Flexing

> **"You weren't set free to shine—you were set free to serve."**

Real leadership doesn't take advantage of freedom—it *uses* it to advance others.

Humility Isn't a Weakness—It's a Weapon

Scripture tells us to serve one another **humbly in love.** That word "humbly" punches the pride straight in the mouth.
Because humility doesn't mean thinking less of yourself—it means thinking of yourself **less.**
It's using your gifts for the good of the group, not the glory of self.
And in a world full of arrogant, power-hungry leadership, humility becomes your **superpower.**
Jesus, the King of Kings, washed feet. And He told us, *"I have set you an example that you should do as I have done for you."* (John 13:15, NIV)

Servant leadership doesn't just tolerate humility—it wields it.

Galatians 5:13 calls us to *"serve one another humbly in love."* That word—*humbly*—is a divine rebuke to the prideful systems of the world. It punches entitlement in the mouth and flips the power dynamic upside down. Because **humility doesn't mean you're less capable—it means you're more surrendered.** It doesn't erase confidence—it sanctifies it.

C.S. Lewis famously wrote, *"Humility is not thinking less of yourself, but thinking of yourself less."* That's more than clever theology—it's elite leadership strategy. In a world addicted to self-promotion, humility makes space for others to rise. It silences the need for applause so that **others can find their voice**. It doesn't withhold strength—it **redirects strength for the good of the group**, not the glory of the leader.

In business, humility drives performance. According to Owens & Hekman (2012), organizations led by humble leaders experience stronger collaboration, higher employee engagement, and healthier team dynamics. Why? Because humility creates **relational safety and sustainable influence**—two things ego can never deliver. Humble leaders aren't passive. They're powerful without being prideful.

Jesus didn't just teach this—He modeled it. *"Now that I, your Lord and Teacher, have washed your feet, you also should wash one another's feet"* (John 13:14–15, NIV).

CHAPTER 4: Servant Leadership and Organizational Culture

The King of Kings got on His knees, looked His betrayer in the eye, and **served him anyway.** That wasn't weakness. That was Heaven's power wrapped in human restraint.

And it leads us to this: humility isn't the end goal—it's the open door. Because humility without love is empty. But humility soaked in love? That's where everything shifts. That's where leadership becomes transformation. And that's where we go next.

Love That Moves

Every command in these verses is anchored in **love**—not emotion, but **action.**
Love that leads to **devotion**, love that produces **honor**, love that results in **service.**
This isn't theoretical theology. This is **applied leadership.**
Servant leadership isn't about being liked—it's about being **loving**, and love is proven not in words, but in sacrifice.
If we want to lead like Jesus, we must **serve like Jesus**—consistently, courageously, and compassionately.

Every Kingdom command we've explored—honor, humility, devotion, service—is **anchored in love.** But not sentimental, soft-focus, coffee-mug love. No—*this* is love forged in action. Love that endures betrayal. Love that fuels mission. Love that bleeds so others can breathe.

Scripture doesn't invite leaders to *feel* loving. It **commands us to move in love.** Galatians 5:13 doesn't say, "Feel nice things." It says, *"Serve one another humbly in love."* That's not theoretical theology. That's boots-on-the-ground leadership. That's love that shows up at the hospital, the boardroom, the locker room, the classroom, and says, *"I'm here. I see you. I'll carry this with you."*

This kind of love doesn't manipulate—it liberates. It doesn't whisper hollow praise—it **speaks hard truth with soft eyes.** It sacrifices ego, convenience, and comfort to elevate the people God has entrusted to you. Jesus didn't *talk* love—He *became* love, and then told us, "Go and do likewise."

Servant leadership isn't about being liked—it's about being **loving**. And love isn't proven in tweets or titles—it's proven in **sacrifice**. If we want to lead like Jesus, we must *serve like Jesus—consistently, courageously, and compassionately.* That's the kind of love that outlasts trends and shatters strongholds.
And when that love is **embedded in your systems**—when it's the default, the rhythm, the expectation—**movements begin.**

Systems of Honor Create Movements

When Romans 12:10 and Galatians 5:13 are built into the

CHAPTER 4: Servant Leadership and Organizational Culture

system of your organization, the atmosphere shifts. People stop competing and start collaborating. Leaders stop clinging to control and start **cultivating people.**
That's when toxic culture dies and Kingdom culture takes root.
You'll know it when the hallway conversations match the vision statements. That's **alignment through scripture-powered culture.**

Honor isn't just a virtue—it's a **systemic force** that reshapes the spiritual architecture of an organization. When Romans 12:10 and Galatians 5:13 stop being memory verses and start becoming *operating systems*, everything changes. The culture shifts from survival to revival. Scarcity dies. Siloes break. And **competition gives way to collaboration.**

When servant leadership is hardwired into policy, rhythm, and language, **people don't jockey for power—they unleash purpose.** Leaders stop clinging to control and start cultivating courage in others. Teams stop asking, *"What's in it for me?"* and start asking, *"How do we win together?"* This is no longer about maintaining order. It's about **mobilizing a movement.**

That's when toxic culture dies—not from better slogans, but from **systems soaked in Scripture.** When a team walks through Ephesians 4, Romans 12, and Galatians 5 in real time—honoring each other, serving humbly, building each other up—the mission doesn't just

survive...
It multiplies.

And here's how you'll know: the hallway conversations will start to sound like your vision statements. Your onboarding will sound like your altar calls. Your culture will become your testimony.
Because what's been embedded in love will be sustained by Spirit.
And that, my friend, leads us to the ultimate aim of servant leadership:

Leadership That Reflects Heaven.

Ready to build it? Let's go.

Leadership that Reflects Heaven

When we lead with these scriptures as our foundation, we don't just lead well—we lead **like Jesus.**
This isn't about theology for Sunday. It's **strategy for Monday.**
It's about honoring others in the conference room, serving your team on deadline day, and loving your people even when it's inconvenient.
Romans 12:10 and Galatians 5:13 aren't suggestions—they are **leadership marching orders.**
This is the bottom line of servant leadership: **if it doesn't look like Jesus, it's not leadership worth following.**

CHAPTER 4: Servant Leadership and Organizational Culture

When we lead with **Scripture as our standard**, we don't just lead well—we lead *holy*. We lead like Jesus. We stop mimicking corporate power plays and start **mirroring Kingdom purpose**. This isn't about theology for Sunday—it's **battle-tested strategy for Monday.** Because servant leadership isn't just an idea to believe in—it's a **framework to build in.**

This is the kind of leadership that honors others in the conference room, **washes feet in the breakroom**, and prays over decisions when nobody's looking. It's showing up with love when your schedule says "leave." It's stepping into conflict with courage and into failure with grace. It's staying tender in a tough world and faithful in a fast one. *It's servant leadership—and it's divine.*

Romans 12:10 and Galatians 5:13 aren't motivational sound bites. They're **marching orders** for Kingdom-minded leaders who refuse to bow to ego, entitlement, or empire. When we **act justly, love mercy, and walk humbly** into the workplace, we turn cubicles into pulpits and staff meetings into revivals.

Here's the bottom line:
If your leadership doesn't look like Jesus—it's not leadership worth following.
Because in the end, real influence doesn't come from titles—it comes from **the towel and the cross.**

SIDEBAR: The Litmus Test of Servant Leadership

"Ask yourself this: If Jesus walked into your organization today, would He recognize the culture?
Would He say, 'Well done'?
If not, it's time to lead like Heaven—on earth."

Call to Action — Chapter 4: Light the Fire in the Culture

If you want to change your organization, you don't start with a memo.
You start with your **heart.**

Culture isn't created in a conference room—it's created in **how you show up,** how you speak, how you serve when no one's watching.
You can't fake a healthy culture. You either live it—or you poison it.
And here's the truth: **You are the thermostat.** You set the temperature. You decide whether your people walk into a furnace of fear or a fire of faith.

Let Romans 12:10 be the mission. Let Galatians 5:13 be the method.
And let every hallway, email, and meeting be soaked in **purposeful honor, joyful service, and fierce devotion to the mission.**
Do not wait for "them" to do it. *You* are the leader.
You are the turning point. You are the culture shift.

Let your organization become a movement.

CHAPTER 4: Servant Leadership and Organizational Culture

Let your leadership become a ministry.
Let your team become a testimony.

Because servant leadership isn't a slogan on the wall, it's **the fire in your bones.**
Now go light that fire in every room you walk into.

14-Day Culture Firestarter Challenge

Chapter 4 Activation: Build It. Live It. Multiply It.

"You are the thermostat. You set the temperature. You decide whether your people walk into a furnace of fear or a fire of faith."

Day 1: Diagnose the Culture Honestly

Action:
Do a deep audit of your current environment. What's being tolerated? What's being rewarded? Where is fear present? Where is honor missing?

Power Statement:
You can't transform what you won't confront.

Day 2: Define the Core Values That Matter

Action:
Write out 3–5 non-negotiable values that will shape the culture moving forward. Don't copy them from someone else. Make them yours.

Power Statement:
Culture begins with clarity.

Day 3: Repent for What You've Allowed

Action:
Privately reflect on and repent for any way you've contributed to fear, ego, passivity, or cultural confusion—intentionally or not. Own it.

Power Statement:
You can't build revival on top of pride.

Day 4: Go Public with the Mission

Action:
Declare your commitment to servant leadership with your team, staff, or community. Speak the vision. Tell them what's changing—and why.

Power Statement:

CHAPTER 4: Servant Leadership and Organizational Culture

Vision kept quiet creates cultures that drift.

Day 5: Ask for Anonymous Feedback

Action:
Create a safe space (digital or physical) for your people to share what the culture *really* feels like. What needs to change? What's working? What's broken?

Power Statement:
People can't be empowered if they're afraid to speak.

Day 6: Confront a Cultural Violation

Action:
Lovingly—but clearly—address a behavior, process, or norm that violates your servant leadership values. Set the tone for truth + grace.

Power Statement:
What you don't confront, you confirm.

Day 7: Honor Someone Who Reflects the Culture

Action:
Celebrate someone who lives the values. Make it loud. Make it meaningful. Use it to signal what your culture actually rewards.

Power Statement:
People repeat what gets rewarded.

Day 8: Design a Ritual Around the Mission

Action:
Create one consistent rhythm that reinforces the values: a gratitude circle, a culture checkpoint, a weekly recognition moment.

Power Statement:
Repetition turns values into reflexes.

Day 9: Build a Boundary That Protects the Culture

Action:
Establish a clear boundary, something you will no longer tolerate, ignore, or permit. Set it. Announce it. Hold it.

Power Statement:
Honor without boundaries becomes dysfunction.

CHAPTER 4: Servant Leadership and Organizational Culture

Day 10: Tell a Story That Shapes the Culture

Action:
Share a real story (your own or someone else's) that embodies the servant leadership culture you're building. Stories shape belief.

Power Statement:
What's told repeatedly becomes culture instinct.

Day 11: Rework One System to Reflect the Mission

Action:
Pick one system—onboarding, evaluations, meetings, communication—and rebuild it around your servant leadership values.

Power Statement:
If it's not in the system, it doesn't exist.

Day 12: Model Vulnerability in Public

Action:
Share something openly with your team: a failure, a

lesson learned, or an area you're growing in. Show them that safety starts with you.

Power Statement:
Vulnerability is the seedbed of trust.

Day 13: Invest in Someone's Growth Today

Action:
Pour into someone on your team, family, or circle. Offer feedback, mentorship, resources, or prayer. Stretch them with love.

Power Statement:
Servant leaders don't hoard wisdom—they multiply it.

Day 14: Write the Culture Declaration

Action:
Write a bold, 3–5 sentence declaration of the culture you're building. Read it to your team. Hang it up. Live it daily.

Power Statement:
The culture you declare is the movement you lead.

Final Rally:

This isn't a challenge—it's a commissioning.
You are no longer reacting to culture.
You are **creating** it.
You are no longer waiting for leadership to change.
You ARE the leadership that changes things.

Now go—light the fire. And never let it die.

The Greatest Among You

CHAPTER 5: Building Systems That Scale

"If your vision can't survive without you, it was never a system—it was a show. But systems rooted in service don't just scale—they outlive the leader and ignite the legacy."

Culture Without Systems is Just a Mood

You can have passion. You can have purpose.
But without systems? You've got **chaos wrapped in charisma** and set on a ticking clock.
A powerful servant culture can't live on hype—it must be **locked into habits, routines, and rituals that repeat.**

The truth is—**momentum without structure burns out.** Culture without systems is just mood music for a movement that will die when the emotions fade or the leader leaves.

Servant leadership isn't sustained by how loud you preach it—it's sustained by how deeply you build it. **Systems are how values become visible.** They are the hardwiring of humility, the architecture of honor, the repeatable rhythms of revival.

Chapter 4 lit the match with purpose, alignment, and values.
Now Chapter 5 builds the **engine that keeps the fire burning**, day after day, team after team, year after year.

Because without systems, you're not scaling a mission… you're babysitting a vibe.

Scale is the Real Test of Leadership

True leaders **create impact that stretches across departments, campuses, and generations.**
If it only works when you're in the room, it's not leadership—it's babysitting.
Systems let your mission grow **without compromising values**.
Servant leadership isn't about making yourself irreplaceable, it's about making your culture **indestructible**.

Anyone can fire up a room. But can you build a structure that fuels others when you're not there? That's the real test. Leadership is not proven in proximity—it's revealed in your absence. When your culture keeps multiplying long after you've left the building, that's when you've truly led. As Kouzes and Posner (2017) note in *The Leadership Challenge*, "leaders must build commitment and competence in others so that shared values become organizational DNA." If it all crumbles without you, it wasn't leadership—it was dependency dressed up in charisma.

CHAPTER 5: Building Systems That Scale

Servant leadership is designed to scale because it transfers ownership, not just tasks. It empowers others through deeply embedded systems, not surface-level inspiration. Research supports this model: decentralized leadership approaches, especially those rooted in servant leadership—drive innovation, retention, and long-term sustainability (Eva et al., 2019). That means you're not just leading a team; you're developing leaders who will carry the mission forward without diluting the message. As Ralph Nader famously said, "The function of leadership is to produce more leaders, not more followers."

If your leadership only thrives under your direct supervision, it's not a movement, it's a bottleneck. But when you build systems rooted in values, the culture self-corrects, the mission self-replicates, and the organization gains spiritual and structural resilience. As Grand Canyon University teaches in its Colangelo College of Business pillars, leadership should be scalable, servant-centered, and sustainability-driven (Grand Canyon University, n.d.). That's why we scale—not to get bigger, but to get **better** at carrying the weight of purpose. And to do that, we must stop treating **systems as the enemy of the Spirit**—and start seeing them as the **vehicles of mission**.

> *"The function of leadership is to produce more leaders, not more followers."* — **Ralph Nader**

Systems Are Not the Enemy of the Spirit

Some think systems kill authenticity. Wrong.
In servant leadership, systems are not cold mechanics—they're **the vessels that carry heart, humility, and mission to scale.**
Think about Jesus: He didn't just perform miracles—He **built a discipleship model** that multiplied leaders across centuries.
That's not luck—that's a **Holy Spirit-infused strategy.** We're about to do the same for your business, your church, your school, or your team.

In too many organizations, there's a toxic myth that's crippled growth: **that systems and the Spirit are opposites.** That structure restricts freedom. That process stifles passion. But let's be clear—**the Holy Spirit is not afraid of structure.** The same God who created galaxies also created **Sabbath rhythms, Levitical codes, and apostolic churches.** Systems are not the enemy of the Spirit—they are His stage. In servant leadership, systems are not robotic rulebooks—they are vehicles of *radical love, restorative justice,* and *scalable transformation.*

Jesus didn't just inspire people—He **deployed** them. He didn't hoard His power—He built a system of empowerment that turned fishermen into apostles, and enemies into evangelists. That's the gold standard of

CHAPTER 5: Building Systems That Scale

spiritual leadership: **mission with multiplication.** And He did it not with confusion, but with **clarity, process, and intentional succession.** As Greenleaf (1977) taught, "The best test of servant leadership is whether those served grow as persons." That kind of growth doesn't happen on accident. It happens in systems built to steward the calling.

The most Spirit-filled organizations aren't the ones with the loudest worship—they're the ones with the deepest alignment. Systems rooted in servant leadership **don't stifle fire—they sustain it.** They ensure that your values show up in hiring policies, in onboarding experiences, in how meetings are run, and how conflicts are resolved. They create **consistency with compassion**—truth without tyranny. In today's chaotic world, we don't need less structure, we need **more sacred structure**: *systems built on the values of Heaven, designed to scale impact on Earth.* That's what you're about to build—from **the boardroom to the break room.**

From the Boardroom to the Break Room

Real transformation doesn't live in policy—it lives in practice.
You want a culture that scales? Then it needs to exist **at every level**—not just in the boardroom, but in the **break room, the classroom, the locker room, the loading dock.**

That only happens when your servant values are **encoded into onboarding, baked into meetings, reinforced in coaching, and visible in decisions.**
Culture must travel.
And systems are how we give it wheels.

Real transformation never stays stuck at the top—it spreads through the trenches. If servant leadership lives only in executive memos and mission statements, it will die in the daily grind. **True cultural change happens when vision is translated into systems and habits at every level of the organization.** From the C-suite to the front desk, from the corner office to the custodial closet—servant leadership must be seen, heard, and felt in every space where people show up. As Liden et al. (2008) emphasize in their research on servant leadership's organizational impact, **performance and satisfaction increase when leadership values are lived consistently across all levels.**

That means every employee, no matter their title, should be able to answer two questions with clarity: *What does this organization stand for? And how do I live it out here?* That clarity doesn't happen through osmosis—it happens through **strategically aligned systems.** Servant-led organizations design processes that reinforce core values at every touchpoint: onboarding, staff development, feedback loops, crisis response, and recognition structures. It's not about having a charismatic leader at the top—it's about having a **culture that's unmistakable at the bottom.** That's when your values stop being ideals

CHAPTER 5: Building Systems That Scale

and start becoming instincts.

This is where most organizations fail. They silo leadership into departments and isolate culture to HR initiatives. But servant leadership is not a department—it's a **distributed identity.** It's a *way of being* that must be systematized so it doesn't evaporate in stress, turnover, or scale. When your systems reflect the mission, your culture becomes mobile. It starts showing up in locker room speeches, customer service calls, warehouse check-ins, and team huddles. **That's when it spreads. That's when it scales.** And that's when it gets reinforced—because **what gets repeated gets remembered.**

What Gets Repeated Gets Reinforced

If it's not repeated, it's not remembered.
Servant leadership becomes real when it **shows up in your calendar, your job descriptions, your incentives, and your feedback loops.**
That's what we mean by scale: not just doing something once, but building the **scaffolding that lets it stand tall and last long.**
Jesus taught the same lessons over and over—not because His followers were slow, but because repetition **is how transformation sticks.**
You want your people to live the mission? Then build it into their week.

In leadership, memory isn't built by inspiration alone, it's built by repetition. The principle is simple but often ignored: **if it's not repeated, it's not remembered—and if it's not remembered, it's not reproduced.** Repetition creates culture. It turns momentary inspiration into muscle memory. That's why servant leadership must be more than a declaration, it must be a discipline. According to Kouzes and Posner (2017), leaders shape culture by "modeling the way" and reinforcing values consistently through language, behavior, and structure. That means every meeting, email, coaching session, and system is an opportunity to reinforce what matters most.

Jesus didn't teach once and move on—He repeated lessons, re-demonstrated servant posture, and revisited the same truths through parables, actions, and relationships. Not because His disciples were incompetent, but because **transformation requires saturation.** Servant leaders today must adopt that same model. This includes embedding values into job descriptions, aligning performance reviews with character-based metrics, and crafting incentive systems that celebrate collaboration, empathy, and growth—not just output. As Grand Canyon University (n.d.) emphasizes in their servant leadership framework, "transformation occurs when values are consistently modeled, taught, and reinforced." Repetition isn't redundant—it's *revolutionary*.

If you want your team to embody servant leadership, **you have to build it into their week.** Start meetings with

CHAPTER 5: Building Systems That Scale

value alignment moments. Reflect regularly on the mission during 1:1s. Celebrate servant-hearted behaviors publicly. Build feedback loops that reinforce culture. Make your values *inescapable*—not by coercion, but through consistency. Because in servant-led systems, **every repetition is a revival.** Every time a leader models the mission, the culture gets deeper roots. And when repeated enough, that mission begins to multiply—not through your personality, but through the system itself.

That leads to the next truth—**servant leadership isn't about platforming a person.** It's about building a structure that outlives the leader. Because **systems should multiply the mission—not the man.**

Systems Multiply the Mission, Not the Man

You're not trying to be the hero. You're trying to **create a heroic culture.**
Systems ensure that your team doesn't have to wait for you to do it—they're **equipped to carry the torch themselves.**
That's why Jesus didn't stay and micromanage—He empowered others to **lead like Him.**
John 14:12 (NIV)- *"Whoever believes in me will do the works I have been doing, and they will do even greater things than these."*
That's scale. That's legacy. That's the **servant leader's**

endgame.

True servant leadership doesn't crave center stage—it builds a stage where others can shine. At its highest level, leadership is not about accumulation of influence, but about **distribution of purpose**. When a leader becomes the bottleneck, the mission suffocates. But when systems are built around the mission—not the man—**scalability, sustainability, and succession become possible.** This is why Jesus spent more time training disciples than performing miracles. He wasn't trying to impress the crowd—He was building a movement. And movements require systems.

John 14:12 isn't just theological encouragement—it's a leadership blueprint: *"They will do even greater things..."* That's not an ego trip; that's empowerment. **Servant leaders don't build empires—they build engines.** They install repeatable processes for coaching, development, accountability, and celebration that carry the culture even when they're absent. Kouzes and Posner (2017) assert that enduring greatness is found when leaders "enable others to act." That enabling happens most effectively through systems that activate the mission at every level, not just in the C-suite.

Innovative servant leadership systems are flexible but focused. Think modular—not monolithic. A powerful onboarding system could include storytelling modules that share the organization's servant values, paired with case studies of value-driven decision-making. Feedback

CHAPTER 5: Building Systems That Scale

systems might use pulse surveys that ask *"Did you feel seen, heard, and valued this week?"* instead of just *"Was your manager responsive?"* Even rituals like "Mission Mondays" or "Testimony Tuesdays" can embed the heart of service into the rhythm of the week. **Innovation doesn't always mean tech—it means intentionality.**

The most advanced systems don't just maintain—they multiply. A great leader isn't irreplaceable, they are replicated. Every meeting cadence, recognition program, disciplinary structure, and peer review process should whisper the same thing: *"This is who we are. This is what we do. This is why we serve."* (Greenleaf, 1977). When systems communicate what the leader used to say manually, the mission lives independently of charisma. **The system becomes the sermon.**

So, if your vision is worth carrying, it must be engineered for endurance. You're not building for a season—you're building for generations. Servant leadership without systems is like having fire with no furnace. But when the furnace is installed, the heat doesn't fade—it spreads. And that's the next step—because **systems are the bridge from vision to victory.**

Systems Are the Bridge from Vision to Victory

Vision is your fuel, but systems are your vehicle. Without them, your leadership dies with your departure.

This chapter gives you the practical, spiritual, and organizational tools to make **servant leadership the standard—not the exception.**

You're going to learn how to **embed service, humility, honor, and excellence into repeatable, adaptable models** that fit any context.

Because servant leadership isn't fragile—it's **formidable** when rooted in strategy.

Vision is essential—it ignites hearts, unites teams, and inspires action. But vision alone doesn't scale. Systems are the structure that gives vision wings and allows it to outlast the visionary. The difference between a flash-in-the-pan movement and a generational legacy is this: **vision becomes victory when systems are built to carry it.** As Robert Greenleaf (1977) emphasized, the servant leader "begins with the natural feeling that one wants to serve," but the truly effective ones design paths, processes, and protocols so that *others* can serve with power and clarity.

To lead with systems is not to trade spirit for structure—it's to **honor the mission with discipline.** Practical examples include developing value-based hiring matrices, where candidates are evaluated not only on technical competence but on evidence of humility, collaboration, and teachability. Design onboarding journeys that teach the *why* before the *what*, embedding the organization's Kingdom values into the first 90 days of employment. Want to make humility scalable? Build peer-nominated recognition programs where employees

CHAPTER 5: Building Systems That Scale

celebrate each other's servant-hearted wins—making honor part of the rhythm, not just the rhetoric.

System design is also spiritual stewardship. **It's your responsibility as a leader to create environments where love, excellence, and mission aren't just preached—they're practiced.** Create feedback systems where team members regularly reflect on how they've served others that week, or mission metrics that track not only output, but the health of collaboration and psychological safety. Servant leadership isn't afraid of metrics—it redefines them. Excellence isn't just results—it's *how* the results are pursued. A system built on these foundations doesn't just achieve goals; it *transforms people in the process.*

The key innovation here? **Make systems that feel human.** Infuse every form, survey, performance check-in, and staff meeting with mission language. Replace bureaucratic bloat with rhythms that reinforce culture. Build "Mission Blocks" into calendars—a protected hour each week for vision resetting, value reflection, or community service planning. What separates good leaders from great ones is their ability to turn inspiration into institution—without losing the soul of the mission. That's how vision becomes victory.

Buckle Up—It's Time to Build

What follows isn't theory—it's your **operating system upgrade.**

The Greatest Among You

From staff development to hiring, from meetings to measurement, we're going to overhaul the way your organization functions at every level.

So whether you're a CEO, pastor, athletic director, coach, principal, or team leader—**this is how you turn your spark into a wildfire.**

Let's move beyond inspiration and into **installation.** Because if you're building something for eternity, it better be built to scale.

From the Boardroom to the Break Room

What follows isn't theory—it's transformation on wheels. Too many organizations stop at the pep talk. They rally the troops but never rewire the systems. That's why cultures collapse when leaders leave. This chapter is your full-scale blueprint to make servant leadership the infrastructure, not just the inspiration. We're not tweaking cosmetics—we're pouring new concrete. Your systems are either multiplying your mission—or muting it. Let's build ones that roar with purpose.

From staff development to hiring, from communication to crisis response, we're going to do more than adjust. We're going to engineer transformation. You're going to install values into the core code of your organization— where no promotion, pivot, or personnel change can erase them. These aren't tricks. These are time-tested systems backed by scripture, strategy, and sweat. Because if you're building for eternity, mediocrity is not an option.

CHAPTER 5: Building Systems That Scale

Whether you're a CEO shaping a global brand, a principal leading a public school, a coach turning a team into a brotherhood, or a pastor shepherding a congregation—you need systems. And not just systems that manage people—systems that unleash them. Systems that *breathe your mission* into job descriptions, meetings, onboarding flows, team huddles, feedback loops, and conflict resolution. This is the gospel of structure—not to restrict, but to empower.

So buckle up. This isn't a self-help chapter. This is a leadership software upgrade that takes your calling and gives it an engine. We're moving beyond motivation and into multiplication. We're not building *for* hype—we're building for *heaven*. You were born to lead something that lasts. And that requires systems that scale, rhythms that reproduce, and alignment that outlives you.

Let's begin where it matters most—not with power plays in the boardroom, but with *culture codes in the break room*. Because if servant leadership doesn't work on the floor, it doesn't work at all.

Servant Leadership Must Be Everywhere

If servant leadership stays locked in the executive suite, it dies in irrelevance.
For it to transform your organization, it must **travel the halls, walk the warehouse, and speak through the**

lunch line.
It must live where the real work happens—**on the floor, in the field, behind the scenes.**
This is not just about senior leaders—it's about **every leader.**
From the CEO to the custodian, everyone has influence, and every position becomes a platform for impact.

Organizations often fail not because of poor mission statements, but because the mission never reaches the boots on the ground. Leadership cannot be confined to corner offices—it must be contextualized into breakrooms, classrooms, team huddles, and loading docks. As Greenleaf (1977) asserted, the servant leader's task is not to command but to *grow other servants*—and that growth must be omnipresent, not elite. When your culture empowers every employee to lead with humility, you activate decentralized leadership that multiplies impact at scale.

Research by Eva et al. (2019) supports this deeply—servant leadership at all organizational levels significantly improves trust, job satisfaction, and team performance. It's not just the managers who matter—it's the mentors in the margins. Your night shift janitor, your delivery driver, your cafeteria team—they are all culture carriers. If they experience the values of love, humility, and empowerment in how they're treated, they will spread those same values in how they serve. Organizations that overlook this relational ripple effect build cultures that are top-heavy, brittle, and shallow.

CHAPTER 5: Building Systems That Scale

So how do you scale it? First, flip your training model. Don't just train executives on leadership principles—equip *everyone* with the mindset of service, stewardship, and shared mission. That means onboarding should be soaked in servant values. Middle managers must be mentored in empathy and accountability. Even your customer service scripts can be rewritten with servant-first language. As Spears (1995) noted, institutions that adopt servant leadership as a *shared language* create "ethical climates that support sustainable success and human flourishing."

Second, audit your systems. Do your performance reviews reward only individual outcomes, or do they celebrate collaboration, service, and cultural contribution? Do your incentives reinforce humility and initiative, or do they breed selfishness and silence? Servant leadership must show up in how you measure success, not just how you preach it. System-wide leadership models must reflect biblical truths like Philippians 2:3—"Do nothing out of selfish ambition... but in humility value others above yourselves." If Jesus empowered fishermen to lead a movement, you can empower your cafeteria staff to carry your mission.

Finally, lead visibly in the trenches. Executives must visit classrooms, sweep floors, and listen without agenda. This is not symbolic—it's systemic. When top leaders walk among their teams and model servant-hearted leadership, they dismantle hierarchy and ignite legacy. True influence is not measured by how many people serve you—but by how many people are transformed because you served them. That's leadership built to last. That's the mission of this book.

Culture Is Caught, Not Just Taught

You can preach vision from the podium, but if it's not visible in the hallway, it's just noise.
People don't follow what you say—they follow what you **consistently live.**
If your frontline managers don't reflect servant values, the culture stops at the surface.
This chapter is about turning your entire team—from executives to interns—into **culture carriers.**
We're about to break the cycle of positional power and raise up a generation of **servant-hearted influencers.**

You can't teach culture through a slide deck. Culture is transferred by proximity. When people witness consistent servant-hearted behavior—in stress, in meetings, in hallway conversations—that's when it becomes real. Leadership behaviors are contagious; research by Kouzes and Posner (2017) confirms that "modeling the way" is one of the most powerful drivers of leadership credibility and cultural replication. If you preach integrity but model impatience, you've already lost. Inconsistency isn't just hypocrisy—it's sabotage.

That's why servant leadership demands radical congruence. You don't just say the right thing—you *live it until it echoes.* Every frontline manager, team lead,

CHAPTER 5: Building Systems That Scale

coach, assistant, and staffer must embody the mission with authenticity. According to Liden et al. (2008), servant leadership's greatest impact is seen when mid-level and emerging leaders carry its principles into daily operations. That means the real change happens not in the boardroom but in the everyday choices made in emails, one-on-one meetings, lunchroom conversations, and crisis responses.

To make this shift, you must re-engineer your leadership development pipeline. Move beyond technical competencies—train for character, humility, empathy, and service orientation. Use 360-degree feedback tools to highlight alignment with cultural values. Promote based not just on results, but on how those results were achieved. And most importantly, *coach your culture in real time*. Great cultures are not managed—they are *mentored*. Build reflection into your rhythms. Debrief after conflict. Praise small acts of service loudly. Culture thrives when it's named, noticed, and nurtured.

Don't underestimate the power of micro-behaviors. Studies on organizational behavior show that the "informal curriculum"—the attitudes and actions that aren't officially part of training—shape more of the workplace atmosphere than any policy ever could (Schein, 2010). If leaders gossip, team members will too. If leaders serve, others will follow. That's why Jesus didn't just lecture about leadership—He grabbed a towel and washed feet. He let His life *teach*. Your staff are watching far more than they're listening. Your culture isn't what you announce. It's what you allow, affirm, and repeat.

Finally, be ruthless about alignment. If someone refuses to carry the culture—no matter how talented—they cannot stay in a servant-led organization. Your mission is too important to be sabotaged by ego. Remember this truth: *Culture is either reinforced or eroded every single day.* The most dangerous people in your organization are not the ones who fail—it's the ones who succeed while poisoning your values. Hold the line. Shape the tone. And build a movement where leadership isn't a title—it's a testimony.

7-Day Leadership Mirror: Culture is Caught Challenge

Purpose: To transform leadership from theory to daily visibility. If you want to build a servant leadership culture that lives beyond slogans, this challenge is non-negotiable.

Day 1: Audit Your Atmosphere

Walk through your workplace—hallways, meetings, break rooms, Zoom calls. Observe *what's actually happening*. Where is the culture showing up? Where is it leaking? Take notes, not excuses.

CHAPTER 5: Building Systems That Scale

Day 2: Spotlight Servant Behavior
Call out one act of humility, empathy, or service you witnessed from someone else today. Publicly. Loudly. Repetition + recognition = reinforcement.

Day 3: Model the Hard Thing
Do something inconvenient that demonstrates servant leadership. Help with a task "beneath" your role. Apologize first. Serve silently. No announcement—just obedience.

Day 4: Feedback Fuel
Ask three team members one simple but courageous question:

> **"What's one thing I do that either strengthens or weakens our culture?"**
> **No defending. Just listening. Real culture carriers seek real input.**

Day 5: Remove a Toxin
Confront one behavior, policy, or habit that contradicts your stated values. Don't just notice it—address it. Quiet compromise is loud culture erosion.

Day 6: Mentor the Mission
Find one rising leader. Don't give them a to-do list—give them your time. Pour into them with a 30-minute conversation about servant leadership. Share your mistakes. Model your mission.

Day 7: Live It When It's Hard
Pick the most frustrating part of your role and go serve *there*—with joy. Let your posture preach louder than your position. If you can't carry the towel under pressure, you're not ready to lead with it in peace.

> **"If you don't model the mission when it's inconvenient, you're not building culture—you're staging a performance."**

Hierarchies Don't Create Movements—Servants Do

The most powerful leaders aren't always the ones with the titles.
They're the ones who show up early, lift others, take responsibility, and make the team better. That's what Jesus modeled—**impact through**

CHAPTER 5: Building Systems That Scale

humility, not hierarchy.
Philippians 2:7 reminds us: *"He made himself nothing by taking the very nature of a servant."*
This chapter will equip you to **decentralize power and multiply purpose.**

Most organizations are built like pyramids—power at the top, obedience at the bottom. But true Kingdom-aligned leadership flips that model upside down. Servant leadership decentralizes control and empowers individuals to lead from wherever they stand. Greenleaf (1970), the father of modern servant leadership, asserted that leadership is first and foremost a choice to serve, not a position to hold. In this view, movements don't begin with power—they begin with purpose, lived out by people willing to lead through love.

Movements are fueled by those willing to sacrifice ego for impact. Philippians 2:7 tells us Jesus "made himself nothing by taking the very nature of a servant," showing us that influence doesn't require a throne—just a towel. Leaders who release authority, delegate with clarity, and champion others build organizations that move with agility and passion. Research from Spears (1995) reinforces this, showing that trust, listening, and empowerment are the keys to scalable influence. Servant leadership isn't about relinquishing control for chaos—it's about replacing command with conviction and contribution.

Hierarchies tend to slow innovation and choke

collaboration. When only those at the top are "allowed" to lead, the majority of your talent sits on the bench. Servant leaders create systems where ideas flow upward, not just downward, and influence is earned through character, not job title. Kouzes and Posner (2012) emphasize that leaders who foster participatory environments see higher commitment, performance, and retention. In short: people work harder when they feel heard and valued—not bossed around.

To decentralize power is not to diminish authority—but to *distribute* it. That means empowering department heads, coaches, teachers, and team leads to carry the mission with full ownership and full alignment. The result? Cultural consistency without micromanagement. Your people don't just follow—they initiate. As academic literature from van Dierendonck (2011) explains, servant leadership enhances psychological empowerment and collective efficacy, building organizations that scale from the inside out.

Jesus didn't create a global movement by managing a corporate structure—He empowered ordinary people to lead in extraordinary ways. Twelve disciples. No title. No platform. But their servant-hearted obedience changed history. That's the model. That's the movement. And if your organization wants to outlive the founder and multiply its mission? It starts by raising up leaders who *serve first and lead strong*—at every level.

SIDEBAR: THE MISSION ISN'T TOP-DOWN—IT'S

CHAPTER 5: Building Systems That Scale

INSIDE-OUT

If your mission dies the moment you leave the room, you don't have a movement—you have a bottleneck.

Here's what legendary servant-led organizations do:

- **They flatten ego, not structure.** Titles don't grant authority—trust does.
- **They train culture-carriers at every level.** Every role is sacred when every person carries the mission.
- **They define leadership as responsibility, not rank.** You're not climbing ladders—you're lifting others.
- **They design systems that empower contribution.** Feedback flows both ways. Ownership is shared.
- **They celebrate the unnoticed.** The janitor who sets the tone in the morning is just as important as the CEO who casts the vision.

"Movements that last are always born from the bottom up, not the top down. That's not rebellion—that's revival."

Let the pyramid crumble. Let the Kingdom rise.

Every Level Needs the Language

If your line staff doesn't speak the language of servant leadership, your organization has a **communication gap** that kills alignment.
We're going to change that.
We'll show you how to **translate values into vocabulary**—so that from onboarding to executive meetings, everyone's speaking the same mission-driven dialect.
When everyone knows what "serve first" looks like in their role, they begin to **own the mission personally.**
And that ownership? That's when revival hits the workplace.

Language is not a side issue—it is the DNA of culture. In organizations where servant leadership thrives, phrases like *"serve first," "model the way,"* and *"listen to understand"* aren't just slogans—they are spoken expectations. Shared language bridges departments, connects hierarchies, and empowers everyone to act with clarity and conviction (Kouzes & Posner, 2017). When the vocabulary is consistent, so is the behavior.

But servant leadership language isn't just about clarity—it's about culture transfer. Leaders must model, teach, and reinforce the terms and behaviors that reflect the mission. This begins in onboarding and continues through meetings, recognition systems, and even conflict resolution. Every communication touchpoint becomes a discipleship moment. As Blanchard & Hodges (2005)

CHAPTER 5: Building Systems That Scale

affirm, "Language either reinforces or resists the culture you're building." That means every sentence you speak is either kingdom-building or culture-breaking.

Servant leadership multiplies when frontline staff, not just executives, can articulate and embody the values. This happens when language is localized: what does "serving with excellence" look like in the kitchen? At the call center? In the locker room? Translate the mission to match the moment. The best organizations take the big vision and make it bite-sized for every context (Greenleaf, 1977; Van Dierendonck, 2011). That's not watering it down—that's making it accessible.

Here's how you build it: create a "Servant Leadership Language Manual." Populate it with mission-driven phrases, biblical references, and behavior definitions that connect belief to behavior. Train managers to use this language in coaching. Turn values into acronyms, visual cues, and verbal mantras. And most importantly, **never allow cultural slang that contradicts servant values** to go unchallenged. Language creates loops of behavior that either anchor your vision or sink it.

Finally, remember: language builds legacy. A legacy culture isn't built through one-off speeches or hype videos—it's built through everyday words spoken with eternal weight. When your team learns to speak the servant language fluently, they won't just repeat it—they'll live it. And when they live it, **they'll teach it to others.** That's how movements are born. That's how legacies are forged.

Coaches, Not Commanders

If you want a servant-led culture, you don't need more bosses—you need more **coaches.**
Coaches walk alongside, develop others, and call out greatness.
We'll teach you how to build **coaching systems** that create leaders who **don't control but cultivate.**
This is how you build **people developers**, not power hoarders.
Your mid-level managers are either multiplying the mission—or muting it. This chapter equips them to **multiply.**

The age of command-and-control leadership is dead. What today's teams need—what they *crave*—are coaches, not commanders. Coaches don't bark orders. They build people. They don't just manage tasks; they unlock potential. This is the heart of servant leadership: to walk alongside, develop others, and call out greatness that even the individual may not see in themselves (Greenleaf, 1977). When leaders commit to coaching, they don't just grow employees—they cultivate disciples of the mission.

Coaching-centered leadership changes how decisions are made, how feedback is delivered, and how excellence is pursued. According to Ellinger, Beattie, and Hamlin (2010), when leaders coach instead of command,

CHAPTER 5: Building Systems That Scale

it results in "significantly improved organizational performance, learning, and engagement." This isn't theory—it's reality. Servant leadership reframes middle management from a layer of control to a launchpad of development. The manager becomes a multiplier, not a monitor. And in this model, you don't lead with fear—you lead with belief.

Jesus was the ultimate coach. He didn't just teach principles—He walked with people, challenged them, corrected them, empowered them, and then sent them out. In Luke 10, He sends out the 72—giving them real responsibility, room to fail, and a mission to fulfill. That's what coaching does. It doesn't hoard influence. It equips and releases it. As Spears (1995) identified in his framework of servant leadership, "developing others" is a foundational pillar—and that's exactly what coaches do.

To implement this, organizations must rewire how they develop their people. That means equipping managers with coaching frameworks: how to hold developmental conversations, how to offer feedback that builds without breaking, and how to measure success beyond numbers—by growth, by initiative, by the internalization of values. Systems should reward coaching behavior, not just bottom-line performance. When managers are evaluated by how well they empower others, not just what they control, a cultural shift begins to take root (Crane, 2002).

The result? An army of mission-aligned leaders at every

level—not just at the top. The future of leadership doesn't belong to micromanagers—it belongs to servant-hearted coaches. Leaders who pour in, build up, and send out. It's time to stop producing positional leaders and start multiplying culture carriers. This isn't soft. It's strategic. It's the kind of leadership that scales purpose, not ego—and changes the game forever.

Pipelines of Purpose

Organizations rise and fall based on the quality of their pipelines.
Not just talent pipelines—but **character pipelines.**
We'll show you how to identify, develop, and launch servant leaders from **every department**, so the culture doesn't rely on one person at the top.
Think of it as leadership succession that's **mission-aligned, values-anchored, and biblically sound.**
This is how legacies are built. Not by accident—but by a **servant-first strategy.**

Great organizations don't just fill positions—they cultivate purpose. They don't just hire talent—they steward character. The strength of a servant-led organization lies not in its headcount, but in the clarity and intentionality of its leadership pipeline. As Greenleaf (1977) asserted, "The best test of a servant leader is whether those served grow as persons." That's the gold standard. And that growth can't be left to chance. It must be engineered into the DNA of the culture—starting with how you spot and shape leaders across every level.

CHAPTER 5: Building Systems That Scale

Servant leadership pipelines aren't about fast-tracking charisma. They're about identifying individuals whose hearts beat with humility, empathy, and courage. It's about building systems that recognize not just what someone can *do*, but *who they are becoming*. Character-based succession planning ensures that when leadership is passed on, the mission is never diluted. According to research by Ready and Conger (2007), organizations with values-aligned leadership pipelines outperform those with performance-only models in long-term growth and cultural cohesion. Why? Because character compounds. And in a servant-led system, character *is* the culture.

This model isn't confined to the executive track. Every department, every shift, every role becomes a launchpad for leadership. Janitors, assistant coaches, administrative aides—all can be leaders if we have the eyes to see and the courage to invest. Jesus didn't recruit from the temples—He called fishermen, tax collectors, and zealots. He looked for obedience over credentials, willingness over polish. In the same way, our pipelines must reflect a commitment to discovering hidden potential and developing it faithfully (Luke 16:10, NIV).

To build this, organizations must institutionalize mentorship, feedback, and experiential development. Regular check-ins with potential leaders should focus not just on performance metrics but on spiritual maturity, emotional intelligence, and alignment with the mission. Leadership academies, stretch assignments, and peer coaching must be seen as essential, not optional. As Van

Dierendonck and Patterson (2015) found, servant leadership flourishes when development is intentional and relational, not transactional.

This is how legacies are formed—not by waiting for the "next great one," but by investing in many who can carry the flame. A pipeline of purpose doesn't just prevent gaps in leadership—it prevents gaps in culture. And when done well, it ensures your mission won't end with you—it will echo through generations of leaders who serve first, love deeply, and lead with conviction. That's not just sustainability. That's succession by design. And it's the only way to build a servant-led movement that lasts.

From Jesus to Jack Welch

This isn't just theory—it's proven.
Faith-driven leaders like **Dan Cathy (Chick-fil-A)** and **James Sinegal (Costco)** didn't just talk servant leadership—they **built billion-dollar brands on it.**
And guess what? Even in secular spaces, servant leadership **outperforms** command-and-control models over time.
Because people don't quit companies—they quit cultures.
We're about to show you how to create one they'll never want to leave.

Servant leadership isn't a niche doctrine—it's a time-tested system. From the basin and towel of Jesus to the boardroom playbooks of billion-dollar brands, this

CHAPTER 5: Building Systems That Scale

approach consistently outperforms traditional leadership paradigms in both moral authority and organizational outcomes. While Jesus washed feet and multiplied movements through humility (John 13:12–15), modern marketplace leaders like Dan Cathy of Chick-fil-A and James Sinegal of Costco scaled with similar principles—by putting people first and profits second, only to see both multiply. Cathy famously closed his restaurants on Sundays and empowered teen workers to grow in character as well as competence. That's not weakness—that's values-based, system-backed, high-performance leadership (Spears, 2010).

Even Jack Welch—long associated with GE's hard-driving, results-first culture—evolved his philosophy late in life. He began to champion leadership built on candor, transparency, and empowering others, even admitting that his earlier "rank and yank" model had limits. In a 2009 *Harvard Business Review* interview, Welch noted, "Before you're a leader, success is all about growing yourself. When you become a leader, success is all about growing others." That's the shift servant leadership requires—and rewards. As Kouzes and Posner (2017) emphasize, the best leaders "enable others to act." Power that multiplies people, not manipulates them, creates movements—not just metrics.

Faith-based companies aren't the only ones reaping the rewards. According to research by Hunter et al. (2013), servant leadership in secular organizations leads to higher employee satisfaction, lower turnover, and better team performance. Why? Because servant leaders create psychological safety, trust, and purpose—all vital for long-term engagement. That's why organizations like Marriott International, Southwest Airlines, and TDIndustries have all leaned into servant-led cultures and reaped the benefits. They don't just hire smart—they hire aligned. They don't just scale revenue—they scale values.

This is what modern leaders must understand: servant leadership isn't soft. It's strategic. It's how you retain top talent in a mobile economy. It's how you attract values-aligned partners in a cynical world. It's how you build organizations people don't just work for—but believe in. As Greenleaf (1977) wrote, "A servant-leader focuses primarily on the growth and well-being of people and the communities to which they belong." When you make that your blueprint, you don't just build a business—you build a legacy.

So yes, Jesus shaped eternity—and so can you. But He didn't do it with power plays. He did it with towels, tables, and time spent developing twelve people who would go on to change the world. Your organization may not be a church—but it can still become a launching ground for Kingdom-minded, purpose-driven leadership. Whether you're in the C-suite, on the court, or in the classroom, the mission is the same: serve people, develop people, send people. That's how movements are born. And that's how they endure.

CHAPTER 5: Building Systems That Scale

Ready to Equip a Revolution

This chapter is a **battle plan**—a tactical, faith-fueled, leadership-on-fire blueprint.
Get ready for stories, drills, examples, and action steps that will **change your staff meetings, your hiring, your coaching, and your bottom line.**
The boardroom may cast the vision, but the break room carries it forward.
And once servant leadership saturates both, you've got more than an organization—you've got a **movement.**
Let's go build one that can't be shaken.

This chapter is not just a collection of ideas—it's a leadership revolution disguised as a playbook. The systems and strategies that follow are designed to do more than spark conversations; they're designed to disrupt the status quo. Servant leadership is not a feel-good side note in today's competitive marketplace—it's the competitive edge. And the time has come to equip every department, every manager, every intern, every board member with the mindset, language, and daily practices that make servant leadership not only visible—but viral. As Northouse (2021) affirms, "Servant leadership is not about control, but about the unleashing of potential through relational trust and consistent modeling." That's the goal. That's the revolution.

And make no mistake—this revolution requires precision and practice. Vision without execution is just a fantasy. That's why this chapter doesn't just inspire—it instructs.

You'll see how to redesign your hiring process to screen for humility. You'll learn how to turn team meetings into discipleship environments that reinforce mission and multiply ownership. You'll adopt frameworks that elevate coaching conversations from compliance checks to transformational moments. And all of it is rooted in the servant-first philosophy of leadership giants—from Jesus Christ to modern pioneers like Greenleaf, Covey, and Kouzes & Posner (Kouzes & Posner, 2017; Greenleaf, 1977).

Every room matters. Your boardroom sets the vision, but if that vision dies in the hallway, you've built a monument—not a movement. The key is saturation. Servant leadership must saturate the org chart. It must be seen in how the CEO makes decisions, how the team lead gives feedback, and how the receptionist treats a vendor on a Friday afternoon. When the break room conversations match the boardroom commitments, you're no longer building an organization—you're building a living, breathing culture of care, purpose, and performance. That's how movements move: from top to bottom, and back up again.

And don't miss this: movements are messy—but they are magnetic. They require courage, consistency, and a refusal to bow to the idol of short-term efficiency. As Sipe and Frick (2009) note, "Servant leaders create cultures of accountability by fostering environments that align people's actions with the mission, not with fear or pressure." These next sections are built for exactly that.

CHAPTER 5: Building Systems That Scale

It's time to weaponize kindness. To operationalize humility. To structure success around sacrifice and service. Because when people see a model worth following, they'll run through walls to protect it.

So buckle up, builder. You're not just reading a leadership book. You're arming yourself for an uprising of influence that starts in your department and echoes into your community. The world has enough bosses. What it needs is a blueprint for servant-led, systems-based, faith-infused culture that cannot be shaken. And that's exactly where we're going next—into the tools and tactics for *Creating Servant Leaders at Every Level.*

Creating Servant Leaders at Every Level

From the New Generation of Greenleaf Thinkers—For a World That Desperately Needs Better Leaders.

If you're only building servant leadership at the top, you've already lost. Movements don't explode from the boardroom; they rise from the trenches. That means if the intern isn't empowered, the culture isn't real. If the night shift manager doesn't carry the mission, the leadership is a lie. This isn't about creating more policies—it's about creating more people who bleed mission in everything they do.

We need leaders at every level, people who take

ownership without needing authority. People who lead themselves first, and others second. The frontline staffer who chooses integrity when no one's watching? That's a servant leader. The custodian who creates safety and joy for others? That's a culture builder. You don't have to wait for a title to lead—you just need permission. And as of this moment, **you have it.**

To build a culture like this, you need replication systems—not just inspiration moments. Servant leadership must be embedded into *onboarding*, reinforced in *training*, modeled in *coaching*, and tested in *evaluation*. If you want people to lead this way, **train them**. Walk them through how to ask better questions. Teach them how to serve under pressure. Show them how to turn correction into coaching and competition into collaboration. It's not enough to tell people to lead like Jesus—you have to build them into it.

This is where innovation meets implementation. Don't just promote your best performers—elevate your best servants. Create an internal leadership academy where your next wave of managers are chosen not by popularity, but by purpose and humility. Build peer coaching programs where employees lead one another. Create systems where the dishwasher becomes the trainer, the admin becomes the influencer, and the security guard becomes the culture champion. *Every level. Every voice. Every room.*

Because here's the truth: **when servant leadership lives**

at every level, toxicity can't survive. Gossip dries up. Turf wars disappear. People don't just stay, they grow, lead, and multiply. You're not just building a better company. You're building a better future. And it starts with creating an army of servant leaders who know the mission, love the people, and live the values.

Leadership Isn't a Title—It's a Posture

The lie the world tells us is that leadership starts with authority.
But **true leadership starts with responsibility**, taking ownership not just of your work, but of the people around you.
You don't need a fancy office or a corner suite to be a leader. You need **a servant's heart, a warrior's grit, and a commitment to lift others up.**
Every person in your organization, from the janitor to the CFO, can be a leader if they understand that **service is power.**
As Jesus said in Matthew 23:11 (NIV), *"The greatest among you will be your servant."*

The most dangerous myth in leadership today is that influence flows from authority. That lie has poisoned boardrooms, schools, churches, and locker rooms for decades. But you're not here for that old model. You're here to disrupt it. True leadership doesn't start with a title—it starts with a *towel*, like the one Jesus used to wash feet before He went to the cross. Leadership is not about status. It's about *stance*. It's a posture of service, sacrifice, and sacred responsibility for the people around you.

Don't wait for permission to lead. Own the hallway. Own the break room. Own the mission, even when you don't have the microphone. The greatest leaders in history didn't wait for someone to hand them a badge—they became the thermostat, not the thermometer. They walked into a toxic culture and brought peace. They saw disconnection and built bridges. They noticed pain and met it with purpose. That's what servant leadership looks like when it's alive at ground level.

So here's your directive: **stop thinking like an employee and start thinking like a leader**—right where you are. Do others feel lighter after being around you? Do your words build people up or tear them down? Are you stepping over others to be seen—or stepping under burdens to lift someone else? *That's* the audit. That's the assignment. Servant leaders ask: "What can I give?" not "What can I get?" And that posture doesn't require a title, it requires courage.

Now, if you're responsible for others, whether as a coach, manager, principal, or supervisor—your job is to call out that posture in the people you lead. Build systems that empower *everyone* to lead from wherever they stand. Don't just reward output—celebrate initiative, care, character, and responsibility. Give people platforms to

CHAPTER 5: Building Systems That Scale

influence beyond their job description. Turn your team into leaders who lead without needing a badge to prove it.

Because the future doesn't belong to the most powerful voice in the room, it belongs to the most *purposeful posture*. The kind that stoops to serve, rises to lift, and stays low enough to hear what others miss. As Jesus taught: "The greatest among you will be your servant" (Matthew 23:11, NIV). We're not just reclaiming that truth—we're installing it in every hallway, every meeting, and every mission we lead.

SIDEBAR: Tools to Build Leadership Posture at Every Level

- **The "No Title Needed" Challenge**
  Have team members write down 3 ways they can lead today *without* authority. Share stories in weekly meetings.

- **Posture Checkpoints**
  Add 5-minute posture check-ins to meetings: How did we serve? Where did we take ownership? What did we lift?

- **Leadership Spotlights**
  Celebrate unsung heroes who led with character, not control—janitors, interns, volunteers.

- **Team Devotions on Posture & Power**

Teach through Matthew 23:11 and John 13. Use it to shift mindset from power-over to power-through-service.

This isn't motivational fluff—it's your formation strategy.
Train posture. Celebrate it. Multiply it.
Because **that's how you build a servant-led movement that doesn't need a title to lead or a stage to shine.**

Culture is Carried, Not Just Created

You can have the best values on your website, but if **your people don't carry them**, your culture collapses. Leadership development can't stop at the executive team—it must **saturate the break rooms, training sessions, team huddles, and customer interactions.** Every level of your organization needs to see themselves as **mission-bearers**.
You don't build a movement with a few elites—you build it when **everyone owns the vision and lives the values.** When the person who stocks the shelves understands they're *serving a greater purpose*, you've got more than an employee—you've got a **servant leader in action.**

Culture doesn't live on a vision statement—it lives in people. Real culture is *carried*, not just crafted in a conference room. You can brand your values, print them on lanyards, and mount them in the lobby, but if they aren't embedded into your people—they're nothing but decoration. A servant-led culture doesn't rise from a

CHAPTER 5: Building Systems That Scale

boardroom brainstorm—it spreads through contagious conviction, shared language, and lived example at *every level*. This is where most leaders fail: they create culture at the top and assume it will trickle down. But servant leadership flows *from the inside out* and *from the ground up*.

Let's be real: your front desk clerk sets the temperature faster than your C-suite. Your night shift team builds your brand just as much as your marketing exec. You don't build a movement by training the elite—you build it by *activating the everyday*. The apostle Paul didn't write letters to just pastors—he wrote to *churches*. Entire communities. Why? Because everyone carries the Kingdom. The same applies here. Your custodians. Your interns. Your drivers. *They are culture carriers*. And if you want to build a servant-led organization that lasts, *they must be equipped and empowered like it*.

So what's the game plan? **Start with identity.** Teach every person that their role has *purpose*. That culture isn't "theirs"—it's *ours*. Then, **infuse language.** Use words and phrases that echo your values in every department. Every meeting, every form, every feedback loop should reflect the mission. Third, **train and model**. Run micro-trainings, story spotlights, and leadership devos that reinforce servant-hearted behavior. And lastly, **build feedback loops** where anyone can call out culture wins—and culture drift.

Because here's the truth: You're not just training

managers. You're raising *mission-bearers*. And when every team member sees themselves as a carrier of purpose, culture becomes a *living organism*, not a laminated document. That's how you move from *organization to organism*—from brand to *body*. From slogans to *servants*. You stop building for scale and start building for *soul*.

Culture Carrier Toolbox

- **Walk the Halls with Intentionality**
  Every leader should spend one hour a week on the front lines. Ask, "What do you need to thrive?" Model proximity. Carry the culture *with* your people.

- **Culture Ripple Stories**
  Start meetings by celebrating everyday actions that reflected your values—no matter how small. Small acts create cultural waves.

- **Give Everyone a Voice**
  Install "Culture Pulse" surveys and storyboards where *anyone* can share moments when the mission was lived.

- **Servant Leadership Scorecards**
  Create department-specific behaviors tied to core values. Let team members *self-assess* how they're carrying the mission weekly.

CHAPTER 5: Building Systems That Scale

Here's the rally cry:
You don't build legacy through leadership *titles*. You build it through leadership *transfer*.
Don't just create culture—train your people to *carry it* like fire.
Because if every role is sacred, then every person becomes a revolutionary.

Let me know when you're ready for the next section:
We're Building a Movement, not a Machine.

The Power of the First Follower

We glorify the charismatic leader, but movements begin with the **first follower**, the one brave enough to follow the vision before it's popular.
Empower your team to be that follower. Equip them to model service, joy, and excellence even when the spotlight isn't on them.
This kind of influence spreads like wildfire.
When a middle manager leads by serving their staff, **a ripple effect begins that transforms teams from the inside out.**
Great cultures aren't built by command, they're built by **commitment to others.**

We talk a lot about leaders—but here's the truth: **no movement starts without a first follower.** Leadership is just a lone act until someone chooses to follow—and *not* because they're told, but because they *believe*. That first follower is the hinge point between a moment and a *movement.* They're the person who steps forward before it's fashionable, before it's comfortable, and says, "I'm in."

And that decision changes *everything*.

Simon Sinek said it best: "The first follower transforms a lone nut into a leader" (Sinek, 2009). But we're not building hype around eccentricity, we're building legacy around *servanthood*. And that means your first follower must embody what the movement is truly about. Their posture *teaches others how to engage*. If they lead with ego, ego spreads. If they lead with honor, *honor* catches fire. The first follower gives permission to the second, the third, the tenth. They signal, "It's safe here. It's *right* to serve. Let's go."

So how do you find them? You don't look for the loudest. You look for the **most aligned**. Watch for the team member who asks deeper questions, who stays behind to help without being asked, who honors people in private as well as in public. They may not be the flashiest, but they are *anchored*. They don't chase praise, they chase *purpose*. That's your first follower.

Now here's the danger: the wrong first follower can *corrupt* the culture. If someone steps up but carries insecurity, bitterness, or pride—they won't multiply mission, they'll manipulate it. So test alignment. Don't hand influence to someone just because they want it. Test it in the trenches: *Are they living the values when no* one's watching? Are they inviting others in with grace, not force? Are they carrying the vision in spirit—not just in words?

When you *know* you've found the right one—**equip them like a general.** Give them language. Let them in on the why. Coach them to coach others. Most importantly, *bless them publicly.* The more visible your belief in them, the more confidence they'll give others to rise. Your first follower becomes a *model*, a mirror, and a *magnet*—reflecting the mission and attracting people with the same DNA.

First Follower Activation Plan

- **Identify Aligned Behavior**
  Look for people who already embody the mission before you ever announced it. People who live the values instinctively.

- **Test Through Trust**
  Give them micro-ownership. A small project, a mentorship moment, a culture checkpoint. Watch how they steward influence.

- **Coach in Private, Celebrate in Public**
  Equip them behind closed doors, but honor them in front of the team. This sets the tone for what leadership *looks like here.*

- **Multiply the Model**
  Use the first follower as a case study. Break it down in team meetings. Tell the story. Let others see *what it looks like to serve with fire.*

Quote to Burn Into Your Brain:
"The first follower is the spark that makes the flame safe to join. Without them, you just burn alone."

This is how servant-led revolutions begin. Not with a platform. Not with applause. But with a **willing follower who steps forward in faith.** When you empower that person, *the culture you've dreamed about becomes contagious.*

You Don't Have to Wait to Lead

Too many organizations make leadership a destination you arrive at after promotions.
But servant leadership flips the script: **you lead right now, right where you are.**
That cafeteria worker who smiles and knows every student's name? That's a servant leader.
The entry-level employee who trains new hires with patience and love? That's leadership, not just labor.
If you want to build an army of servant leaders, start by **telling everyone they already have permission to lead.**

Servant leadership annihilates that myth. It says leadership is not about position—it's about posture. And posture is something you can choose today.

CHAPTER 5: Building Systems That Scale

Leadership isn't locked in a job title—it's unleashed in your daily choices. That cafeteria worker who knows every student's name and treats them with dignity? That's not just good service—it's a masterclass in influence. The entry-level employee who patiently trains the new hire with care and encouragement? That's not just onboarding—that's grassroots leadership development.

You want to ignite a servant-led culture? **Tell your people they don't need permission to lead.** Teach them that every interaction is a moment to lift, to serve, and to shape the atmosphere. A janitor who chooses joy is creating psychological safety. A receptionist who listens with empathy is modeling emotional intelligence. Culture shifts when people realize they already have the power—they just need to activate it.

Example:
In a manufacturing company in the Midwest, the transformation didn't begin in the C-suite—it started when a forklift operator began hosting 5-minute morning huddles to check in on coworkers' mental health. Within months, that spirit spread across departments and productivity shot up. He didn't have a leadership title. **But he changed the culture.**

Here's How to Lead Now:

- **Start with service.** Ask: *Who can I help today? Who needs encouragement?* Make that your daily mission.

- **Model what you want multiplied.** Integrity. Gratitude. Accountability. If you live it, others will catch it.

- **Speak life.** In every meeting, conversation, or email, look for a chance to build someone up.

- **Take initiative.** You don't need a memo to solve problems. If something's broken, fix it—or start the conversation to get it fixed.

- **Stay consistent.** Leadership isn't proven in big moments—it's cemented in small, repeated acts of love, truth, and service.

You don't need a corner office to be a culture-shifter. You don't need an invitation to be a servant leader. You need **vision**, **courage**, and **a commitment to lift others—right now, right here.**

Challenge Box:
For the next 7 days, choose **one daily act of servant leadership** that doesn't require permission. Smile at the custodian. Help the overwhelmed new hire. Speak up in the meeting to defend someone else's idea. Keep a journal of how it felt, how others responded, and how the culture shifts around you.

Develop People, Don't Just Deploy Them

Leaders aren't born—they're **developed with intentionality and love.**
If you're only using your people for their skills, you're missing their potential.
Every meeting, every correction, every coaching moment is a chance to **shape someone's identity as a servant leader.**
Don't just manage tasks—**build people.**
Because when you invest in hearts, not just hands, you unlock a **culture of multiplication**, not just maintenance.

You are not in the business of efficiency. You are in the business of transformation.

Too many organizations treat their people like chess pieces—deployed for strategic gain, then discarded or sidelined when their immediate utility ends. But the servant leader rejects that model. **You don't just deploy people—you develop them.** That's the difference between leadership and stewardship. One sees people as resources. The other sees them as *revelations* of untapped greatness.

Leadership is not about extracting performance; it's about expanding potential. And research continues to affirm this: according to Kouzes & Posner (2017), leaders who invest in personal development and model the behaviors they expect see exponentially higher levels of trust, commitment, and innovation among their teams. Servant leaders don't ask, *"How can I use this person?"* They ask, *"Who is this person becoming—and how can I help them get there?"*

Every coaching moment becomes a crucible of identity formation. When you challenge someone, you don't just correct their behavior—you elevate their belief in who they are and who they can become. When you offer feedback with clarity and compassion, you teach them to lead with truth and grace. When you give away real responsibility—not just tasks, but ownership—you're saying, *"I trust you to carry the mission forward."* That's developmental leadership. And it's rare.

Academic Insight: Greenleaf (1977) noted that the best test of a servant leader is whether those served *"become healthier, wiser, freer, more autonomous, more likely themselves to become servants."* That's not deployment. That's discipleship. That's building *legacy leaders*—the kind who don't just replicate systems but *replicate spirit*.

Here's How to Develop Servant Leaders in Practice:

- **Embed development into your rhythms.** Use 1-on-1s, team huddles, and even email feedback as consistent platforms for growth conversations—not just task updates.

CHAPTER 5: Building Systems That Scale

- **Create stretch opportunities.** Give people projects that challenge them beyond their comfort zone and then *walk with them* through it. This is where real formation happens.

- **Coach identity, not just behavior.** When correcting or guiding, affirm who they are becoming. Say things like, *"This isn't who you are—we believe in better because we see it in you."*

- **Model vulnerability and growth yourself.** Leaders who admit they're still learning create space for others to do the same.

- **Recognize invisible progress.** Not every win is visible. Celebrate growth in confidence, integrity, emotional intelligence, and spiritual maturity.

Servant leaders are not empire builders—they are *soul shapers*. They aren't afraid to slow down the system to speed up the person. Because they understand the truth: **a developed leader will always outperform a deployed robot.**

Quote to Frame This Section:
"The job of a leader is not to be in charge—it's to take care of those in their charge." — Simon Sinek

Sidebar: Greenleaf's Gold Standard

In *Servant Leadership*, Robert Greenleaf challenged organizations to evaluate themselves not by profit margins, but by *who they were becoming*. Ask yourself:

- Are the people in my care becoming more autonomous?

- Are they becoming servant leaders themselves?

- Are they thriving beyond this organization because of what they learned within it?
  These are the questions that forge enduring, people-first legacies.

Accountability with Compassion

Creating servant leaders doesn't mean lowering standards—it means raising **expectations with grace.**
Hold your people accountable not out of anger, but out of belief in their potential.
Servant leaders challenge others because they care too much to let mediocrity slide.
You don't avoid hard conversations—you **anchor them in dignity and love.**
That's how you build a leadership culture where **truth and trust walk hand-in-hand.**

Accountability is not the enemy of love—it's the evidence of it.

CHAPTER 5: Building Systems That Scale

True servant leaders **do not coddle comfort—they cultivate character**. And that means building a culture where high standards are non-negotiable, but *so is human dignity*. You don't lead people by excusing their failures—you lead them by **believing they're capable of greatness and holding them to it**. As Brené Brown (2018) asserts, *"Clear is kind. Unclear is unkind."* Accountability with compassion is the clearest kindness of all.

Compassionate accountability means you correct without condemnation and confront without crushing. You don't sweep failure under the rug—but you don't weaponize it either. Instead, you use it as a **mirror**—to reflect both the misstep and the potential waiting underneath it. The goal isn't to punish, it's to **call out the gold beneath the dirt**. As Philippians 1:6 (NIV) reminds us, *"He who began a good work in you will carry it on to completion."* A servant leader leads from that assumption.

Here's How to Deliver Compassionate Accountability That Transforms:

1. **Prepare Spiritually, Not Emotionally.**
   Before a tough conversation, check your heart. Are you trying to *fix*, or are you trying to *form*? Anger leads to shame. Compassion leads to breakthrough. Pray. Reflect. Anchor your identity in humility first.

2. **Use the Two-Sided Mirror Technique.**
   Begin with *reflection* ("Here's what happened and why it matters.")
   Then pivot to *projection* ("But here's what I believe you're capable of.")
   This lets the person see both the reality and the redemptive path forward.

3. **Set Expectations That Empower, Not Intimidate.**
   Don't just say, "You need to do better." Say, "Here's the standard. I believe you can meet it, and I'm here to walk with you to get there."

4. **Follow Through Without Flinching.**
   Compassionate accountability doesn't mean avoiding consequences. It means *delivering them with clarity, consistency, and care*. Boundaries create safety. Follow-through builds trust.

Academic Anchor: Research by Kim Cameron (2012) in *Positive Leadership* found that "organizations that hold people accountable within a culture of compassion and affirmation perform significantly better on measures of profitability, productivity, and engagement."

Example: The Missed Deadline

An employee misses a major deadline that affects multiple departments. Here's how a servant leader responds:

CHAPTER 5: Building Systems That Scale

"I want to talk to you about the impact of missing that deadline. It created real stress for others who had to scramble, and that's not the standard we're about. But I also know this isn't who you are. You've shown responsibility and care before. I'm calling you to step back into that. I'm not mad—I'm invested. Let's talk about what happened, and how we fix it—*together*."

That kind of leadership doesn't produce shame—it **produces growth**. It turns mistakes into milestones, and underperformers into culture-shapers.

"Grace is not the absence of standards—it is the fuel for people to reach them."
The next generation of servant leadership must be fierce in love and fearless in truth. Leaders who default to silence in the name of "kindness" are robbing their people of the development they deserve.

Challenge Your Organization:

- Are we clear on our behavioral and performance standards?

- Do our people know we'll speak truth when it's needed—but always with their dignity intact?

- Are we more committed to comfort or to character?

If the answer isn't crystal clear, it's time to **build accountability systems that mirror Heaven: full of truth, full of grace, and full of redemption.**

Structure Must Support Servant Leadership

You can't just tell people to lead with love and then reward only results.
Your systems must reinforce your values.
Recognize team members who serve quietly, not just those who shine loudly. Promote those who **elevate others**, not just those who hit metrics.
This is where HR, training, rewards, and performance reviews must all **point in the same direction: servant leadership.**
"People do what you inspect, not what you expect"—so inspect for service, humility, and others-first action.

You can't preach purpose while promoting pride.
You can't tell people to serve and then reward selfishness.
If the structure doesn't support the values, the culture will collapse.

Far too many leaders *declare* servant leadership from the stage while their systems scream the opposite. You say "put people first," but your performance review rewards only profit. You say "teamwork matters," but your incentives elevate individual stars and ignore the glue of culture. That disconnect? It **destroys trust** and sabotages alignment. Structure is not just support—it's the scaffolding that determines what kind of leadership stands.

Innovation No One's Talking About: The Inverted Scorecard

Most organizations track what people *produce*. But servant-led organizations also track how people *contribute to others*.

Create an inverted scorecard where 50% of the evaluation is based on:

- How you elevate your team

- How you embody the organization's values

- How you handle conflict, feedback, and failure

- How you lead when no one is watching

Example: A department lead who delivers solid but not spectacular numbers—yet consistently coaches, mentors, and supports everyone else—should be scored *higher* than a lone superstar who hits metrics but erodes culture. The former builds systems. The latter builds silos.

Academic Insight: Cameron & Lavine (2006) found that organizations rooted in "positive deviance"—those who intentionally reward values-based behaviors—outperform those driven by metrics alone. This supports a systemic shift toward value-centered assessments that prioritize both culture and results.

How You Build a Structure That Supports Servant Leadership

1. Redesign Your Recognition System

- Celebrate "invisible wins": the employee who stayed late to help a teammate, the leader who turned down credit and passed it to their team, the support staff who quietly carried the weight.

- Create a *"Servant of the Month"* award—not based on production, but on **people-centered action**. Let peers nominate each other.

- Publicly recognize acts of humility, inclusion, and sacrifice. That tells your team: *this is what we praise here.*

2. Rewire Your Performance Reviews

- Add categories like *emotional intelligence, empathy in conflict, service orientation, and peer feedback.*

CHAPTER 5: Building Systems That Scale

- Let team members rate their own alignment with organizational values—and support them with coaching plans to improve.

- Include *"How did you help someone grow this quarter?"* as a mandatory reflection item.

3. Promote Based on Fruit, Not Flash

- Don't promote based on charisma. Promote based on **cultural contribution**. Ask: *Does this person multiply mission, or just manage tasks?*

- Tie promotions to their track record of empowering others. Jesus didn't give keys to the loudest disciple—He gave them to the one who confessed, failed, returned, and was *ready to serve.*

4. Equip HR and Training to Be Mission Carriers

- HR isn't just policy—it's prophecy. They shape who gets in, who grows, and who stays.

- Train HR staff to interview for servant values. Ask: *"Tell us about a time you put someone else's success ahead of your own."*

- Onboarding should feel like discipleship: *This is who we are. This is how we serve. This is why it matters.*

Quote for the Wall:
"If your structure promotes selfishness, don't be shocked when your culture does too."

Next-Level Practice: The Legacy Table

Create a quarterly leadership roundtable. At it:

- Invite 5–7 staff members from all levels.

- Each shares *one way someone served them* and *one way they served someone else.*

- Leadership listens, affirms, and identifies blind spots in the structure.

Do this regularly, and the *structure becomes the sermon*—a visible reinforcement of your culture.

Final Word

If you reward hustle and ignore humility, you'll breed burnout and bitterness.
If you elevate results and ignore relationships, your people will produce—but they won't stay.
But if your **structure honors servant leadership**, you

won't need hype.
Your system will carry the vision. Your culture will echo Heaven.

The Movement Starts with You

If you want servant leaders at every level, you must be one.
The tone you set becomes the tone they spread.
Every hallway conversation, every feedback loop, every decision you make must bleed the **DNA of service.** When people see you serving with joy, owning your mistakes, lifting the lowest, and cheering others forward—**they will follow.**
Because servant leadership isn't a class. It's not a slogan. It's a **contagious fire that spreads when one person decides to live like Jesus.**

Every revolution has a spark. Every culture shift begins with one person refusing to lead the way the world taught them—and choosing instead to lead like Jesus. That person? It's you. Don't wait for a memo, a position, or a bigger platform. **The moment you start living the mission, the movement begins.**

We cannot outsource culture. We cannot delegate servant leadership. **It doesn't scale through policies—it scales through people.** And that means the person reading this—*you*—are not just a participant in this transformation. You are the instigator. You are the thermostat. You set the temperature. Your courage to serve, to sacrifice, and to speak truth with love becomes the model that others will mirror.

Leadership Is Caught Before It's Taught

Culture is contagious. People watch your tone in meetings more than your mission statement. They watch how you treat the admin assistant, how you respond when challenged, how you handle credit and blame. The question is not **if** you're being watched—it's **what** you're showing. The essence of servant leadership isn't displayed in speeches—it's revealed in the hallway, in the email reply, in the unscripted moments. The moment your behavior matches the belief, you become the example that gives others permission to rise.

"The most powerful form of leadership is demonstration." – (Spears, 1995)

When your staff sees you empty the trash before a meeting, they notice. When you show up early to support a teammate, they remember. When you own a mistake publicly and protect someone else privately, they follow. And when you cheer for others' success louder than your own? They catch fire. That's how a movement starts—not with charisma, but with consistency.

Modeling Drives Culture

According to Kouzes & Posner (2012), "Model the way" is one of the five practices of exemplary leadership. In fact, leaders who consistently model values in action have **25% higher engagement scores** across teams. Servant leadership is not theoretical—**it is observable, measurable, and repeatable.** When you live it out visibly, you make it tangible. When you embed it personally, it multiplies professionally.

What to Do Starting Today:

1. **Audit Your Own Leadership:**

    - Ask yourself: *Where do I lead with service? Where do I lead with control?*

    - Make a list of leadership moments this week that could be more others-focused.

2. **Schedule One Act of Visible Service Per Day:**

    - Refill the coffee pot. Write a handwritten thank-you note. Cover a shift. Stay late to listen.

    - Let your team *see* you lead with your hands, not just your voice.

3. **Publicly Celebrate Values-Based Wins:**

    - Catch someone in the act of serving others—and tell the whole team.

    - This signals what matters most and gives others a template to follow.

4. **Admit a Failure. Own a Miss.**

    - Next time you get it wrong, **go first.**

    - Vulnerability builds trust faster than perfection.

5. **Invite Accountability:**

    - Ask a peer or team member to call you out when you drift from servant leadership.

    - Create a culture where the leader is coachable.

Quote for the Wall:
"Don't wait for culture to change, become the culture worth repeating."

Next-Level Tool: *The Mirror Moment*

CHAPTER 5: Building Systems That Scale

Once a week, ask yourself three questions:

1. *Who did I serve this week—without being asked or recognized?*

2. *Did my leadership make someone else better?*

3. *If my team led exactly like me, would we be healthier?*

Write down the answers. Reflect. Adjust. **Because culture follows the leader—and the movement starts with you.**

Coaching Your Team to Serve Others

Servant leadership doesn't scale through slogans—it scales through **coaching**. And if you're serious about building a culture of impact, you must become more than a manager. You must become a **servant coach**—a developer of people who multiplies purpose through personal investment.

Let's be clear: *you're not just leading projects—you're shaping hearts*. Coaching your team to serve others isn't a one-off seminar or a nice quarterly retreat. It's a **lifestyle of leadership development** embedded into how you speak, train, evaluate, correct, and celebrate. And the secret weapon? **Consistency over charisma**.

"The test of true leadership is this: do those served grow as persons? Do they, while being served, become healthier, wiser, freer, more autonomous?"
— Robert Greenleaf, 1970

Start with" Heartset", Not Just Skillset

Most companies train employees *what* to do. Servant leaders coach them on **who to become**. Before you train skills, build a foundation of values. Teach them the "why" behind the "what."

Practical Steps:

- Start meetings with short "mission moments" that highlight acts of service.

- Incorporate reflection into onboarding: "What does service mean to you?"

- Ask, *"What would this task look like if Jesus was doing it?"*

That's not fluff. That's **identity-based coaching**, and it's how you raise up people who lead from the inside out.

CHAPTER 5: Building Systems That Scale

Use the I-Do, We-Do, You-Do Model

One of the most effective models to coach behavior is the *I Do, We Do, You Do* approach:

- **I Do**: Model servant leadership clearly and visibly. Show your team what radical empathy and mission-driven excellence look like.

- **We Do**: Invite them into the process. Serve *with* them. Reflect together. Share wins and mistakes.

- **You Do**: Empower them to lead. Give them space to serve without micromanagement—and celebrate their growth.

Example:
You're leading a customer service team. You *model* a conversation where you resolve a complaint with grace (I Do). You then handle a call together (We Do). Then you empower your team member to take the next one solo, and afterwards, you debrief (You Do). That's **servant coaching in action.**

Create Feedback Loops that Build Culture

Correction without coaching leads to resentment. Coaching without clarity leads to confusion. You need **feedback loops that reinforce both service and** accountability.

- **Train managers to give praise for servant-hearted behaviors,** not just high performance.
- **Debrief tough situations** by asking, *"How did we reflect our values here?"*
- **Invite upward feedback:** ask your team how *you* can serve *them* better.

This kind of transparency builds **psychological safety**, which research consistently ties to stronger performance and innovation (Google's Project Aristotle, 2015).

Develop Peer Coaches to Multiply the Mission

Don't make servant coaching a top-down task. **Create peer coaching circles** where team members sharpen each other. This decentralizes the growth process and turns the whole culture into a coaching engine.

Toolkit:

- Set up monthly "Service Spotlights" where peers nominate each other for servant leadership moments.

- Train a few team members to become *Values Champions*—peers who lead by influence, not title.

CHAPTER 5: Building Systems That Scale

- Pair new hires with seasoned servant leaders for *shadow and serve* mentorship.

Remember: **movements don't grow through control—they grow through shared ownership**.

Turn Every Touchpoint into a Teaching Moment

Every one-on-one, every huddle, every email is a chance to coach servant leadership.
Ask questions that rewire mindset:

- *"Who can you lift up this week?"*

- *"What does success look like for the person you're serving?"*

- *"What's one small act of service you can do today that no one expects?"*

That's how you transform duty into **discipleship**, transactions into **transformation**, and tasks into **testimonies**.

SIDEBAR: The Servant Coaching Creed

- I don't train followers. I multiply leaders.

- I don't control—I cultivate.

- I don't hoard wisdom—I hand it off.

- I model it, I teach it, I repeat it.

- I coach for the Kingdom, not for the credit.

Bottom Line

You are not just managing a team.
You are **discipling a movement** of servant-hearted warriors who lead with honor, love with grit, and serve with fire.
And that doesn't happen by accident. It happens when you **coach them to serve others—daily, visibly, and intentionally.**

Let's go make coaching the new currency of leadership.

Coaching Isn't Correcting—It's Cultivating

If your idea of coaching is just fixing mistakes, you're not a coach—you're a mechanic.
True servant coaching is about **cultivating growth**, not just correcting behavior.
It's about calling people into greatness, not just pointing out what they did wrong.

CHAPTER 5: Building Systems That Scale

Jesus didn't just rebuke His disciples—He **walked with them, explained parables, washed their feet, and gave them room to fail forward.**
If you want a culture of servant leaders, then **coach with patience, clarity, and purpose**, not punishment.

If your idea of coaching is limited to fixing flaws or pointing out performance gaps, then you're not coaching—you're managing deficiencies. You're a mechanic working on machines, not a mentor raising up leaders. Servant leadership demands something far greater. **Coaching is not about compliance—it's about cultivation.** It's the intentional, relational, day-by-day investment in people's potential. You're not just correcting what's wrong—you're calling forth what's right but buried.

"True coaching doesn't focus on who someone is now—but who they're becoming. That's why it requires both courage and compassion."

From Feedback to Formation

Most feedback models revolve around evaluation. But servant coaches don't just evaluate—they **form character**. Jesus didn't just correct His disciples when they failed—He used each failure as fertile ground to plant deeper wisdom. When Peter sank in the water, Jesus didn't shame him—He lifted him. When Thomas doubted, Jesus didn't dismiss him—He gave him evidence. That's **formational coaching**: where feedback is sacred and forward-focused.

Try this model:

- **Ask**: "What did you learn from this?"

- **Reflect**: "How did this reflect our values?"

- **Challenge**: "What will you do differently next time?"

- **Affirm**: "I see growth, and I believe in you."

This kind of coaching doesn't produce compliance—it produces commitment.

See the Seed, Not Just the Soil

Groundbreaking coaches are not obsessed with current performance—they're obsessed with **unrealized potential**. You coach based on what you *see* in them, not just what they show you today. This is why Jesus was able to call Peter "the rock" long before he acted like one (Matthew 16:18). **Servant coaches speak to the future self of their team members**—and by doing so, they accelerate transformation.

The greatest gift a coach can give is belief—spoken aloud and lived consistently (Spears 1995).

Train your eye to spot *seeds* of greatness, not just *symptoms* of mistakes.

Coaching Requires Rhythms, Not Randomness

You don't cultivate a garden by checking in once a quarter—you do it daily, with intention and rhythm. Servant coaching must be **systemized**, not sporadic. Set rhythms of reflection, feedback, shadowing, and stretch assignments.

Your Coaching Rhythm Blueprint:

1. **Weekly 1-on-1s**: Not to assess KPIs—but to ask, "How are you growing?"

2. **Monthly Peer Coaching Circles**: Where culture-bearers encourage and sharpen each other.

3. **Quarterly Stretch Projects**: To test values under pressure and reveal leadership capacity.

4. **Annual Servant Review**: Not just what they *did*—but how they *served*.

This creates a **living laboratory of growth**, not a stale hierarchy of fear.

Coach With Fire and Grace

There's a difference between soft leadership and servant leadership. Servant coaches do not lower standards. They raise them—with fire in the belly and love in the delivery. You confront when needed. You challenge often. But you always coach **with restoration in mind, not rejection**. Jesus flipped tables when the temple was desecrated—but He also restored Peter after denial with a meal and a mission.

Correction without care is cruelty. But care without correction is compromise.
Servant coaches hold both in holy tension.

Your team doesn't need perfection from you. They need consistency, clarity, and care.

Coach to the Whole Person, Not Just the Performer

Servant coaches don't just coach behavior. They coach **belief, mindset, mission, identity**, and **habits**. You're developing whole people—not just productive employees. That means asking deeper questions:

- *What's getting in the way of your growth?*

- *What's going on outside of work that I should know?*

CHAPTER 5: Building Systems That Scale

- *Who do you want to become over the next year?*

- *How can I serve that dream while still pushing the mission forward?*

That's where loyalty is born. That's where real transformation begins.

SIDEBAR: The Servant Coach's Checklist

- I coach potential, not just performance.
- I give feedback that forms, not just fixes.
- I reflect and challenge in love.
- I establish rhythms of growth.
- I lead coaching conversations with restoration, not retribution.
- I hold people accountable because I believe in who they can become.

Final Charge

Coaching the servant way isn't about being soft—it's about being strategic. It's about building people who build the culture that builds the mission. You are not just a supervisor. You are a cultivator of calling. And when you take that seriously, your team stops surviving and starts **soaring**.

This isn't management.
This is multiplication.

And it's time to coach like Jesus and build like fire.

Model Before You Mentor

You can't coach your team to serve others if you're not *already serving them.*

People don't respond to what you say—they respond to **what you live.**

If your team sees you showing up early, jumping into the trenches, picking up trash, praying over people, and never seeing any job as "beneath you"—they'll follow.

Coaching begins with modeling: servant leadership must be **seen before it's spoken.**

As Paul wrote in 1 Corinthians 11:1 (NIV), *"Follow my example, as I follow the example of Christ."*

Create a Culture of Coaching

Coaching can't just be a one-on-one meeting—it has to become **part of your culture.**

That means leaders coach leaders. Peers coach peers. Veteran employees coach rookies.

You should hear phrases like "That's not how we do it here," or "We lift each other up," **on every floor, at every desk, in every department.**

Culture is shaped by what gets corrected and what gets celebrated.

So celebrate servant-hearted behavior like it's an Olympic gold medal.

CHAPTER 5: Building Systems That Scale

Coach the Why, Not Just the What

Many leaders make the mistake of coaching for performance instead of **purpose.**

Don't just tell your people *what* to do—show them **why it matters.**

Serving customers, encouraging teammates, going the extra mile—these aren't tasks. They're **reflections of your mission.**

Coaching with purpose means **connecting the dots between action and impact.**

Purpose is what fuels consistency when the motivation fades.

Most managers train behavior. Servant leaders transform belief.

And that transformation only happens when you **coach the why.**

Yes, performance matters. But purpose fuels performance long after motivation runs dry. According to Sinek (2009), "People don't buy what you do; they buy why you do it." The same is true of your team—they don't just follow tasks, they follow meaning. When you coach from a deep "why," you're not just shaping action—you're shaping identity. You're not creating robots—you're calling forth revolutionaries who lead with purpose.

Reframe Every Task Through Purpose

It's not just **"greet customers"**—it's **"make every person feel seen and valued."**
It's not just **"run the team meeting"**—it's **"set the tone for how we serve one another."**
It's not just **"clean the workspace"**—it's **"honor the environment where mission work happens."**

When you coach this way, you elevate even the smallest actions into acts of service. Suddenly, employees aren't just working for a paycheck—they're **anchored in purpose**. And that anchoring leads to higher engagement, deeper satisfaction, and a stronger emotional connection to the mission (Grant, 2008; Kouzes & Posner, 2017).

Make "Why" Part of the Rhythm

Most teams are drowning in checklists and starving for meaning. Fix that.
In every coaching conversation, start with this question:

"Why does this matter?"
Then follow with:
"How does this connect to who we are and what we value?"

Better yet—teach your team to ask those questions

CHAPTER 5: Building Systems That Scale

before they act. Train them to **self-coach the why**, and you'll build a team that's intrinsically aligned with the mission—not just externally compliant.

Coaching Framework: The "WHY-WHAT-HOW" Model

When you're coaching, use this 3-step model to embed purpose in performance:

1. **WHY** – *"Why does this task or behavior matter to our mission and values?"*

2. **WHAT** – *"What specific behaviors or outcomes are expected?"*

3. **HOW** – *"How will you carry this out in a way that honors our culture and values?"*

Example: Don't just say, "You need to be on time to meetings."
Say: "When you show up on time, you show respect for your team's time and contributions. That's how we honor one another."

Purpose drives consistency. It creates emotional buy-in. It replaces micromanagement with ownership. (Lencioni, 2002; Patterson, Grenny, Maxfield, McMillan, & Switzler, 2012).

Why Coaching the Why Builds Leaders

When people understand the deeper meaning behind their work, they stop needing constant motivation. Instead, they develop self-leadership.
This is how you **scale servant leadership**—not by controlling every outcome, but by shaping **how people think and feel about their role** in the larger story.

Jesus didn't just say, *"Feed my sheep."* He said, *"Do you love me? Then feed my sheep"* (John 21:15-17). He connected action to affection—task to heart—*what* to *why*.

This is what separates **mechanical managers from movement-makers**.

SIDEBAR: 5 Questions That Coach the Why

- Why does this task matter to our mission?

- Who is impacted by how well we do this?

- What value does this action reflect?

- How does this connect to our story as a team?

- What's at stake if we do this poorly—or with

excellence?

Final Charge

If you want a team that shows up with fire instead of fatigue, stop drilling tasks.
Start cultivating purpose.
Let every coaching session become a reminder of the mission—not just the metrics.
Let your people see themselves not as cogs in a machine, but as **ambassadors of a vision** that's bigger than them.

Because when the "why" becomes clear, the "what" becomes unstoppable.

Use Story as a Coaching Tool

Want to inspire your team to serve? Tell stories that move them.
Use real examples of service in action—stories of sacrifice, compassion, excellence, and impact.
When you coach through story, you **connect hearts to behavior**, not just brains to checklists.
Jesus taught in parables because He knew that stories stick when rules don't.
If you want to shape how your team thinks, tell them stories that show **who you want them to become.**

If you want to create a culture that breathes service—not just performs it—you need more than rules. You need

stories. Because stories don't just inform people—they **transform** them.

Cognitive science backs this up. Research shows that when we hear stories, our brains light up as if we're experiencing the events ourselves (Zak, 2015). Unlike lists, policies, or bullet points, **stories activate emotion, empathy, and memory.** They create neural resonance. That's why Jesus didn't lecture—He told parables. He taught the Kingdom through narrative because He knew the human heart isn't changed by instruction alone. It's changed by invitation into a story.

Why Story Works in Servant Leadership

- **Neuroscience confirms it**: When we hear stories, our brains simulate the experience (Zak, 2015). This "neural coupling" creates empathy, emotion, and memory—three pillars of transformational leadership.

- **Jesus modeled it**: He didn't hand out manuals. He told parables. Why? Because stories don't just inform—they **invite transformation.**

- **Culture is built through narrative**: Rules create compliance. Stories create conviction. If you want a team that breathes service—not just performs it—embed stories into your leadership DNA.

CHAPTER 5: Building Systems That Scale

How to Use Story to Build Servant Leaders

1. **Collect Stories of Service**
   Gather real examples from your team, community, or history. Look for moments of:

   - Sacrifice for others

   - Compassion in action

   - Excellence that uplifts

   - Impact that ripples outward

2. **Tell Stories with Purpose**
   Don't just entertain—**educate and inspire**. Frame each story around a core servant leadership value:

   - *Empathy*: "Here's how one coach listened deeply and changed a life."

   - *Stewardship*: "This athlete used their platform to serve their neighborhood."

   - *Commitment to Growth*: "This leader invested in others and built a legacy."

3. **Coach Through Story**
   Use stories in:

   - **Team meetings**: Start with a story that sets the tone.

   - **One-on-ones**: Share a narrative that mirrors the challenge your team member is facing.

   - **Training sessions**: Replace bullet points with story arcs.

4. **Invite Reflection and Action**
   After sharing a story, ask:

   - "What part of this story resonated with you?"

   - "How can we live this out in our team?"

   - "Who do you want to become because of this?"

Make Your Culture Legendary

Every organization has stories. The question is: **Are they worth telling?**

If someone went on a "culture tour" of your company,

CHAPTER 5: Building Systems That Scale

school, or team—what stories would they hear whispered in the halls? Who gets honored? Who gets celebrated? What gets repeated?

Great servant leaders **curate, craft, and circulate** stories that reflect the values they want multiplied. Stories about the employee who stayed late to help a struggling teammate. About the coach who noticed a quiet player and changed their trajectory. About the janitor who led with excellence so powerful it inspired an entire department. These stories become the **unofficial curriculum of culture.**

Why This Works

- **Culture is shaped by what gets repeated.** If you want service, humility, and excellence to thrive, you must **amplify the stories that embody them**.

- **Behavior follows belief.** When people hear stories of servant leadership, they begin to believe that service is not just allowed—it's expected, honored, and celebrated.

- **Stories create identity.** Neuroscience shows that stories activate the brain's empathy and memory centers (Zak, 2015). They don't just inform— they **transform**. They help people see themselves in the narrative and ask, *"How can I live that story too?"*

How to Make Your Culture Legendary Through Story

1. **Identify Your Cultural Heroes**
   Look for individuals—regardless of title—who embody servant leadership. These are your culture carriers. Highlight:

   - The employee who stayed late to help a struggling teammate.

   - The coach who noticed a quiet player and changed their trajectory.

   - The janitor whose excellence inspired an entire department.

2. **Tell Their Stories Loudly and Often**
   Use every channel available:

   - Staff meetings

   - Newsletters

   - Social media

   - Wall displays

   - Onboarding materials

CHAPTER 5: Building Systems That Scale

Make these stories **part of your organizational lore**. Repeat them until they become legend.

3. **Tie Stories to Core Values**
   Don't just tell what happened—explain **why it matters**. Connect each story to a servant leadership principle:

   - *Listening*: "This leader heard what others missed."

   - *Empathy*: "This teammate stepped into someone else's shoes."

   - *Commitment to Growth*: "This mentor invested in someone's future."

4. **Create a Story-Sharing Culture**
   Invite others to share stories. Ask:

   - "Who inspired you this week?"

   - "What act of service did you witness?"

   - "What story needs to be told?"

When storytelling becomes communal, culture becomes contagious.

Tactical Coaching Strategy: Story-Driven Culture Loops

Here's a coaching method that scales:

1. **Start every staff meeting with a story.** Not a quote. Not a stat. A *story* of service.

2. **Embed storytelling in reviews.** Ask: "Tell me about a time you saw someone else live our values."

3. **Turn feedback into narrative.** Don't say, "Do better." Say, "Let me tell you about a moment when someone embodied this value—and how it changed everything."

4. **Use storyboards in training.** Replace bullet points with case studies, parables, and real-life culture wins.

This practice is grounded in adult learning theory, which emphasizes experience, reflection, and relevance as keys to long-term growth (Knowles, Holton, & Swanson, 2015). Stories do all three.

CHAPTER 5: Building Systems That Scale

Jesus Wasn't Just a Teacher—He Was a Master Storyteller

Let's be clear: Jesus didn't need to use stories. He could've delivered theology like a courtroom prosecutor. But He chose parables. Why?

Because stories draw people in. They bypass resistance. They invite ownership. He said, *"There was a man with two sons..."* and the crowd leaned in. Not to memorize—they leaned in to **see themselves** in the narrative.

Do the same with your team. Let the story be the mirror and the map. Show them who they are—and who they can become.

SIDEBAR: 5 Story Types Every Servant Leader Should Tell

1. **The Sacrifice Story** – Someone who gave up comfort for the mission.

2. **The Redemption Story** – A failure turned into transformation.

3. **The Silent Leader Story** – A background role that had front-line impact.

4. **The Ripple Effect Story** – A small act that changed everything.

5. **The "Caught, Not Taught" Story** – When someone lived the values without being told.

Final Charge

If you want to **coach with depth, lead with fire**, and **build a culture that doesn't quit**—don't just train behaviors.
Tell stories that shape identities.
Stories make culture contagious. They make service legendary. They turn values into vision and vision into movement.

Because when the story hits the soul—**behavior follows without being forced.**

Encourage Progress, Not Perfection

Coaching servant leadership is **not about creating perfect people**—it's about **developing consistent ones.**
Encourage your team when they show growth, even if it's small.
Call out effort. Call out heart. Call out grit.
The more your team sees that **serving is noticed and valued**, the more they'll double down on it.
Servant cultures don't grow from fear—they grow from **hope, encouragement, and honest praise.**

Servant leadership is not about creating flawless performers—it's about developing faithful cultivators. In

CHAPTER 5: Building Systems That Scale

today's high-pressure, perfection-obsessed world, leaders often confuse excellence with **errorlessness**. But perfection is a myth. Progress, however—that's where transformation lives.

Research in developmental psychology and organizational behavior is clear: people thrive in cultures that celebrate *growth*, not just outcomes (Dweck, 2006). A fixed mindset leads to fear, burnout, and stagnation. A growth mindset, rooted in **grace and grit**, produces resilience, ownership, and innovation. Servant leaders coach with this understanding. They know that a single act of growth—showing empathy, pausing to listen, owning a mistake—is cause for celebration. Why? Because cultures change **one small faithful step at a time**.

Call Out the Climb

Want a culture that multiplies service? Then *affirm the climb,* not just the summit.

The team member who once ignored feedback but now leans into coaching? Praise that.
The employee who used to rush through tasks but now pauses to ask how they can help? Celebrate that.
The leader who used to dominate meetings but now makes space for others to speak? Shine a spotlight on that.

Those aren't small wins—they're **cultural**

breakthroughs. And when your people see that effort is seen, valued, and honored, they begin to chase **internal alignment**, not just external applause.

The servant-leader is servant first. It begins with the natural feeling that one wants to serve, to serve first. And if you want your people to serve first, you must **see them first**—not just when they win, but when they grow.

Step 1: Spot the Shift

Servant leaders are cultural archaeologists. They dig beneath the surface to find the gold of transformation. Look for:

- The team member who used to dodge feedback but now leans into coaching.

- The employee who once rushed through tasks but now pauses to ask, "How can I help?"

- The leader who used to dominate meetings but now makes space for others to speak.

These aren't small wins—they're **cultural breakthroughs**. They're signs that the soil is fertile and the seeds of servant leadership are sprouting.

Step 2: Build a Ritual of Recognition

Greenleaf believed that servant leadership is sustained through **intentional reinforcement**. So make celebration a system, not a surprise.

- **Create a "Climb Wall"**: A physical or digital space where you spotlight growth moments. Not just results—*resilience*.

- **Start meetings with "Climb Shoutouts"**: Let peers nominate each other for moments of growth.

- **Use story-based praise**: Don't just say "Good job." Say, "Last month, you struggled with delegation. Today, you empowered your whole team. That's leadership."

Step 3: Make Effort the Currency

In a servant-led culture, **effort is honored as much as excellence**. Why? Because effort is the evidence of transformation.

- Praise the process, not just the product.

- Reward the risk, not just the result.

- Celebrate the courage to change, not just the comfort of competence.

When your people see that effort is seen, valued, and honored, they begin to chase **internal alignment**, not just external applause.

Step 4: Tell the Climb Stories Loudly

Greenleaf taught that *"the best test of a servant-leader is: do those served grow as persons?"* So tell those stories. Often. Loudly.

- Share growth stories in newsletters, team huddles, and onboarding.

- Let your culture echo with transformation tales.

- Make the climb contagious.

Because when people hear that growth is celebrated, they'll start climbing—not for credit, but for character.

Final Charge from Greenleaf's Spirit:

"The servant-leader lifts others not by demanding greatness, but by recognizing the seeds of it—and watering them with honor."

So go ahead—**call out the climb**. Make growth visible. Make effort sacred. And watch your culture rise, one courageous step at a time.

CHAPTER 5: Building Systems That Scale

Don't Just Praise—Be Precise

Generic encouragement is background noise. Precision is what makes praise powerful.

Instead of saying, "Good job," say,

"I noticed you stayed late to help your teammate even when your task was done. That's servant leadership in action."

Instead of saying, "You're doing better," say,

"The way you handled that difficult client with patience and empathy showed maturity and growth."

This kind of feedback becomes a **mirror of identity**. It says: *"I see who you are becoming, and it matters."*

Build a Progress Recognition System

1. **Create a "Culture Wins" Channel** – Digital or physical space where leaders and peers can recognize servant leadership behaviors.

2. **Weekly Progress Check-Ins** – In meetings, ask: "Where did someone live our values this week?"

3. **Progress Journals** – Encourage team members to

track how they are growing in specific servant leadership traits (empathy, humility, courage).

4. **Celebrate Progress in Public, Coach in Private** – When growth happens, honor it where everyone can see.

According to Kouzes and Posner (2017), the act of **recognizing contributions and celebrating values in action** is one of the five practices of exemplary leadership. It builds morale, deepens trust, and creates forward motion.

The Jesus Model

Jesus never demanded perfection. He invited *progress*.

He didn't fire Peter when he denied Him—He restored him.
He didn't scold Thomas for doubting—He invited him closer.
He didn't dismiss His disciples' failures—He turned them into *foundations*.

This is the heart of servant leadership: **meeting people where they are, and walking with them until they rise.**

SIDEBAR: 5 Phrases That Build Progress Culture

- "I see growth in you."

CHAPTER 5: Building Systems That Scale

- "That took courage—and I'm proud of you for it."

- "You're not there yet, but you're further than you were."

- "This might seem small, but it's a big deal."

- "Keep going—I'm walking with you."

Final Charge

Stop trying to build perfect teams. Build **faithful ones**.

Teams that don't shrink in failure.
Teams that don't fake strength to avoid judgment.
Teams that know growth is the goal—and that every inch forward is sacred ground.

Because when servant leaders encourage progress, they don't just change people's work.
They resurrect people's worth.

Make Coaching an Expectation, Not a Favor

Too many leaders treat coaching like a bonus. Wrong.
It's a **non-negotiable**, especially in a servant-led organization.
If you don't have time to coach your people, you don't

have time to lead.
Schedule it. Systematize it. Build it into your **daily and weekly rhythm.**
Because coaching your team to serve others is how you **build the leaders who will carry your vision forward.**

Servant leadership is not about creating flawless performers—it's about developing faithful cultivators. In today's high-pressure, perfection-obsessed world, leaders often confuse excellence with **errorlessness**. But perfection is a myth. Progress, however—that's where transformation lives.

Research in developmental psychology and organizational behavior is clear: people thrive in cultures that celebrate *growth*, not just outcomes (Dweck, 2006). A fixed mindset leads to fear, burnout, and stagnation. A growth mindset, rooted in **grace and grit**, produces resilience, ownership, and innovation. Servant leaders coach with this understanding. They know that a single act of growth—showing empathy, pausing to listen, owning a mistake—is cause for celebration. Why? Because cultures change **one small faithful step at a time.**

Coaching Creates a Chain Reaction

One servant-coached leader turns into five. Then ten. Then a department. Then a campus. Then a movement. **Coaching multiplies culture.**
It raises standards. It builds confidence. It eliminates

CHAPTER 5: Building Systems That Scale

confusion.

When you coach with purpose, passion, and consistency, your team becomes **a living, breathing embodiment of servant leadership.**

And in that moment, **you're not just managing people—you're releasing leaders to change he world.**

How to Build a Servant-First Pipeline

"Don't build pipelines that produce power-hungry climbers—build pipelines that unleash purpose-driven warriors. The next generation doesn't need more bosses in suits. They need builders of people, carriers of mission, and servants who lead with fire."

Start Early, Start Often

The servant-leadership pipeline doesn't begin when someone lands a promotion—it begins **the moment they walk through your door.**

Whether it's a new hire, intern, volunteer, or first-time team leader, **you need to plant the seed of service from day one.**

Don't wait to teach values—embed them in **onboarding, orientation, and early team experiences.**

If you start shaping hearts early, you won't have to repair behavior later.

As Proverbs 22:6 (NIV) reminds us: *"Start children off on the way they should go, and even when they are old they* will not turn from it."

Create a Culture of Mentorship

Your pipeline won't grow unless today's leaders are committed to developing tomorrow's.
This means mentorship must be **built into the rhythm of your organization**—not optional, but *expected*.
Every leader should have someone they're lifting. Every rising leader should have someone lifting them.
When mentorship becomes a norm, not a novelty, you'll see a **generational chain of service** that strengthens your core.
Remember: the best leaders don't leave legacies—they leave **leaders**.

Rotate and Expose

Don't trap potential servant leaders in one department or duty—**rotate them.**
Expose them to multiple teams, perspectives, and challenges.
Stretch them. Give them **service-based projects that force growth**.
Southwest Airlines is known for cross-training and rotating leaders to ensure they understand how the whole system serves the mission (Collins, 2001).
You're not just building experts. You're building **well-rounded, self-aware, others-focused leaders.**

Build in Feedback Loops

A healthy servant pipeline requires **constant evaluation and recalibration.**
Your future leaders need real-time feedback—*not just about results, but about how they serve.*
Are they empowering others? Are they modeling the values?
Use 360-degree reviews, peer feedback, and even customer insights to **fuel their development.**
Great pipelines are **built on feedback, not favoritism.**

Create Small Leadership Labs

You don't need giant programs to grow servant leaders—you need **small, intentional labs** where people can practice.
Create spaces where emerging leaders **try, fail, reflect, and grow.**
Run internal service challenges. Assign group projects with servant values at the core.
When people see leadership as a laboratory, they stop waiting for perfection and start **engaging with passion.**
Remember: **experiences transform faster than lectures.**

Celebrate Pipeline Progress

Publicly celebrate servant leadership in development, not just in action.

Highlight your team members who are **growing**, not just those who've "arrived."

Create monthly shout-outs, internal awards, or spotlight stories that **honor the process.**

When people see that becoming a servant leader is *celebrated*, they'll chase it.

What you **celebrate gets repeated**—so celebrate the climb, not just the summit.

Build It To Outlive You

The ultimate test of your servant-first pipeline? **It thrives without you.**

You're not building followers—you're building **future leaders who build more leaders.**

This means documenting values, codifying processes, creating handbooks, running succession planning, and **embedding service into every level.**

If your leadership dies when you leave, it was never servant leadership—it was personal control.

Legacy leaders don't build empires. They build **ecosystems of empowerment.**

Action Plan — Weekly "Lead Like Jesus" Drills

You don't transform a culture through intention—you do it through repetition, reflection, and responsibility.

I'm telling you this plainly: **culture is not built by chance—it's drilled by design.** Just as elite athletes don't become great through one practice session,

CHAPTER 5: Building Systems That Scale

servant leaders don't emerge from a single team meeting. They are **formed in the trenches** of consistent, intentional training.

These "Lead Like Jesus" drills are weekly, high-impact exercises designed to help your team **move from belief to behavior, and from behavior to breakthrough.** Each drill develops spiritual posture, emotional intelligence, cultural awareness, and execution aligned with the values of Christ-like leadership.

WEEKLY DRILLS FRAMEWORK

1. Monday Morning Alignment: Start With Scripture

- Begin the week with a 5-minute reflection on a scripture about service, humility, or leadership. Example: *Mark 10:45 — "For even the Son of Man did not come to be served, but to serve..."*

- Ask each team member: *"What does this verse mean for how we treat each other this week?"*

- Write responses on a shared board or digital space. Review them Friday.

2. Tuesday Storytelling Session: Real Heroes, Real Impact

- Share a story from within the team (or another

organization) where someone modeled servant leadership.

- Discuss what made the behavior powerful. Tie it back to your values.

- Ask: *"What behavior in that story do we need more of in our culture?"*

3. Wednesday One-on-One Walks

- Managers take 15 minutes for a walk-and-talk with each team member.

- Ask two servant-focused questions:

    1. *"How can I serve you better this week?"*

    2. *"Is there someone on the team you think deserves to be honored?"*

- Use these moments to **model listening, build psychological safety**, and foster dignity.

4. Thursday Challenge: One Act of Radical Service

- Every team member must perform one act of radical service for a teammate, customer, or community member.

- No recognition, no announcement—just impact.
- Friday meeting includes optional story sharing.

5. Friday Feedback Loop

- End the week with a 30-minute debrief.
- Discuss what was learned, what was hard, and what surprised people.
- Reinforce wins. Celebrate quiet victories. Close in reflection or prayer (if appropriate to your context).

SIDEBAR: Why Drills Work

Modern research on behavioral change and organizational culture proves that **repetition builds retention** (Duhigg, 2012; Clear, 2018). Teams that engage in regular behavior modeling are **3x more likely** to develop shared ownership of values (Lencioni, 2002). Jesus trained through repetition—feeding the 5,000, washing feet, healing in public—not to impress, but to **imprint a pattern of leadership on His followers**. These drills follow the same model.

"Great cultures aren't caught by accident—they're caught by example, and cemented through action."

The Greatest Among You

From the Sermon to the System

Most leadership values die because they're talked about in one meeting and never practiced again.
But not this time.
"Lead Like Jesus" drills are **weekly rhythms of servant leadership training**—short, powerful, culture-changing exercises that turn belief into behavior.
They're designed to be 20-minute micro-lessons that **fit into any staff meeting, huddle, or shift kickoff.**
You're not just learning—you're **conditioning** a team to think, act, and love like Christ.

Drill 1: Foot Washing Fridays

Jesus washed feet. Not as a gimmick—but as a model of leadership (John 13:14-15, NIV).
Create a "Foot Washing Friday" moment where team members **serve one another in small, tangible ways**—cleaning someone's workspace, writing notes of gratitude, covering a tough shift.
This isn't symbolic—it's **sweaty, sacrificial, sacred service.**
Start or end your week reminding everyone: **leadership begins where comfort ends.**
Your culture will transform when people stop asking, *"Who serves me?"* and start asking, *"Whose feet can I wash?"*

CHAPTER 5: Building Systems That Scale

Drill 2: The 3-10-1 Challenge

Have your team each week:

- Speak encouragement to 3 people,

- Ask how they can help 10 people,

- Serve 1 person in a way that costs them something.
  It rewires the brain from self-protection to **kingdom impact.**
  Track it. Share wins. Watch your team get addicted to **intentional service.**
  Jesus didn't measure greatness by titles—He measured it by **how many people you lift.**
  (Matthew 23:11)

Drill 3: The Interruptible Leader

Pick a leader each week to carry the **Interruptible Leader badge**—their job is to be *intentionally available* to whoever needs them.
No door closed. No task too urgent. No question too small.
It teaches humility, accessibility, and patience—the core

of servant leadership.

If Jesus could pause to heal a bleeding woman while on His way to raise the dead (Luke 8:43–48), **you can stop and serve too.**

Train your leaders to lead like they're **interruptible by heaven.**

Drill 4: Cross-Carrying Conversations

Create a 15-minute team devotional each week around this question:

"What cross are you carrying this week—and who are you helping carry theirs?"

Let people share victories, struggles, and prayers.

It doesn't have to be church—it just has to be **real.**

This develops **psychological safety**, spiritual depth, and relational glue that makes teams unstoppable.

Remember: *"Carry each other's burdens, and in this way you will fulfill the law of Christ."* (Galatians 6:2, NIV)

Drill 5: The Secret Service Mission

Each week, assign team members a "secret mission" to bless someone without getting caught.

Pay for a lunch. Leave a note. Send flowers anonymously.

Then share stories (without names) at the end of the

week.
It makes service **fun, mysterious, and contagious.**
In a world obsessed with recognition, raise up **invisible heroes.**

Drill 6: Legacy Journals

Have team members keep a "Legacy Journal" where they reflect on:

- Who they served,

- What they learned,

- How they lived out the mission.
  Make space once a week to share insights.
  This **builds reflection and intentional growth**—the mark of a mature servant leader.
  Jesus didn't just rush from task to task—He **withdrew, reflected, and prayed** (Luke 5:16).

Discipline Builds Disciples

The only difference between a value and a virtue is **repetition.**
If you want servant leadership to define your

organization, then **train it like it's sacred.**
Weekly drills move people from inspiration to transformation.
They make "servant leadership" not just your mantra—but your **muscle memory.**
These drills won't just change your week—they'll build **servant leaders for life.**

Light the Fuse — Build the Movement

You've read the blueprints. You've felt the heat. You've stood at the intersection of conviction and execution. Now it's time to **step into the fire** and **build systems that scale**, not egos that swell.

You don't need a new policy.
You don't need a fancy title.
You need **boldness**, **discipline**, and a **heart that beats for others**.
From the boardroom to the break room, from the corner office to the loading dock—**leadership begins when you decide to serve, today.**

Don't wait. Don't wish. Don't water it down.
The world is suffocating from corporate narcissism, soul-sucking systems, and bottom-line obsession. But the servant leader? They rise with a towel, not a throne. They're *the ones who flip the script*, who coach with compassion, who drive profit without poisoning the

CHAPTER 5: Building Systems That Scale

people.

This is the moment you stop talking and start building. This is the week you launch your **"Lead Like Jesus" drills**, build your **servant-first pipeline**, and unleash a **culture that serves itself into greatness**.

The world doesn't need another boss.
It needs you.
The builder. The torchbearer. The servant.

Let's build systems that **outlive our titles and outshine our resumes**.
Let's raise up a new generation of leaders who don't seek applause, but impact.
This is how movements begin—one act of humble, daily, scalable service at a time.

Now go build it.
This is your time.
This is your **legacy in motion**.

SIDEBAR: The 10-Minute Culture Shift

"You don't need an all-day seminar to change your culture. You need **10 minutes of consistency** every week."

- Begin your weekly meeting by honoring someone who served quietly.

The Greatest Among You

- Share a 2-minute story about a servant leader from scripture or real life.

- Challenge your team to do one invisible act of service before Friday.

- End by asking: "Who did you lift up this week?"

That's it. Ten minutes. Do it for 12 weeks, and you won't recognize your culture.

CHAPTER 6: The Faith Factor

"The truest form of leadership was not theorized in ivory towers or written in leadership manuals—it was demonstrated when the Son of God knelt to wash the feet of broken men. Servant leadership is not a strategy; it is the incarnation of divine authority wrapped in humility. To lead like Jesus is to reject the illusion of power and embrace the redemptive force of love in motion."

There's a reason why servant leadership isn't just another corporate trend—it's a divine calling.
This movement doesn't originate in business books or boardrooms. It began with a Carpenter-King who washed feet instead of commanding thrones.
When Jesus said, *"The greatest among you will be your servant"* (Matthew 23:11, NIV), He wasn't giving a metaphor—He was flipping the world's leadership model on its head.
The **faith factor** isn't optional. It's the **engine** behind everything we've built so far.

What separates **Christ-centered leadership** from human-centered strategy is its **source of power**.
The world builds influence through manipulation, fear, and control. Jesus built His through sacrifice, truth, and grace.
The faith factor teaches us that leadership isn't about raising yourself up—it's about **lowering yourself in love**.
That truth changes how we coach, how we delegate, how

we speak, and how we confront.

When faith is woven into leadership, the mission stops being profit—it becomes **purpose**.

Faith-rooted leadership makes **prayer the first strategy, not the last resort.**

It connects purpose to people, and profit to eternity.

It teaches leaders to pause, listen, and follow—because no matter your title, **you're not the ultimate leader—He is.**

Luke 22:26-27 reminds us: *"The greatest among you should be like the youngest, and the one who rules like the one who serves... I am among you as one who serves."* (NIV)

In a culture obsessed with climbing, Christ-centered leaders descend—into compassion, into character, and into obedience.

Faith-based leadership is not just spiritual—it's **high-impact, high-reward, and high-accountability.**

When you start with prayer, lead with humility, and serve with excellence, you build trust that can't be faked and culture that can't be bought.

Your decisions align with your convictions.

Your team begins to **feel the Gospel before they ever hear it.**

That's not just leadership. That's **kingdom culture at work.**

Organizations led by Christ-following servant leaders often outperform their competitors—not because they're

CHAPTER 6: The Faith Factor

chasing profits, but because they're **chasing people's hearts.**

They retain talent, inspire innovation, and earn trust that lasts.

You can see it in companies like **Chick-fil-A** or **Interstate Battery**, where values aren't just posters—they're practiced, every day, at every level.

Why? Because their leaders are **anchored in something eternal.**

Their compass isn't quarterly returns—it's the **cross.**

When you integrate **prayer, purpose, and people**, you start leading on holy ground.

You begin asking: *Who am I serving? Why does this matter? How is Christ honored in this?*

You stop hiding your faith behind professional polish and start living it through **quiet, courageous, consistent acts of service.**

That's how faith becomes leadership: not through domination, but **through daily, disciplined submission.**

When Jesus said *"follow me,"* He meant **in boardrooms, break rooms, and beyond.**

But let's be real—faith-centered leadership isn't easy.

It demands prayer when you're tired, integrity when it's costly, and mercy when you'd rather fire someone than forgive them.

But that's the difference. That's the **faith factor.**

It strengthens your spine while softening your heart.

It makes you the kind of leader who builds teams that not only succeed—but leave people **changed.**

This chapter isn't just about adding a Christian label to corporate culture.
It's about living out a leadership legacy rooted in the life, death, and resurrection of Jesus.
It's about becoming a **living Gospel**, not just a leader with goals.
If you dare to embrace the **faith factor**, your leadership will not only transform your company—it will transform **eternity** for the people you influence.
Now let's go deeper—because **Christ-centered leadership changes everything.**

Why Christ-Centered Leadership Changes Everything

Leadership without Christ is like a compass without true north—it may spin, but it never leads.
Christ-centered leadership doesn't simply improve an organization—it **redefines it** from the inside out.
When Jesus becomes the model, the motive, and the mission, everything changes—priorities shift, egos shrink, and service rises.
Leaders begin to measure success not by how many follow them, but by how faithfully they follow Him.
As Paul says, *"Follow my example, as I follow the example of Christ"* (1 Corinthians 11:1, NIV)—that's the gold standard of leadership.

The business world often demands compromise. Christ-centered leadership demands **conviction**.

CHAPTER 6: The Faith Factor

It calls you to remain honest in the face of shortcuts, gracious in moments of conflict, and humble when victory is won.

It turns performance reviews into *restoration opportunities* and staff meetings into *ministry moments*.

Christ isn't a department head—He's the CEO of the soul.

And when He leads the way, **love becomes your culture**, not just your company value.

Worldly leadership says, "How can I use people to accomplish my goals?"

Christ-centered leadership asks, *"How can I serve people to fulfill God's calling?"*

That single mindset shift changes how you hire, train, correct, and elevate your team.

You stop using people to build your platform—and you start using your platform to **build people.**

That's how teams are healed. That's how cultures are transformed.

When you lead like Christ, you stop chasing applause and start **seeking obedience.**

You're no longer the center of the mission—God is.

This kind of leadership doesn't just thrive in the light, it walks with integrity in the shadows.

You make decisions that are *eternally wise*, not just **temporarily beneficial.**

"Do nothing out of selfish ambition or vain conceit. Rather, in humility value others above yourselves."
(Philippians 2:3, NIV)

Christ-centered leaders don't avoid confrontation—they **redeem it.**
They don't manipulate with fear—they lead with faith.
They don't seek to be served—they *show up first, stay the latest, and wash feet in the middle of chaos.*
When your identity is rooted in Christ, leadership becomes less about control and more about calling.
That calling says: *"Serve. Love. Die to self. And lead others to do the same."*

In crisis, worldly leaders panic. Christ-centered leaders **pray.**
In pressure, they press in—not to their pride, but into God's promises.
They create environments where **grace is policy, excellence is worship,** and **truth is never for sale.**
They model a strength that doesn't dominate—it dignifies.
And that strength, rooted in the Spirit, **cannot be faked or broken.**

This is not soft leadership—it's **sacrificial leadership.**
It bleeds, it bends, it builds.
And because it is rooted in eternity, it produces **fruits that outlive profits, titles, or trends.**
Jesus didn't climb the ladder—He **carried the cross.** And in doing so, He gave us the blueprint for leadership that will *never fail.*
As Galatians 5:13 says: *"Serve one another humbly in love."*

CHAPTER 6: The Faith Factor

Christ-centered leadership changes everything because **Christ changes everything.**
He redeems broken systems, repairs fractured teams, and reignites tired leaders with *resurrection power.*
When Jesus is your model, your mission, and your message—*you stop trying to be great, and start becoming good and faithful.*
That's the type of leader the world is desperate for.
And that's exactly the leader **you're becoming.**

Integrating Prayer, Purpose, and People

Prayer isn't a formality—it's a **foundation**.
Too many leaders treat it like a morning checkbox instead of a constant lifeline.
But Jesus didn't lead without praying, even for those who betrayed, abandoned, or doubted Him.
If Christ—the Son of God—**needed prayer to lead**, how much more do we?
When leaders build prayer into their habits, huddles, and heartbeats, they unlock spiritual clarity that **strategy alone can never produce.**

Prayer anchors your purpose in something deeper than KPIs and performance reviews.
It aligns your vision with the **Author of Vision.**
It removes selfish ambition and sharpens God-given direction.
When a servant leader prays before hiring, firing,

launching, or pivoting, decisions are made with both boldness and **biblical grounding**.
"Commit to the Lord whatever you do, and he will establish your plans" (Proverbs 16:3, NIV).

But prayer isn't passive—it ignites **purpose**.
It turns mundane tasks into ministry and ordinary meetings into **divine encounters**.
Purpose is what keeps people in the fire without getting burned.
It reminds the leader and the team: *We are not here just to produce. We're here to serve.*
And purpose rooted in heaven fuels endurance on earth.

Purpose alone, however, means nothing without **people**.
You can have the most inspiring mission statement in the world—but if your people feel invisible, broken, or used, it's all noise.
God's entire redemptive plan was built on relationships. Christ didn't die for corporations—He died for souls.
So servant leaders must elevate people above process, *honor over hurry, and belonging over bureaucracy.*

True leaders **don't just care about their people's performance—they care about their souls.**
That starts with prayer and continues with personal investment.
Ask yourself: *When was the last time I prayed for my team by name? When did I last ask them about their dreams?*
If your people feel seen, heard, and lifted—they'll run through fire for the mission.

CHAPTER 6: The Faith Factor

Why? Because **servant leadership turns a job into a calling.**

Integrating prayer, purpose, and people means creating a culture that is spiritually alert, emotionally engaged, and missionally focused.
It's not just a "Jesus fish" on your logo—it's the posture of your leadership.
You invite God in not just for wisdom, but **to take the lead.**
You align every role, process, and product with the greater calling: *to love, to serve, to glorify Him.*
When you do that, even your Monday staff meeting becomes holy ground.

There is no more powerful strategy than a leader who walks the halls praying silently for wisdom...
...who meets confrontation with grace instead of pride...
...who reminds every teammate that they are not a tool, but a **treasure.**
Prayer is the *oil*, purpose is the *engine*, and people are the *vehicle*.
Without one, the others fail. But together—they **move mountains.**

Integrating prayer, purpose, and people isn't just a tactic—it's a **testimony.**
It shows the world that leadership can be holy. That business can be beautiful.
That a faith-driven leader doesn't just manage assets—they *shepherd hearts*.

Let your team feel the power of your prayers, the clarity of your purpose, and the dignity of your love.
Because when prayer, purpose, and people collide—
heaven comes to work.

Living Out the Gospel Through Service

Jesus didn't just *talk* about servant leadership—He *embodied* it.
On the night He was betrayed—when most men would be concerned about self-preservation—He **grabbed a towel and washed feet** (John 13:3-5).
He didn't just preach sermons; He touched lepers, wept with mourners, fed crowds, and **restored dignity** to the discarded.
Every step of His ministry screamed: *"I did not come to be served, but to serve"* (Mark 10:45, NIV).
And if the Son of God chose the path of service, how can any leader dare to choose otherwise?

The Gospel isn't just about salvation—it's about *transformation*.
And when leaders live it out through service, they bring heaven into **boardrooms, break rooms, classrooms, and courtrooms**.
It's not just about sharing Bible verses—it's about carrying burdens, noticing needs, and creating systems where **love leads the way**.
Living out the Gospel means opening your calendar, your

CHAPTER 6: The Faith Factor

wallet, and your heart.
It means you stop asking, *"How can they help me?"* and start asking, *"How can I help them become who God created them to be?"*

Gospel-centered service dismantles hierarchy.
You stop seeing titles—you start seeing **souls.**
You stop measuring influence by control and start measuring it by compassion.
When a leader chooses to serve first, it removes fear and replaces it with **freedom**.
And in that freedom, your team begins to flourish—not for your glory, but for *His*.

Living out the Gospel through service is not about playing nice—it's about **changing culture**.
Culture doesn't shift by slogans or staff retreats—it changes when **leaders kneel before others and lift them up.**
Your people don't need another memo—they need a mentor.
They don't need more rules—they need someone willing to listen, care, and lead with *kingdom courage*.
Because when love is in motion, even the hardest hearts begin to soften.

In a world of burnout, bullying, and brokenness, Gospel-driven service is **radical resistance.**
It says: *"You matter. Your story matters. You are more than your productivity."*
When a leader lives that truth, it doesn't just impact one

person—it **multiplies across teams, families, and entire communities.**
It's how Christ changed the world—**one towel at a time.**
And it's how we'll do it, too.

Make no mistake—this kind of leadership will **cost you.**
It's slower, harder, and rarely applauded in the short term.
But servant leadership is *eternal leadership*—and the legacy it creates will outlive every metric, meeting, and milestone.
Your team may not always remember what you said, but they will **never forget how you made them feel** when you served them like Christ.
That's how you lead people to Jesus—**not by command, but by compassion.**

When you build service into your leadership DNA, everything starts to align—hearts, habits, and **heaven's purpose.**
You'll find yourself praying in meetings, encouraging the discouraged, and staying late not to prove a point, but to *lift a burden.*
You'll become the leader who knows birthdays, mourns losses, and **fights for justice in quiet, powerful ways.**
The Gospel in action looks like everyday service fueled by **supernatural love.**
And that kind of love **can't be ignored.**

This is the Gospel lived—not just believed.
When the world sees leaders serve with humility,

strength, and grace, it sees a glimpse of the **Kingdom of God.**
So go ahead—wash feet, lift heads, carry crosses, and build people.
That's not weakness. That's *what victory looks like in the Kingdom.*
And that's how you, brother, will change the world.

Scripture: Matthew 23:11, Luke 22:26–27

"The greatest among you will be your servant" (Matthew 23:11, NIV).
Let that sink in—not the most powerful, not the richest, not the one with the biggest office or loudest voice.
Jesus flipped the leadership model upside down and said, *"You want to be great? Then grab a towel, not a title."*
That single verse obliterates every worldly definition of success.
True greatness isn't measured by how many serve you—it's measured by how many you're willing to serve.

In a world obsessed with influence, Jesus calls us to intimacy.
While others climb over people, He calls us to *kneel beside them.*
He didn't say servant leadership was a nice idea—He said it's the very **definition of greatness.**
This wasn't weakness. It was **divine strength under control.**

The Greatest Among You

And when we lead like this, we stop imitating the world and start *reflecting the King.*

Luke 22:26–27 puts it even more plainly:
"The greatest among you should be like the youngest, and the one who rules like the one who serves... I am among you as one who serves."
These are Jesus' words at the Last Supper—on the brink of betrayal, He reminded them **not to lead with a throne, but with a towel.**
He modeled servant leadership not when things were easy, but when His **world was about to collapse.**
That's the power of Gospel-driven leadership—it stands firm in crisis because it's **rooted in calling, not control.**

Jesus wasn't vague. He didn't just say to "try your best."
He said, *"I am among you as one who serves."*
That's not symbolic. That's **directional.**
It means your role as a leader is to walk into the room and ask: *Who can I lift today? Who needs my hands, my words, my presence?*
That's how you become great in the eyes of God—not by commanding, but by **compassionately contributing.**

This is where titles die and legacies are born.
Because nobody remembers the org chart from 10 years ago—but they'll never forget the leader who **showed up when it mattered most.**
Jesus never held a formal title, never led a corporation, never had LinkedIn followers... but His impact shattered empires.

CHAPTER 6: The Faith Factor

Why? Because He led with a *cross, not a crown.*
And when you lead like that, heaven moves.

When Christ says, *"The greatest shall be your servant,"*
He's inviting you into a leadership model that **heals instead of harms.**
No manipulation. No intimidation. Just **influence born out of love, sacrifice, and daily, deliberate humility.**
This isn't about passivity—it's **warfare against ego.**
It's the kind of leadership that costs you everything... and **gives you back your soul.**
Because the true throne room of leadership is found in the hearts of those you serve.

The church needs this. The marketplace needs this. Your team needs this.
Because when leaders start loving like Christ and serving like Christ, **revival starts in the workplace.**
Jesus didn't outsource servanthood to HR departments or church volunteers.
He did it Himself. He lived it. And He told us to **go and do the same** (John 13:15).
This is your call to *lead the way, love the people, and live the Gospel out loud.*

Matthew 23:11 and Luke 22:26–27 are not spiritual wallpaper.
They are the *battle anthem of the bold*, the blueprint for kingdom-minded executives, pastors, teachers, coaches, and dreamers.
These words are sacred fire—meant to burn away selfish

ambition and ignite **servant revolutionaries**.
So let's rise—not by elevating ourselves, but by *lifting others higher than we ever dreamed possible*.
This is your moment. **Lead like Jesus—and never look back.**

This Is the Way

You've heard His voice. You've felt the pull.
Now it's time to rise—not in title, but in **testimony.**
The world doesn't need another self-appointed boss barking orders from a throne.
It needs *you*—a **blood-bought, Spirit-filled, servant-hearted warrior** who's willing to pick up the towel and **change the world from the inside out.**

You were never meant to lead like everyone else.
You were meant to lead like **the King.**
And our King? He *washed feet*.
He *broke bread*.
He *took lashes and carried a cross*, not because He had to—but because **love leaves the throne to lift the broken.**

That's your calling now.

You, CEO.
You, coach.
You, teacher.
You, pastor.
You, young leader who doesn't yet have the title but has

CHAPTER 6: The Faith Factor

the *fire*—this is your moment.

The world may not understand it.
Some will mock it.
The insecure will try to silence it.
But when **Jesus-style leadership** hits the ground, *hell trembles.*
Because nothing disrupts darkness like a leader filled with **light, humility, courage, and conviction.**

So go.
Lead like it's **holy ground**—because it is.
Serve like eternity depends on it—because it does.
And never forget:

"The greatest among you will be your servant." — Matthew 23:11

Now grab your towel, pick up your cross, and **ignite the revolution.**

This is the way.

The Greatest Among You

CHAPTER 7: Obstacles to Servant Leadership

The War Within, The War Around Us

Servant leadership is **not for the faint of heart**.
It's easy to post about. Easy to hashtag. Easy to slap on a mission statement.
But to *live* it—to die to ego, reject comfort, and lead with sacrifice—that takes a kind of holy courage this world can't manufacture.
This chapter is about what stands in the way—*inside of us* and *around us*.
Because every movement that transforms the world must first confront the monsters that hide in plain sight.

The biggest obstacle to servant leadership isn't external—it's internal.
It's not policy. Not budget. Not even your team.
It's your **ego.**
That still, whispering voice that says, *"You deserve more. You're above this. Let them serve you."*
But make no mistake: ego is the enemy of elevation. If Jesus laid His down, so must we (Philippians 2:5–8, NIV).

Then comes **control.**
Control masquerades as leadership, but it's rooted in fear.
It says, *"If I don't do it, it won't get done right."* It bulldozes collaboration and buries creativity.

Leaders addicted to control suffocate their people—and often don't realize it until the best ones are gone.
You cannot raise servant leaders if you insist on being the only voice that matters.

And behind both ego and control is the roaring lion called **fear**.
Fear of losing relevance. Fear of vulnerability. Fear of being seen as "less than."
But Scripture reminds us: *"God has not given us a spirit of fear, but of power, love, and self-discipline"* (2 Timothy 1:7, NIV).
Fear-based leadership creates shells of teams—burned out, checked out, and clocking out.
Servant leadership is the cure, but fear must be dragged into the light first.

And then there's the culture.
Let's be real—**most organizations reward ego, not humility.**
They celebrate dominance, not empathy.
They promote the loudest, not the wisest.
But when culture is toxic, no leader can thrive unless they're willing to *wage war against the norm*.

These toxic cultures don't just happen—they're **built**.
Built on bad habits. On unchecked pride. On leaders who forgot who they were called to be.
And if we don't intentionally build something better, we will unintentionally become the very thing we once swore we'd never be.

CHAPTER 7: Obstacles to Servant Leadership

You can't detox a culture until you detox the leadership. And that starts with *you*.

Servant leadership is **inconvenient.**
It demands your time, your heart, your availability.
It asks you to show up when you're tired. To listen when you'd rather speak. To carry weight that's not in your job description.
But here's the truth: *anything that changes the world will cost you something*.
And those willing to pay the price will inherit a legacy nothing can tarnish.

This chapter is a mirror and a match.
A mirror to reveal what's in the way—and a match to set it on fire.
If you've been leading out of ego, fear, or control, **repent and rebuild.**
If you've been crushed by a toxic culture, **rise and resist.**
Because the world doesn't need more leaders in love with their own image. The world needs leaders who look like *Jesus*.

Ego, Control, and Fear

The Unholy Trinity of Toxic Leadership

Let's start with **ego**—that seductive whisper that tells a leader, *"You are the reason this place works."*
Ego doesn't care about people. It doesn't build teams. It builds kingdoms—**tiny, fragile kingdoms**—on the backs

of burnt-out employees.

The egotistical leader surrounds themselves with yes-men, silences dissent, and demands praise like oxygen.

But Scripture couldn't be clearer: *"Pride goes before destruction, a haughty spirit before a fall"* (Proverbs 16:18, NIV).

Ego is the first domino in the downfall of every self-serving empire.

When I started working at age 15, I met these leaders.

They didn't lead—they lorded.

They wore their title like a crown and their power like a sword.

They belittled, barked, and bossed just to feel tall.

And every time I brought a new idea to the table, they swatted it down like a fly—because "it wasn't their idea."

Ego was their god, and they worshiped themselves.

Next up: **control**.

Control is the silent killer of innovation, collaboration, and team ownership.

The leader who must approve every decision, oversee every detail, and micromanage every move isn't building excellence—they're building a cage.

You can't empower your team if you chain them to your perfectionism.

"Where the Spirit of the Lord is, there is freedom" (2 Corinthians 3:17, NIV)—and servant leaders bring that freedom into every room they lead.

Control is rooted in fear.

CHAPTER 7: Obstacles to Servant Leadership

Fear that someone else might do it better.
Fear that letting go means losing relevance.
But control doesn't make you stronger—it isolates you.
And isolated leaders always collapse under the weight of their own insecurity.

Now let's name it outright—**fear** is the master puppeteer.
Fear says: *"Don't trust your team. Don't show weakness. Don't lead with vulnerability—it'll get you eaten alive."*
But here's what fear won't tell you: **it's a liar**.
The greatest leaders I've ever known—coaches, CEOs, pastors, parents—weren't fearless. They were **courageous** enough to lead *through* the fear.
Servant leaders walk into the unknown and declare:
"Even if it costs me everything, I will lead with love."

Fear-based leaders manipulate with silence.
They keep people guessing. They lead through intimidation, not inspiration.
They thrive on chaos and use it as a smokescreen to avoid accountability.
And the cost? **Trust dies. Loyalty crumbles. Culture collapses.**
"There is no fear in love. But perfect love drives out fear..."
(1 John 4:18, NIV)—and servant leadership is the weapon that casts it out.

When ego, control, and fear rule the throne, you get **high turnover, low trust, and wasted potential.**
You get environments where people clock in physically but check out emotionally.

Where creativity is crushed, boldness is buried, and vision becomes a faded plaque on the break room wall.
No one *wants* to work for these kinds of leaders—they just *survive* under them.
But this book, this movement, is about **ending the tyranny** and restoring leadership to its divine calling.

Let this be your moment of reckoning.
If any part of this section punched you in the gut—it was supposed to.
Because only when we face the monster can we kill it.
And the death of ego, control, and fear is where **real leadership begins.**
Pick up your towel. Drop the mask. And step into the fire of **authentic, Jesus-modeled leadership.**

Toxic Cultures and How to Detox Them

Exposing the Rot and Planting New Roots

Toxic cultures don't announce themselves—they sneak in like a parasite.
At first, it's subtle. Eye rolls at vulnerability. Backhanded comments about "soft" leadership. Little punishments for speaking up.
But soon it spreads: good people leave, great people shut down, and mediocrity becomes the norm.
And the worst part? These places still post #Teamwork on LinkedIn while bleeding their people dry.

CHAPTER 7: Obstacles to Servant Leadership

A toxic culture doesn't just happen—it's **allowed** to happen.

Let's call out the warning signs.
Gossip is currency. Turnover is high. Employees are promoted for loyalty to power, not competence.
Ideas are squashed if they don't come from the top.
Mistakes are punished, not learned from.
These are the markers of dysfunction—and they **never fix themselves.**
A toxic culture will rot from the inside out unless a leader walks in with a sword and says, "Not on my watch."

The real poison in toxic cultures is **fear**—fear of speaking truth, fear of being authentic, fear of being disposable.
People in these environments *don't feel safe*.
And when people don't feel safe, they stop caring.
They disengage, they coast, or they quietly plan their escape.
"Where there is no vision, the people perish..." (Proverbs 29:18, KJV)—and toxic cultures kill vision with a thousand tiny cuts.

Here's the part no one wants to admit:
You can have a toxic culture **with nice people.**
You can have "Christian values" on the wall and **absolutely zero Jesus** in the way people are treated.
Culture is not what you say—it's what you **tolerate.**
And servant leaders don't tolerate disrespect, dishonor, or disconnection. They shine a light on it—and burn it out.

So how do you detox a toxic culture?
Step one: name it. Stop pretending. Call it what it is.
If you walk into a building and it smells like death, don't light a candle—**clean the rot.**
Have the hard conversations. Tear down the old idols. Strip the varnish off the fake "family" culture and deal with what's really happening.
You can't fix what you won't face.

Step two: rebuild with truth.
Every great culture begins with one question: *How do we treat people here?*
And if the answer isn't rooted in honor, empathy, and responsibility, **you're not ready to rebuild.**
Start by modeling it. The culture begins with the *leader*, not the HR department.
If you want people to care, serve, and grow—**you go first.**

Step three: protect the new culture like it's sacred.
Because it is.
You'll face resistance. You'll face eye rolls. You'll face people so steeped in dysfunction that they don't know how to work in freedom.
Detoxing a culture is *not* a one-time meeting—it's a daily battle.
But if you stay faithful to the process, you won't just fix a workplace—you'll **resurrect a mission.**

The world is done with fake cultures.
With pizza parties instead of pay raises. With "family" talk while layoffs hit. With diversity statements and no

CHAPTER 7: Obstacles to Servant Leadership

inclusion.

The kingdom culture is different. It's servant-led. It's Spirit-powered. It's unshakeable because it's built on truth.

You want to change the world? Start by changing your culture.

Light a match. Burn the old ways. Build the kind of organization that makes heaven proud.

How to Build a Legendary Servant Culture

Step 1: Define What Heaven Honors

Before you build, you must know what you're building toward. Ask:

- What does God celebrate in leadership?

- What kind of stories would Jesus tell about your team?

- What values do you want whispered in the halls?

Write down 3–5 **core servant leadership values**. These are your cultural anchors—truths that won't bend under pressure.

Examples:

- Radical empathy

- Excellence without ego

- Sacrifice for the sake of others

- Listening that leads to transformation

- Stewardship of influence

Step 2: Find the Stories That Prove It's Possible

Culture isn't built by slogans—it's built by stories.

Look around your organization. Who's already living the values you want multiplied? Find the janitor, the coach, the quiet leader who's making heaven proud.

Document their stories. Interview them. Celebrate them publicly. These stories become your **unofficial curriculum**—the lessons people remember long after the training ends.

"Culture is not taught. It's caught. And stories are the net."

Step 3: Circulate the Stories Until They Become Legend

CHAPTER 7: Obstacles to Servant Leadership

Don't let these stories die in a meeting. Make them part of your rhythm:

- Share one story at every team meeting.

- Post them on walls, websites, and onboarding packets.

- Use them in coaching conversations.

- Let them shape your hiring, your promotions, your rewards.

Repetition builds reputation.
The more you tell the right stories, the more your culture becomes real.

Step 4: Align Every System to Serve

Culture isn't just what you say—it's what you **systematize**.

Audit your organization:

- Do your rewards honor servant leadership?

- Do your policies reflect empathy and inclusion?

- Do your leaders model what they preach?

If not, **burn the old ways**.
Rewrite the playbook.
Build systems that serve people, not just profits.

Step 5: Teach Others to Build What You've Built

Servant leadership multiplies. It doesn't stop with you.

Train your team to:

- Spot servant leadership in action

- Tell stories that shape culture

- Coach others through narrative

- Build systems that reflect Kingdom values

Give them the tools. Give them the authority.
Then watch the culture spread like wildfire.

Why Servant Leadership Is the Only Model That Works

Because it's not built on charisma—it's built on character.
Not on control—but on compassion.
Not on hype—but on humility.

CHAPTER 7: Obstacles to Servant Leadership

Servant leadership works because it's **aligned with truth**.
It honors the image of God in every person.
It builds cultures that don't just perform—
they **transform**.

And when you build a culture like that?
You don't just change your organization.
You change the world.

The Courage to Serve When It's Inconvenient

Because greatness never asks for permission.

Everyone wants to serve when the lights are on, the cameras are rolling, and the room applauds.
But servant leadership isn't forged in spotlights—it's forged in shadows.
It shows up at 5:00 AM to clean the mess no one else sees.
It sacrifices credit, comforts, and convenience for the good of others.
"Even the Son of Man did not come to be served, but to serve..." (Mark 10:45, NIV)—and He didn't wait for ideal conditions.

Inconvenience reveals character.
Anyone can serve when it's easy. But **who are you when it's messy, hard, and thankless?**

The Greatest Among You

I've seen leaders disappear during crisis—silent, hidden, waiting for PR to fix what their integrity couldn't.
And I've seen others wade into the fire with their sleeves rolled up and their hearts wide open.
Servant leadership doesn't run from chaos—it runs toward it.

Courage is not the absence of fear—it's the **decision to show up anyway.**
When the numbers aren't good, when morale is low, when you're exhausted and unappreciated—**that's the battlefield.**
Servant leaders walk into the storm, not because it's easy, but because *people are counting on them.*
They anchor the ship when the waves are high.
"Be strong and courageous… for the Lord your God goes with you; he will never leave you nor forsake you" (Deuteronomy 31:6, NIV).

Convenient leadership is built on preference.
Courageous leadership is built on conviction.
Preference asks, "What's best for me right now?"
Conviction asks, "What's right—even if it costs me everything?"
Servant leaders answer to a higher call—and that call doesn't care about your calendar or your comfort.

I've worked under leaders who vanished the moment the pressure rose.
Leaders who handed off the mess, blamed their teams, or retreated behind bureaucracy.

CHAPTER 7: Obstacles to Servant Leadership

And I've worked under a few who got on the floor with us—who mopped, packed, lifted, and stood shoulder to shoulder when we were drowning.
Those are the leaders people *bleed* for.
Not because they're perfect—but because they're **present when it counts.**

Serving when it's inconvenient isn't just a heroic moment—it's a lifestyle.
It means being available when you'd rather be alone.
It means mentoring a struggling employee instead of writing them off.
It means speaking truth when silence is safer.
And it means leading with your hands, not just your mouth.

Jesus didn't serve when it was convenient.
He washed feet hours before being betrayed.
He forgave while being crucified.
He didn't wait for applause—He embraced the **mission of messy, inconvenient love.**
And if you want to lead like Jesus, you better get used to *sweat, blood, and surrender.*

The world is hungry for **leaders who show up when it's hardest.**
That's when loyalty is earned, cultures are transformed, and trust becomes unbreakable.
Convenient leadership is everywhere—and it's failing.
What the world needs now are **warrior-servants**, those who kneel with courage and rise with grit.

You want to lead a revolution? Start by serving when every excuse tells you not to.

Rally Cry: We Serve—And We Never Surrender

This world has had enough of empty suits, ego-fueled emperors, and boardrooms ruled by fear.
It's sick of "leaders" who hide behind their title, who use people instead of *raise* them.
It's tired of toxic policies, fake cultures, and work environments where souls go to die.
We're done.
And we're not asking for permission—we're declaring a revolution.

We are the **servant leaders**.
We lead from the front lines, not from the corner office.
We carry towels, not crowns. We lift others instead of lifting ourselves.
We **listen**, we **care**, we **act**—and when it's hardest to lead, we lean in harder.
We don't wait for applause. We bleed for the mission.

This isn't weakness. This is **warrior strength.**
It takes zero courage to boss people around.
But it takes a lion's heart to wash feet, to build trust, to lead through storms without needing the credit.
We don't want to be *seen* as great—we want to **serve** so others can become great.

CHAPTER 7: Obstacles to Servant Leadership

We don't build empires—we build legacies that last.

To every leader who's afraid to serve because it might look "soft"—wake up.
There is nothing soft about sacrifice.
There is nothing weak about love.
And there is nothing small about putting people first.
That's not soft leadership—it's **sacred leadership.**

So rise up.
Tear down the old systems that rot from within.
Rebuild cultures with truth, trust, and the unstoppable power of purpose.
Don't just read this chapter—**live it.**
Because the world doesn't need more bosses. It needs **servants who lead and leaders who serve.**

Let's go.

The Greatest Among You

CHAPTER 8: Servant Leadership in Schools, Sports, and Nonprofits

"If you want to raise the next generation of leaders, don't build empires—build people. The scoreboard, the budget, the test scores—they'll fade. But the way you served? That echoes in eternity."

If you want to change the future, stop waiting for someone else to do it.
Step into the schools, onto the fields, and into the nonprofit trenches—*because that's where the soul of society is being formed.*
The greatest CEOs, coaches, and leaders of tomorrow are sitting in desks right now—waiting for someone to **believe in them, serve them, and show them what leadership really looks like.**
They don't need more rules—they need **real examples.**
They don't need perfection—they need your *presence.*

We aren't just teaching students, athletes, or volunteers—we're shaping **destinies.**
Servant leadership in these arenas is not optional—it's **critical.**
Because the habits they learn now—how to treat others, how to handle adversity, how to lead with love—those

become the scaffolding of their future character.
And in a world drowning in selfishness, **purpose-driven leaders don't emerge by accident.**
They are *forged* in servant-led environments.

I have walked this path.
I have stood in front of classrooms filled with kids who had given up on school and turned them into believers in themselves.
I have coached soccer teams from the bottom of the standings to champions—not by yelling, but by *serving*.
I have pulled greatness out of kids who didn't see anything great in themselves.
And this chapter is a call to every educator, coach, mentor, and nonprofit leader to do the same.
The stats don't lie—youth mental health is in crisis.
Isolation, anxiety, and a loss of purpose are *devouring this generation.*
What they need now more than ever is **connection with servant-hearted adults** who see beyond behavior and into the battle within.
They need schools that feel safe, teams that feel like family, and organizations that give more than they take.
They need servant leaders who show up every day with grit, grace, and *gut-level belief* in their potential.
Servant leadership in schools isn't just about teaching standards—it's about **raising standard-bearers.**
In sports, it's not about wins—it's about **winning souls to a bigger vision of what life can be.**
In nonprofits, it's not about charity—it's about **changing**

CHAPTER 8: Servant Leadership in Schools, Sports, and Nonprofits

communities one relationship at a time.
This is the work that doesn't make headlines but builds heroes.
And we desperately need more of it.

Scripture hits it hard:

"Start children off on the way they should go, and even when they are old they will not turn from it." — Proverbs 22:6 (NIV)
This isn't just a parenting principle—it's a **servant leadership mandate.**
Every moment you invest in a child, a student, a young athlete—it echoes in eternity.
It's time we took this charge seriously, not just as leaders but as *disciples*.

And whatever you do in the classroom, in the huddle, in the nonprofit boardroom—

"Work at it with all your heart, as working for the Lord, not for human masters..." — Colossians 3:23 (NIV)
This isn't about applause—it's about **assignment.**
God didn't put you where you are so you could coast—He placed you there to *serve like Jesus and lead like fire*.
You are the model. You are the culture. You are the movement.

This chapter is more than words—it's a *torch*.
It's for every exhausted teacher, every underpaid nonprofit warrior, every coach pouring heart and soul into kids who barely say thank you.
You matter.
Your leadership matters.
And if you serve like Jesus—even when no one sees—it **will change the world.**

Building Future Leaders Through Education and Coaching

The future doesn't arrive by accident—it's *shaped,* day by day, leader by leader, classroom by classroom, practice by practice.
Our schools and sports fields are not just institutions for learning—they are **factories of future leadership.**
And every coach, teacher, and mentor is a *spiritual architect*, building frameworks of character, courage, and conviction into the lives of young people.
What's being modeled today will be **multiplied tomorrow**—for better or worse.
And if we're not intentional about building servant leaders now, we are planting seeds for a leadership crisis later.

Leadership doesn't start with titles—it starts with **training.**

CHAPTER 8: Servant Leadership in Schools, Sports, and Nonprofits

It begins when a kid learns to speak truth with kindness, take responsibility with humility, and serve others with joy.

That's not taught in a textbook.

It's **caught from the leaders** who show up every day, who give grace when it's hard and push for greatness when it's uncomfortable.

This is where *real* education and coaching ignite lasting transformation.

Research confirms it: leadership development begins in adolescence and is highly influenced by mentorship and adult modeling (Murphy & Johnson, 2011).

When youth are empowered with leadership roles and coached by servant-minded adults, they develop stronger social-emotional skills, better academic outcomes, and greater long-term career success.

This isn't just theory—it's **data-driven truth.**

The earlier we build servant leadership into their DNA, the stronger our teams, companies, and communities become in the future.

It's ROI with eternal impact.

Education isn't just about standardized testing—it's about **standard-bearing character.**

When schools prioritize values like empathy, collaboration, and service, they produce students who aren't just smart, but **significant.**

Coaching isn't just about wins and losses—it's about

forming resilient, selfless young people who learn to lead with purpose.

The best programs today—the ones producing world-class citizens—are **anchored in servant leadership principles.**

That's not a coincidence—it's a choice.

But here's the hard truth: **you can't lead someone where you've never gone.**

If our educational and coaching environments are filled with burned-out, bitter adults who've never been *led with love*, how can we expect them to raise up future leaders?

This is why **investing in adult servant leadership training is essential.**

Principals must serve teachers. Athletic directors must serve coaches. Nonprofit directors must serve volunteers.

When leadership becomes service at every level, it creates a **culture of influence that outlasts any curriculum.**

The greatest leaders of history—from Jesus to Mandela to Coach Wooden—understood this: **coaching is discipleship.**

It's long, patient, frustrating work. But it's also **world-altering.**

Jesus took twelve unqualified, ordinary people and changed the world by *serving them relentlessly* until they learned to lead others.

CHAPTER 8: Servant Leadership in Schools, Sports, and Nonprofits

That's the blueprint. That's the model.
We don't need more charismatic speakers—we need *consistent coaches* who serve from the inside out.
This is especially crucial in underserved communities. Studies show that students in high-risk environments who have at least one consistent, supportive adult are far more likely to graduate, avoid incarceration, and become contributing members of society (Search Institute, 2022). That adult doesn't have to be rich, famous, or brilliant—they just need to **serve with heart.**
Education and coaching—when done right—aren't just jobs.
They're **lifelines.**

If you're a leader in education, sports, or the nonprofit world, hear this: *you are holding the future in your hands.* What you model, they mirror. What you tolerate, they absorb. What you celebrate, they become.
Don't waste the opportunity.
Build them. Teach them. Coach them. Serve them.
And one day, they'll lead with fire, with faith, and with the same servant heart you showed them.

Creating Purpose-Driven Environments for Youth

Purpose is the heartbeat of transformation. Without it, kids drift. They go through the motions, float from class to class, from practice to practice, *surviving* but never truly living. But when youth are placed in environments where purpose is clear, modeled, and expected, they don't just participate—they **ignite.** Purpose-driven environments tell every child: *You matter. You were made for something great. And your leadership starts today.*

This generation isn't lost—they're **looking.** They're starving for truth, meaning, and identity. But the world keeps feeding them distraction, vanity, and empty applause. That's where **servant leadership environments change the game.** When youth are surrounded by leaders who serve, sacrifice, and model integrity, they begin to believe that life isn't about fame—it's about **faithfulness.**

Studies show that youth who connect to a purpose greater than themselves are more resilient, perform better academically, and are more likely to become positive contributors to their communities (Damon, 2008). Purpose doesn't eliminate pain, but it gives it meaning. It transforms obstacles into opportunities and setbacks into stepping stones. That's what every school and sports program should be doing—**lighting torches of vision** in every young person they encounter.

Creating these environments starts with *culture.* And culture is built by **what we model, tolerate, and celebrate.** If we model kindness, tolerate growth, and celebrate service—we create a culture that breathes purpose. But if we model control, tolerate ego, and celebrate only winning, we produce performance-

CHAPTER 8: Servant Leadership in Schools, Sports, and Nonprofits

obsessed robots who burn out before they bloom. We must **choose our culture intentionally.** Because culture always wins.

A purpose-driven environment doesn't mean soft discipline or low expectations. It means high expectations with **high support.** It means saying: "I believe in you too much to let you quit." It's calling kids *up* instead of calling them *out.* It's servant leaders getting in the trenches, walking beside them, and saying: *"Let's build something together."* It's not rules first—it's *relationship first.*

Athletics, classrooms, and nonprofit programs are the new **battlegrounds of belief.** If we don't define what matters most, TikTok, peer pressure, and culture wars will do it for us. Purpose-driven environments give kids a compass when the world offers a maze. We show them who they are, Whose they are, and *why* they're here. And when they understand that, they begin to **lead with fire and follow with faith.**

One of the most powerful ways to build these environments is through **shared mission.** Whether it's "Serve first," "Leave it better," or "Lift others up"—a compelling mission gives meaning to every drill, every lesson, every huddle. It becomes more than a poster on a wall—it becomes a **pulse** in the building. The greatest programs in the world don't just teach—they train for life, through values that endure long after the final whistle.

If we want to raise servant leaders, we have to build environments where kids see service as strength and purpose as power. This doesn't happen by accident—it's the **result of vision, passion, and daily intentionality.** We don't wait for them to "figure it out." We create environments that *show* them the way. And when we do, we don't just prepare them for careers—we prepare them for **kingdom impact.** That's leadership that lasts.

Stories from Life: Coaching, Teaching, and Leading

I had never even *heard* of servant leadership until I became a student at Grand Canyon University—and when I did, something inside me roared to life. It wasn't a new concept; it was a name for what had always burned inside me. Finally, someone gave language to the way I had always believed leaders *should* lead. GCU didn't just educate me—it **activated** me. And for that, I'll be forever grateful.

Before servant leadership had a name in my mind, it had a place in my heart. I saw what leadership *wasn't* long before I saw what it could be. I worked under bosses who wore their title like a crown of thorns—painful for everyone but themselves. They used fear instead of faith, control instead of care. And every time I watched someone get torn down for being bold, creative, or human, I whispered to myself, *"If I ever get the chance to lead... I will never lead like that."*

CHAPTER 8: Servant Leadership in Schools, Sports, and Nonprofits

When I began coaching soccer, I didn't walk into the role thinking, "I'm a leader now." I walked in thinking, *"These kids need someone who sees them."* I pushed them hard—we ran, we sweat, we competed—but I never forgot they were somebody's son or daughter. And I treated them the way I wished I'd been treated when I was their age. I didn't know it then, but I was living out the heart of servant leadership: **demanding excellence while delivering dignity.**

There was a fire in me that couldn't be smothered by bad bosses or broken systems. It's the fire that told me *real leadership doesn't look like domination—it looks like dedication.* Servant leadership isn't soft. It's sacrificial. It's showing up early, staying late, knowing names, seeing pain, and never using authority as a weapon. When my players failed, I carried the weight with them. When they succeeded, I stepped back and let them shine.

In the classroom, that same fire followed me. Every student who walked into my room wasn't just a name on a roster—they were *mine.* I taught every kid like they were my own child. Because I've seen what happens when students are dismissed, labeled, or neglected by prideful "professionals" who care more about power than purpose. And I promised myself: **"My classroom will be different. My leadership will lift."**

What I learned over time is this: **you can't fake care.** Kids know. Athletes know. Employees know. You either serve them or you use them—there is no in-between. Servant leadership means rejecting ego, fighting apathy, and choosing to *see* people instead of simply managing them. And when you do that consistently, you don't just earn respect—you earn *legacy*.

I didn't invent servant leadership. I *discovered* it in action—in locker rooms, on fields, in classrooms, and in conversations with students and athletes who didn't need a boss... they needed a believer. Every win on the scoreboard was built on something deeper: **relationship.** When my players and students came back years later and told me I changed their life, it wasn't because of a worksheet or a formation—it was because I led with heart.

Now I know this truth like it's written in my DNA: servant leadership isn't a buzzword—it's a calling. And it's a calling worth fighting for. I lived under tyrants and rose to lead as a servant. I've coached teams no one believed in, taught students others wrote off, and watched purpose bloom in impossible places. And now, my mission is simple: **pass it on.** If we want to build the future, we better start *serving* it.

Scripture: Proverbs 22:6, Colossians 3:23-24

"Start children off on the way they should go, and even when they are old they will not turn from it." (Proverbs 22:6, NIV)
This verse isn't a suggestion—it's a strategy. It's not just for parents; it's for teachers, coaches, mentors, and

CHAPTER 8: Servant Leadership in Schools, Sports, and Nonprofits

leaders who understand that every investment made in a child is a down payment on the future. If you're molding young minds, you're not babysitting—you're *blueprinting destiny.* Servant leaders know that true influence doesn't start in boardrooms, it starts in the hearts of the next generation. What we train now echoes for decades.

This isn't about behavior management—it's about heart formation. Proverbs 22:6 calls us to shape the whole person: their character, conviction, confidence, and compassion. You don't do that with shouting, shame, or fear. You do it by modeling what leadership looks like when it kneels down, locks eyes, and says, *"I see greatness in you."* Servant leaders don't just point to the path—they *walk* it with those they lead.

Now flip the script with Colossians 3:23-24: *"Whatever you do, work at it with all your heart, as working for the Lord, not for human masters... It is the Lord Christ you are serving."* (NIV)
This is servant leadership in a single breath. No matter your title, your task, or your timeline—*you're serving Jesus.* That means the mop in your hand is holy. That means the spreadsheet on your screen is worship. When you get this deep in your soul, every action becomes purpose-fueled and eternity-anchored.

These verses collide to create a framework that cannot be shaken: train the next generation with intention, and do it with the kind of effort you'd give if Jesus Himself was in your classroom, your locker room, or your office.

Because guess what? *He is*. Servant leadership means we don't take shortcuts. We don't clock in and out emotionally. We show up full-throttle, because the work is too important and the stakes are eternal.

This kind of leadership builds legacy. When you pour into others like this, you don't just teach skills—you build spiritual DNA. People remember who loved them, who believed in them, and who refused to give up on them when they were still figuring it out. Proverbs 22:6 is a promise, but it's also a challenge: are you shaping lives for *temporary gain* or *eternal impact*? Servant leaders always play the long game.

Colossians 3:23-24 destroys the idea that we can be passive or mediocre in our leadership. It says *whatever* you do—*whatever*—do it with all your heart. So yes, that means showing up for the early shift. That means writing the extra note of encouragement. That means saying, *"I've got your back"* to a student, employee, or teammate when they feel like no one else does. Every small act becomes sacred when it's done for the glory of God.

These scriptures don't let leaders hide. They don't let us blame culture, politics, or policy. They call us higher. They say: *"You want to lead like Jesus? Then serve like Jesus."* That means consistency. That means character. That means caring when it's inconvenient, hard, or unnoticed. But here's the secret—those are the moments when Heaven is watching most closely.

CHAPTER 8: Servant Leadership in Schools, Sports, and Nonprofits

So whether you're a coach in cleats, a principal in dress shoes, or a CEO in loafers, these verses set your standard. Start them young. Serve with heart. Do it all as if you're on Kingdom assignment—because you are. Let Proverbs 22:6 shape your mission, and let Colossians 3:23-24 fuel your execution. This is servant leadership with a cross in your heart and fire in your soul.

Building Future Leaders Through Education and Coaching

Education is not just about academics—it's the launching pad for legacy. Servant leaders see every classroom, every practice, and every hallway conversation as a chance to shape the next generation of world-changers. You aren't just filling minds with facts; you're lighting hearts with fire. The student in the back row, the benchwarmer on the sideline, the shy kid who won't speak up—they're all waiting for someone to see *them*. That's what servant leadership does—it *sees*, it *believes*, and it *builds*.

The greatest leaders of tomorrow are being formed in the hearts of coaches, teachers, mentors, and directors who choose service over status. You can teach a playbook, sure—but can you teach purpose? You can assign homework—but are you awakening hope? When you lead with love and lead by example, young people learn the most valuable lesson of all: that real leadership is not about rising above others—it's about lifting them. Every servant leader becomes a carpenter of character, chiseling away insecurity to reveal greatness.

There is overwhelming research showing that students who have a trusted adult mentor are more likely to succeed in school, avoid destructive behaviors, and aspire to higher goals (Rhodes, 2002). Servant leaders fill this gap—not by force, but by presence. They don't just cheer from the stands—they stand beside. They don't lead with ego—they lead with empathy. They create relationships where students don't just feel instructed—they feel *known*.

Coaching, too, is sacred. It's not about shouting commands—it's about modeling character. Great coaches know the scoreboard will fade, but the way you made your players feel will echo forever. Servant leaders teach kids that greatness is found in effort, not entitlement. That losing doesn't mean failure if you showed up with heart. That character always outlasts talent. You're not just developing athletes—you're developing warriors of wisdom, grit, and grace.

We've got too many adults trying to be in charge without knowing how to lead. True leadership is caught, not just taught. When students watch us *serve*, they start to understand what greatness really looks like. When we let them lead—through group projects, team decisions, or class responsibilities—they don't just learn power. They learn *purpose*. Every moment we model servant

CHAPTER 8: Servant Leadership in Schools, Sports, and Nonprofits

leadership, we plant seeds of transformation.

Our world is starving for future leaders who aren't driven by ego or applause but by mission. Servant leadership in education and sports rewires their thinking early—it teaches them to win with humility, to speak with honor, and to serve with joy. They don't grow up chasing the spotlight; they grow up *becoming the light.* That's the future we need. That's the army we're building—one lesson, one locker room, one kid at a time.

When educators and coaches embrace servant leadership, they become the bridge between potential and destiny. They don't just see what a student *is*—they see what they *can become.* That kind of vision is contagious. It makes young people stand taller, speak louder, and dream bigger. They don't just graduate with a diploma—they graduate with *direction.*

So yes, this work is hard. And yes, it's holy. If you're shaping minds or molding hearts—if you're building leaders one child at a time—*you are on divine assignment.* Servant leadership isn't an option for our future; it's a *requirement.* And the classroom, the court, and the community center? They're your battlefield. Now get back in there—and lead like someone's future depends on it. Because it does.

Creating Purpose-Driven Environments for Youth

Purpose is the compass that gives direction to potential. Without it, kids drift—tethered to nothing, pulled by whatever current is loudest or nearest. When servant leaders step into their lives, they anchor them with meaning. We don't just teach content—we cultivate calling. Creating a purpose-driven environment means helping students and athletes see *why* their lives matter, not just *what* they can achieve.

In a world screaming for attention, youth are silently begging for significance. Social media tells them they're not enough unless they're seen, liked, followed. But purpose flips that script—it says, "You were made for more than likes. You were made for *legacy*." When classrooms and locker rooms are infused with this truth, everything changes. Purpose becomes the power that makes effort sustainable and growth irresistible.

Studies show that adolescents who develop a strong sense of purpose are more resilient, better at coping with adversity, and more likely to thrive academically and socially (Damon, 2008). This isn't theory—it's transformation. Purpose-driven environments reduce behavioral issues, increase student engagement, and strengthen mental health. Servant leaders aren't just fixing problems—they're planting purpose. And when that seed takes root, kids start showing up differently.

Purpose is contagious—once a young person finds it, others around them catch fire. We must create ecosystems—classrooms, teams, and clubs—that breathe meaning into every conversation, every challenge, every win and every loss. You don't need a fancy curriculum to do this. You need leaders who are intentional, encouraging, and who speak identity into the next generation. The spark of belief from one leader can ignite the whole room.

A purpose-driven environment isn't soft—it's sacred. It holds students accountable because their dreams demand it. It disciplines with love because it sees who they can become. It sacrifices ego and control in favor of growth and development. Servant leaders don't coddle—they *call up*. They set the bar high, not to break kids, but to build them.

Sports are an especially powerful arena for purpose. The team becomes a family. The grind becomes a proving ground. The scoreboard becomes a mirror of discipline and drive. Coaches who serve with intention turn every drill into a lesson and every setback into a story. They help young people see that hard work honors God, and purpose fuels perseverance (Colossians 3:23–24, NIV).

Education, too, must be infused with destiny. Students who see their learning as connected to a deeper mission don't just memorize—they *internalize*. They don't just pass tests—they pursue truth. Purpose changes posture. It makes students sit up straighter, speak with more confidence, and care more deeply about the world around them.

If we want the next generation to lead with integrity, love with courage, and serve with strength, we must give them the "why" before the "what." We must create environments where they feel safe enough to dream and strong enough to fight for that dream. Servant leadership turns schools, gyms, and community centers into launchpads. Not just for better grades or faster times—but for lives filled with vision, passion, and destiny. That's the power of a purpose-driven environment—and it starts with *us*.

Scripture: Proverbs 22:6, Colossians 3:23–24

"Start children off on the way they should go, and even when they are old they will not turn from it." *(Proverbs 22:6, NIV)* — this is not just advice. It's a divine blueprint. This scripture doesn't promise that the path will be easy, but it guarantees that what's planted in youth *sticks*. That means every moment with a student, every minute with a player, every conversation in a classroom or a practice field is sacred. You're not just teaching a skill—you're shaping a soul.

Proverbs 22:6 is a battle cry for every teacher, coach, mentor, and parent. It demands intentionality. You can't

CHAPTER 8: Servant Leadership in Schools, Sports, and Nonprofits

wing this. You don't *accidentally* raise up world-changers—you raise them by walking beside them, modeling Christ, and making sure they see purpose in themselves before the world tries to tear it out of them. This verse is the foundation of generational leadership.

Colossians 3:23–24 takes it even further: "Whatever you do, work at it with all your heart, as working for the Lord, not for human masters... It is the Lord Christ you are serving." *(NIV)* — That's not just a verse to hang in an office. That's leadership fuel. This scripture destroys every excuse for mediocrity. It says excellence is not about pleasing people—it's about honoring God with your effort, attitude, and integrity.

Servant leaders internalize this truth: *Every task is holy when done for the right reason.* It could be cleaning up after a team meal or preparing lesson plans late at night. When you work as if Jesus Himself signed your paycheck, everything shifts. Entitlement dies. Excellence rises. That's the kind of mindset that transforms an ordinary organization into a mission-driven movement.

Together, these two scriptures form the heart of youth-centered servant leadership. *Proverbs 22:6* shows us the long game—what we plant today will shape tomorrow. *Colossians 3:23–24* keeps our present efforts aligned with eternity. When a coach refuses to scream and instead chooses to teach, when a teacher chooses encouragement over sarcasm, when a director sees their team as ministry, not just labor—that's when heaven invades the workplace. That's when cultures change.

We live in a world obsessed with outcomes. Wins. Grades. Rankings. But scripture shows us that process and purpose *matter more*. If the process honors God, the results will take care of themselves. That's the power of these verses—they reorder our priorities. They remind us that servant leadership isn't about *looking* impressive—it's about *being* faithful.

These verses also liberate our youth from the trap of people-pleasing. When students and athletes internalize that they are serving Christ through their effort, they stop performing for applause and start living for purpose. Confidence is no longer tied to validation from others—it's rooted in God's truth. You can't bully that kind of identity. You can't shake it. That's the kind of mindset that produces fearless, servant-hearted world changers.

Servant leadership, guided by the Word, builds future leaders who are grounded, relentless, and unshakable. Proverbs 22:6 and Colossians 3:23–24 aren't just memory verses—they are blueprints for building culture, character, and calling. They remind us that leading youth is not a side task—it is kingdom work. If we want to see revival in classrooms, teams, and nonprofits, it starts with leaders who *live* these verses. Plant the truth. Work with all your heart. Serve like Jesus. That's the fire that changes the world.

CHAPTER 8: Servant Leadership in Schools, Sports, and Nonprofits

Rally Cry: Raise the Standard, Light the Fire

You were never called to babysit classrooms, run drills, or shuffle papers. You were called to *build futures*. You are not just a teacher—you are a destiny-shaper. You are not just a coach—you are a soul cultivator. You are not just a director—you are a general in God's army, preparing the next generation to rise, stand, and lead.

Enough with playing small. Enough with just surviving the day. Our kids don't need lukewarm lectures—they need *white-hot leadership*. They don't need babysitters—they need fire-starters. You were chosen, *appointed*, and *anointed* to bring purpose where the world brings pressure. You were born for this.

This is not a job—it's a mission field. Every bell that rings, every whistle that blows, every clipboard, every chalkboard, every sideline—it all becomes holy ground when you show up with servant leadership burning in your bones. Show them what love looks like. Show them what humility sounds like. Show them how to lead by washing feet, not flaunting titles.

Raise the standard. *Elevate the culture.* Build environments so filled with purpose that apathy can't survive. Light a fire so hot that ego, fear, and laziness get burned up in the blaze. Let them see what happens when Christ is not just *preached*, but *lived*—through sweat, service, sacrifice, and grit.

You're not just preparing students to pass tests—you're preparing warriors to *transform the world*. You're not just coaching games—you're coaching hearts to hear God's call. This is your battleground. This is your revival ground. This is your moment.

Now go build something eternal. Go unleash a generation of servant leaders with hearts on fire and hands ready to serve. It starts with YOU.

This is the movement. You are the catalyst. Now GO.

14-Day Plan: Building Future Leaders Through Education and Coaching

Day 1: Define the "Why"

- **Objective**: Clarify your personal purpose as a leader.

- **Action**: Write a purpose statement for your role. Why do you teach, coach, or lead? What legacy do you want to leave?

- **Why it works**: Purpose-driven leaders create purpose-driven environments. You must know your "why" before you can help youth find theirs.

Day 2: Speak Identity

- **Objective**: Begin shaping how youth see themselves.

- **Action**: Identify 3 students or athletes and speak life into them. Affirm their strengths, character, and potential.

- **Why it works**: Identity precedes behavior. When young people believe they matter, they begin to act like it.

Day 3: Create a Culture Contract

- **Objective**: Establish shared values.

- **Action**: Collaboratively create a "Culture Contract" with your group. Include values like respect, effort, empathy, and growth.

- **Why it works**: Ownership builds buy-in. When youth help shape the culture, they protect it.

Day 4: Tell a Story of Purpose

- **Objective**: Use narrative to inspire.

- **Action**: Share a personal story or a story from history that illustrates purpose in action.

- **Why it works**: Stories stick. They bypass resistance and awaken imagination.

Day 5: Connect Learning to Legacy

- **Objective**: Link content to calling.

- **Action**: Take one lesson or practice and explicitly connect it to a larger life skill or purpose.

- **Why it works**: Purpose makes effort sustainable. When youth see the "why," they engage more deeply.

Day 6: Model Servant Leadership

CHAPTER 8: Servant Leadership in Schools, Sports, and Nonprofits

- **Objective**: Lead by example.

- **Action**: Serve your students or athletes in a visible way—clean up after them, bring encouragement, show up early.

- **Why it works**: Servant leadership is caught more than taught. Your actions preach louder than your words.

Day 7: Create a Safe Space for Dreams

- **Objective**: Invite vision.

- **Action**: Ask youth to write or share one dream they have for their life. Listen without judgment.

- **Why it works**: Vulnerability requires safety. Purpose grows best in soil rich with trust.

Day 8: Teach Resilience Through Purpose

- **Objective**: Reframe adversity.

- **Action**: Share a story of someone who overcame

hardship through purpose. Then ask: "What's one challenge you're facing right now?"

- **Why it works**: Purpose turns pain into fuel. It gives meaning to the struggle.

Day 9: Celebrate Character Over Achievement

- **Objective**: Shift the scoreboard.

- **Action**: Publicly recognize someone for a character trait—kindness, perseverance, humility—not just performance.

- **Why it works**: What gets celebrated gets repeated. This rewires motivation from external validation to internal values.

Day 10: Build a Purpose Wall

- **Objective**: Make purpose visible.

- **Action**: Create a wall or digital board where youth can post their purpose statements, dreams, or affirmations.

CHAPTER 8: Servant Leadership in Schools, Sports, and Nonprofits

- **Why it works**: Visual reminders reinforce identity. It also builds community around shared vision.

Day 11: Coach Through Questions

- **Objective**: Develop critical thinking and self-awareness.

- **Action**: Ask powerful questions like:

    - "What do you want your life to stand for?"

    - "Who do you want to become?"

    - "What impact do you want to make?"

- **Why it works**: Questions unlock reflection. They help youth own their journey.

Day 12: Create a Challenge with Meaning

- **Objective**: Push growth through purpose.

- **Action**: Design a challenge (academic, athletic, or service-based) that requires effort and ties to a deeper value.

- **Why it works**: Purpose makes hard things worth doing. It transforms tasks into missions.

Day 13: Invite Mentorship

- **Objective**: Multiply influence.
- **Action**: Pair youth with mentors—older students, alumni, or community leaders—who model servant leadership.
- **Why it works**: Purpose is contagious. Mentorship accelerates growth and deepens roots.

Day 14: Reflect and Recommit

- **Objective**: Solidify transformation.
- **Action**: Host a reflection session. Ask:
    - "What have you learned about yourself?"
    - "How has your purpose grown?"

CHAPTER 8: Servant Leadership in Schools, Sports, and Nonprofits

- "What kind of leader do you want to be?"

- **Why it works**: Reflection turns experience into wisdom. Recommitment turns momentum into movement.

- This isn't just a plan—it's a **movement**. You're not managing behavior. You're **cultivating destiny**. Every conversation, every correction, every encouragement is a seed. And when purpose takes root, the harvest is unstoppable.

The Greatest Among You

CHAPTER 9: Leaving a Legacy of Service

"Legacy isn't what you leave behind—it's who you lift while you're here. Service is the only inheritance that multiplies in the lives of others."

Legacy isn't about plaques, paychecks, or platform size. Legacy is about *impact that echoes when you're gone*. It's about the fingerprints you leave on people's hearts, not just your handprints on a whiteboard or clipboard. Real leadership doesn't seek recognition—it seeds *reproduction*. It doesn't terminate in retirement; it multiplies through those you've served, trained, and empowered.

We live in a world obsessed with *now*—quarterly results, instant fame, and rapid influence. But true servant leaders live for what will outlast them. They don't just build programs—they build people. They don't just cast vision—they *plant it deep*, water it with humility, and guard it with faith. The goal isn't to be the hero of the story; it's to *write others into the story of service* so it continues long after your chapter ends.

Your influence is not measured by how much you achieve, but by how much you ignite in others. This is the power of servant leadership: It replicates. It inspires others to lead like Jesus, to carry the torch, to wash the feet you no longer can. It creates a chain reaction of love, humility, and impact that stretches far beyond your lifetime.

Think about the teachers who shaped you, the coaches who believed in you, the leaders who modeled truth when no one was watching. Most of them are never mentioned in news headlines or remembered by masses—but you remember them. Why? Because they left more than a memory—they left a *mark*. And now, it's your turn.

The finish line is not the end of your leadership—it's the launching pad of your legacy. Like Paul, you're called to *"fight the good fight, finish the race, and keep the faith"* (2 Timothy 4:7–8, NIV). This chapter is not about slowing down—it's about *passing the baton* with full strength, full conviction, and full confidence in what God will do through the ones you've mentored.

Servant leadership is not a seasonal fad—it's a *generational flame*. And if you tend that fire well, it will burn brighter in those who follow you than it ever did in you. You may never see the harvest, but you plant anyway. You water anyway. You pray anyway. Because *God brings the growth*—and your faithfulness fuels it.

You are writing eternity with every act of service. Your legacy is not what you build for yourself—it's what you build into others. This is the final charge. The moment where good leaders retire, but *great ones reproduce*. If you're ready to lead a legacy, not a moment—then step

CHAPTER 9: Leaving a Legacy of Service

forward, servant. This final chapter is for *you*.

Let's finish well. Let's multiply. Let's leave a legacy of fire.

Servant Leadership That Outlives the Leader

The measure of a great leader isn't seen in quarterly reports or yearly accolades—it's seen in what *remains* when the leader is gone. Servant leadership doesn't stop at success; it sows seeds for the *next harvest*. It's not about building a brand—it's about building *people* who carry the mission forward with relentless faith and fire. The best servant leaders know their influence isn't meant to center on them—it's meant to multiply in others. Legacy isn't carved in stone; it's written on hearts that were forever changed by love, sacrifice, and vision.

We live in a world obsessed with being *remembered*, but servant leaders are obsessed with *releasing*. They don't hoard influence—they *give it away* like a gift meant to keep growing. True leaders train others to stand on their shoulders and go *further*. It's not about holding the mic—it's about teaching the next person to *sing the anthem of purpose* louder. You don't leave a legacy by dying rich—you leave a legacy by *living poured out*.

Jesus washed feet, lifted heads, and broke bread with the broken. He left no written memoir, no earthly empire—but His *impact endures forever*. His model wasn't domination; it was *devotion*. His goal wasn't followers—it was *disciples who make disciples*. That's the blueprint. Servant leadership isn't built for applause; it's built for *eternity*. The moment we surrender our need to be *the one*, we become the kind of leader who births *many*.

Leaving a legacy means *naming the next generation*. It's calling out destiny in people who don't even know they're chosen yet. It's the coach who sees the kid who never gets playing time and tells them, "You're going to lead this team someday." It's the teacher who notices the quiet student and says, "You have a voice this world needs to hear." Legacy builders *breathe belief* into others until they start to believe in themselves.

But make no mistake—this kind of legacy doesn't happen accidentally. It takes *intentionality*. It takes writing down the values, codifying the vision, and building the kind of systems that don't die when you walk out the door. Every playbook, every staff meeting, every one-on-one becomes a *transfer point*. We're not just managing—we're *mentoring*. We're not just inspiring—we're *equipping*.

A servant leader's job is never done, because legacy is about *what others do after you're gone*. The boardroom you leave behind. The classroom you no longer teach in. The players you once coached who now lead teams of their own. If they're still standing in truth, still loving people, still giving their all—*you did your job*. Your leadership is *alive in them*.

CHAPTER 9: Leaving a Legacy of Service

The greatest compliment a servant leader can receive isn't a statue or a hall of fame induction—it's this: "Because of them, I believed I could lead too." That's the mark. That's the finish line. That's *eternal fruit*. Leaders may retire, but the mission *never does*. Servant leadership is legacy in motion.

So go ahead and *leave the title behind*. Pass the baton. Light the torch in someone else's hands. Let them run farther than you ever dreamed—and *cheer them on like crazy*. That's legacy. That's servant leadership. That's what outlives you.

Mentorship, Multiplication, and Mission

Mentorship is the engine that drives legacy. It's not just teaching—it's *transforming*. A mentor doesn't just share knowledge; they share their life. They let others *into the process*—the scars, the victories, the setbacks, and the lessons that can't be learned from a textbook. Servant leaders don't wait until someone is "ready"—they *walk beside them* until they are.

Multiplication is the *fruit* of true mentorship. It's when your leadership *reproduces leadership*—and not clones, but *champions*. Servant leaders don't create followers; they *create more leaders* who are driven by purpose, humility, and love. This is the Jesus model. He didn't just call the twelve to watch Him—He trained them to *carry the mission* after He was gone. And those twelve multiplied into billions.

In leadership, the greatest compliment is when someone says, "I lead this way because of how you led me." That's multiplication. That's legacy. That's *discipleship in action*. Paul captured it in 2 Timothy 2:2 (NIV): "And the things you have heard me say… entrust to reliable people who will also be qualified to teach others." That's four generations of leadership in *one sentence*—mentor, mentee, multiplier, movement.

Finishing Well

Finishing well isn't about *coasting*—it's about *charging across the line with nothing left in the tank*. True servant leaders don't retire from purpose—they pass it on with *fire*. The greatest legacy isn't in the title you held or the accolades you collected. It's in the lives you transformed, the mission you lived, and the baton you *intentionally* handed off. Finishing well means *finishing strong*—not fading away.

Too many leaders collapse at the end because they lived for position, not purpose. But servant leaders fuel their fire from a *different source*. Their energy comes from *service*, their strength from *sacrifice*, their joy from *multiplying others*. That's why they cross the finish line with passion still burning in their bones. They don't finish to escape work—they finish to *unleash the next generation* with everything they've built.

CHAPTER 9: Leaving a Legacy of Service

Paul modeled this powerfully in 2 Timothy 4:7–8 (NIV): "I have fought the good fight, I have finished the race, I have kept the faith." He wasn't bragging—he was *declaring victory*. That's what finishing well looks like: staying the course, holding the line, refusing to compromise. And because he finished well, his legacy still fuels millions. *We're writing this book on the shoulders of that kind of leadership.*

Finishing well requires *intentional handoffs*. You don't just hope someone takes your place—you *prepare* them to *surpass you*. The greatest leaders aren't afraid of being replaced—they're *excited to be multiplied*. If your ceiling becomes their floor, *you've won*. If your culture outlives your contract, *you've succeeded*. If your team thrives when you're gone, *you led like Jesus*.

Let's be real: ego will fight this every step of the way. Ego wants your name on the banner and your portrait on the wall. But legacy doesn't care about plaques—it cares about *people*. When you finish well, your reward isn't a statue—it's a ripple. A movement. A new generation of servant leaders who carry the torch farther than you ever could. That's *immortality with purpose*.

Finishing well is also about *honor*. It's about looking back and seeing the *faces* more than the stats. It's about remembering the kid you believed in, the coworker you encouraged, the culture you built when no one else would. It's realizing that your real resume is *written in the hearts of people*—and it's read long after you're gone.

The Greatest Among You

Hebrews 13:7 (NIV) says, "Remember your leaders, who spoke the word of God to you. Consider the outcome of their way of life and imitate their faith." That's the kind of leadership people *want* to follow.

Let's bury the lie that finishing well means slowing down. No—finishing well means *showing up*, one last time, like it's your *first* day on fire. It means being the loudest voice cheering on the next leader, the most joyful mentor in the room, the first one to roll up your sleeves and say, "How can I help?" It means becoming the kind of leader whose shadow inspires more light than darkness. That's legacy in motion.

So when your time in the chair ends—when the whistle is hung up, the title fades, and the keys are turned in—don't just walk out... *pass it on*. Leave a team that's stronger, a culture that's healthier, a mission that's clearer. That's finishing well. That's servant leadership. And that... *that is how legends live on*.

But this isn't just about growth for the sake of expansion—it's about *mission*. The mission is the *why* behind the *who*. Great servant leaders pass on a *purpose*, not just a process. They say, "This is why we do what we do. And this is who we do it for." They *breathe mission* into every lesson, every drill, every board meeting, every conversation. Without mission, multiplication is meaningless.

A mission-driven leader multiplies others with *clarity and*

CHAPTER 9: Leaving a Legacy of Service

fire. They don't raise up managers—they raise up *movements*. And movements don't start with megaphones; they start with *mentorship*. One person taking another under their wing. One coach believing in one player. One teacher seeing potential in one student. Multiply that, and you get *a culture of purpose that reproduces itself*.

The world is desperate for servant leaders who will *multiply on mission*. Too many organizations hoard talent instead of *unleashing it*. Too many leaders cling to power instead of *passing it on*. But Jesus didn't build an empire—He *launched a movement*. And it started by spending three years mentoring twelve ordinary men, then telling them, "Go and make disciples of all nations" (Matthew 28:19, NIV). That's servant leadership. That's multiplication on mission.

Mentorship requires *proximity*. It's not just zoom calls and performance reviews—it's coffee shop conversations, shared experiences, and deep trust. It's asking hard questions and offering honest feedback. It's the long game. Servant leaders think generationally. They don't just think about the next quarter—they think about the *next generation*. They mentor like the future depends on it—because it *does*.

If your leadership ends with you, it was never really leadership—it was ego management. But when your leadership *multiplies others*, it becomes a wildfire of purpose. And when that multiplication is *rooted in mission*, your impact becomes unstoppable. That's what servant leadership does. It mentors, it multiplies, and it ignites mission. And in doing so—it builds a legacy that *will not die.*

Leaving a Legacy of Service
Scripture — 2 Timothy 4:7–8, Hebrews 13:7

"I have fought the good fight, I have finished the race, I have kept the faith." (2 Timothy 4:7, NIV) Those are not the words of a broken man—they're the *battle cry of a victor*! Paul didn't just *survive* ministry—he *poured himself out like a drink offering* (v.6). He gave everything. And that's what legacy demands. If we want to leave a mark on this world that glorifies God and multiplies impact, we have to *live and lead like our time is limited, but our calling is eternal.*

Paul's words were forged in blood, sacrifice, sleepless nights, betrayal, prison, and *absolute devotion* to the mission. And yet he didn't sound bitter. He sounded *triumphant*. Why? Because legacy wasn't about how comfortable he became—it was about *how obedient he stayed*. That's the standard of servant leadership: enduring the cost, embracing the pain, and declaring at the end, "I never quit." And when you lead like that, *your story never ends.*

He continues in verse 8: "Now there is in store for me the crown of righteousness, which the Lord, the righteous

CHAPTER 9: Leaving a Legacy of Service

Judge, will award to me on that day..." (2 Timothy 4:8, NIV). Paul didn't run the race for applause—he ran it for the *eternal reward*. The greatest leaders don't serve for earthly crowns—they serve because they know *Heaven is watching*. They understand that the most valuable trophies aren't displayed in glass cases, but in *transformed lives*.

Now bring in Hebrews 13:7: "Remember your leaders, who spoke the word of God to you. Consider the outcome of their way of life and imitate their faith." (NIV) That's the legacy test—*do others want to imitate your faith*? Not your charisma. Not your strategy. Your *faith*. Your *life*. Your *willingness to serve when it cost you*. If your leadership doesn't lead to imitation of Jesus, it's not legacy—it's ego in disguise.

This verse isn't asking us to admire leaders—it's *commanding us to follow the model of their faithful living*. Faith that wakes up when everyone else sleeps. Faith that shows up when no one is watching. Faith that keeps pouring out when your tank is dry, because you *trust the Source won't fail*. And when your life reflects that kind of commitment, your name may not end up in history books—but it *will be known in Heaven*.

Both of these scriptures remind us that the *real finish line is not retirement—it's eternity*. And servant leaders don't lead for temporary gain. They don't hoard power or manipulate people. They lead with open hands, open hearts, and eyes fixed on the One who first served them.

When they leave, they leave behind a legacy of *discipleship, transformation, and holy fire*.

Let's be honest—these verses *aren't soft*. They don't stroke our egos or whisper affirmations. They *call us to war*. They demand that we burn away the fluff, the pride, the excuses, and *lead like Jesus really died for us*. When 2 Timothy 4:7-8 and Hebrews 13:7 become your leadership model, *you don't need a title to lead—you just need a mission*.

So, what will your epitaph say, leader? "He built a business"? Or… "He built people"? "She climbed the ladder"? Or… "She carried the cross"? Let this be the cry that echoes after you're gone: *They fought the fight. They finished the race. They kept the faith. And we are forever changed because they led like Christ.*

Ignite the Movement of Servant Leadership

To every leader reading this—*you were born for more than titles*. You were created for a *purpose bigger than position*. The world doesn't need more bosses, rulers, or commanders. The world is starving—for *servants*. The kind of leaders who wash feet before they give orders. The kind of leaders who would *rather carry the burden than pass the blame*. The kind of leaders who *bleed purpose, not pride*.

CHAPTER 9: Leaving a Legacy of Service

This isn't a suggestion. This is a *summons*. You've seen the brokenness. You've witnessed the burnout. You've felt the sting of toxic cultures and hollow recognition. And now? *Now you know there's a better way.* Christ didn't come to be served, but to serve—and if that was good enough for the King of Kings, it better be good enough for us.

You are the spark. Right now. Not tomorrow. Not after another leadership seminar. Not when your boss gives you permission. *NOW*. Whether you lead a company, a classroom, a team, or a single child—*you are a servant leader in the making*. The moment you choose to stoop low so others can rise, to listen before you speak, to lift someone else's vision higher than your own—*you are building a legacy that will echo in eternity*.

Flip the tables. Tear down the idols of ego. Burn the altars of control and fear. And raise up a banner that reads: **"The greatest among you will be your servant."** (Matthew 23:11, NIV). That's not weak leadership. That's *kingdom leadership*. That's how cultures change. That's how lives are transformed. That's how Heaven gets a foothold in the workplace, on the field, in the school, and in your community.

So go. Lead. Serve. Bleed for your people. Fight for your culture. Love when it's inconvenient. Lead when no one else will. Be the voice in the wilderness crying out, *"There is a better way!"* And then *live it so loud that the world cannot ignore it*.

The Greatest Among You

Because when the fire of servant leadership catches in one heart—it becomes a spark.
When it spreads to a team—it becomes a flame.
When it reaches a school, a business, a nation—it becomes a wildfire.
And that wildfire… is the movement.

You've got the fire. Here's the fuel. Now go light the world.

CHAPTER 10: The Greatest Among You

"The greatest among you will be your servant." — Matthew 23:11 (NIV)

The world has sold us a lie. That greatness is about domination. That it's earned by climbing over others, silencing opposition, winning at all costs. But the truth is louder than the noise: greatness is found in service. Jesus didn't say the servant would be *great* — He said the servant **would be the greatest**. The high places belong to those who stoop low in humility, love, and sacrifice.

We live in a culture obsessed with platform and power, but real legacy isn't built on LinkedIn titles or corner offices. It's built in the hearts of people you've served. You don't build greatness through control — you forge it through compassion. You don't become a legend by being the loudest in the room — you become unforgettable by listening, lifting, and leading with grace. The world measures greatness in numbers; Heaven measures it in obedience.

This book, this movement, this moment — it's all about reclaiming the ancient path of leadership that doesn't burn people out but **builds them up.** The leaders who change the world are the ones who **love people more than profit, mission more than metrics,** and **impact more than image.** They are the ones whose names may never be in headlines, but whose fingerprints are on everything that matters. This is not soft leadership. This is *soul leadership*. And it's the most powerful force the world has ever known.

So what does it mean to be "the greatest among you"? It means choosing the towel over the title. It means showing up early to serve and staying late to care. It means defending those without a voice, empowering those without status, and encouraging those without hope. It's not about how many follow you — it's about how many you've lifted. It's not about having your name on a building — it's about building others to stand tall long after you're gone.

You've read about culture, strategy, systems, community, and the heartbeat of servant leadership — but now we're down to **the decision.** The world is desperate for something real. Your team, your school, your family, your company — they don't need another boss. They need someone who will wash feet, not wave fingers. They need someone who listens first, serves second, and leads third. That person is you.

And don't think for a second this path is easy. It will cost you your ego. It will require your strength. It will test your patience. But it will reward your soul. You will sleep well, knowing your leadership builds people up and makes this world better. You will leave behind more than profits — you'll leave behind a legacy.

CHAPTER 10: The Greatest Among You

Because at the end of your life, it won't be your resume that people remember. It will be your sacrifice. It won't be your accomplishments that echo through time — it will be your acts of service. You were made for more than power. You were made for purpose. You were created to be **the greatest among them.**

The Legacy of Impact: Building What Outlives You

"Your greatest contribution to the kingdom of God may not be something you do, but someone you raise." — Andy Stanley

True greatness doesn't come from what you build *for yourself* — it comes from what you build *into others*. The monuments we build will crumble. The plaques, the titles, the paychecks — they'll fade. But when you pour into a person's life, when you invest your leadership into developing their character, calling, and courage — *that impact never dies.* That's legacy. That's the echo of servant leadership.

Servant leaders don't just shape businesses. They shape hearts, destinies, and generations. They understand that a lasting legacy doesn't depend on visibility — it depends on **intentionality.** It's found in the leaders they mentor, the students they champion, the underdogs they elevate, and the movements they spark. The real scoreboard of your leadership isn't written on spreadsheets — it's written on souls. It's in the quiet moments where you helped someone believe in themselves again.

Look at the life of Jesus — He never ran a company, never held political office, never wrote a book. But He poured Himself into 12 disciples, and through them, changed the world. His legacy was never about buildings or budgets — it was about *people.* As Paul wrote, "You yourselves are our letter... written not with ink but with the Spirit of the living God" (2 Corinthians 3:2-3, NIV). What you build into others is your most sacred architecture.

You don't have to be famous to be faithful. You don't need a stage to make an impact. You just need to show up every day with a heart to serve, a will to sacrifice, and a desire to see others flourish. **Your ceiling should become someone else's floor.** Your wisdom should become their foundation. Your mistakes, their guide. When you lead like this, your legacy isn't a line on your obituary — it's a fire that lives on in every life you've touched.

The greatest leaders are legacy leaders — they *multiply themselves* through others. They don't hoard their knowledge — they share it. They don't protect their power — they release it. They create ripple effects of goodness that stretch beyond their lifespan. The teacher who inspired a student to believe in themselves, the coach who challenged an athlete to chase purpose over popularity, the manager who promoted someone others overlooked — these are the monuments of servant

CHAPTER 10: The Greatest Among You

leadership.

Your legacy isn't found in the applause — it's found in the impact. And here's the powerful truth: you don't get to decide how long you live, but you **do get to decide what lives on after you.** Will it be bitterness and burnout? Or will it be boldness, love, and transformation? Every choice to serve, every moment of sacrifice, every act of compassion — it all becomes part of the eternal story you leave behind.

One day, someone will sit in a chair you built. Someone will carry a torch you lit. Someone will face a challenge and hear your voice in their head: *You were made for this. Keep going.* That's the power of servant leadership. That's the difference between influence and immortality. You're not just leading for today — you're building forever.

So build what outlives you. Love louder. Serve deeper. Give more. And when you're gone, let the world still feel your impact — not because you demanded greatness, but because you *delivered it* through how you lived. **That's the legacy of the greatest among you.**

Multiplying the Mission: Disciples Who Make Disciples

"Go and make disciples of all nations..." — Matthew 28:19 (NIV)

The Greatest Among You

You were never meant to be the end of the story — you're the beginning of someone else's. The final measure of your leadership is not just how many people follow you, but how many are *equipped to lead* because of you. This is multiplication. This is kingdom math. Servant leadership isn't satisfied with creating impact — it creates **impact creators.**

Jesus didn't just make followers — He made *disciple-makers*. He modeled the message, empowered His people, and then sent them out to do the same. He could've done all the ministry Himself, but He chose to invest in 12 — and then trusted them to carry the torch. That's our model. You don't multiply by control. You multiply by *release*.

In your business, your classroom, your team, your church — your mission must be **bigger than you.** The most toxic leaders hoard their knowledge, withhold authority, and create dependency. But the greatest among us *give it away*. They create pipelines, not pedestals. They don't need the spotlight — they shine it on others. Why? Because their goal is *mission, not ego*.

Real multiplication starts when you begin preparing your replacement before you ever step down. When you lead with an open hand, you create a ripple effect of empowered people who go out and *do what you did* — and more. Your courage becomes their conviction. Your sacrifice becomes their strategy. You reproduce a movement, not just manage a team.

CHAPTER 10: The Greatest Among You

In today's world, we don't need more celebrity leaders — we need **legacy leavers.** We need leaders who understand that true success is succession. Every lesson you teach, every opportunity you provide, every hard conversation you lean into — it's all part of *launching someone else's destiny.* And when you do this faithfully, that person will go and launch someone else. That's multiplication.

This mission doesn't stop at retirement. It doesn't end when the job title changes. You multiply until your last breath. Like Paul said in 2 Timothy 2:2 — *"...entrust to reliable people who will also be qualified to teach others."* That's four generations of leadership in one sentence. That's what this world needs: **leaders who make leaders who make leaders.**

Your daily decisions — to serve, to empower, to train, to encourage — they become generational waves of goodness that will outlast you. People you've never met will be blessed by what you built, because you chose to *lead like Jesus.* So don't just fill positions. Don't just grow a team. **Multiply the mission.** Make disciples. Launch leaders. *And change the world.*

The Invitation to Greatness: Will You Answer the Call?

This is the moment of decision. You've walked through the fire of toxic cultures, climbed the mountain of humility, and been drenched in the downpour of purpose. Now the question comes crashing like thunder into your soul: *Will you lead differently?* Will you join the uprising of men and women who refuse to settle for titles and instead choose **transformation**? This isn't a theory—it's a movement. It's the call of Christ.

We live in a world that says greatness is found in likes, leverage, and legacy buildings with your name on the wall. But Jesus flipped the definition. He said the greatest is the one who *serves*. Who bends the knee. Who washes feet. Who gives when no one notices and leads when no one claps. You want to change your school, your business, your community? *Start by serving.*

Servant leadership isn't weak. It's the most courageous form of leadership that exists. It takes guts to lead this way. It takes backbone to sacrifice the spotlight and elevate others. It takes spiritual fire to walk into a room not asking, "What can I get?" but declaring, "What can I give?" If you want safety, this isn't your path. If you want *significance*, saddle up. You're in the right place.

You don't have to be famous. You don't need a perfect past. You need **conviction.** You need a vision that shakes you awake in the middle of the night. A holy fire that burns up your excuses. An obsession with building people and launching dreams and turning cubicles into revival grounds. The world is full of bosses. The world is starving for *servants*.

CHAPTER 10: The Greatest Among You

So what will you do with what you've just read? Will it be another book that collects dust, or will it be the match that lights a wildfire? Will you finish this page and scroll on with your life, or will you tear out the pages and build your battle plan? Jesus didn't invite us to comfort. He invited us to the *cross*. And from the cross, He led the greatest rescue mission in history.

This is your moment. Take everything you've learned—every principle, every conviction, every God-breathed truth—and *live it*. Be the leader your kids will remember. Be the boss who brought healing. Be the coach who didn't just win games but won *hearts*. Be the teacher who planted dreams. Be the director who didn't dominate but *discipled*.

So, will you answer the call? Will you redefine greatness? Will you lead like Jesus?

The world is waiting.

Let's go build the future. Together.

THE REVOLUTION STARTS WITH YOU

"From everyone who has been given much, much will be demanded; and from the one who has been entrusted with much, much more will be asked." — Luke 12:48 (NIV)

The Greatest Among You

This isn't the end—it's the beginning. Right here, right now, you are standing at the line between average and greatness, between status quo and servant revolution. Everything you've read, felt, and wrestled with in these pages has led to this moment. The world doesn't need more managers. It needs leaders willing to serve. Willing to bleed. Willing to pour out their lives so that others might rise.

The revolution doesn't start in Washington or Wall Street. It doesn't start in some corporate boardroom or at a conference with fog machines and fancy lights. It starts in **you**. In your next meeting. Your next conversation. Your next decision to listen instead of lecture, to empower instead of dominate, to serve instead of flex.

Will you be different? Will you be brave enough to live this out when it's not trending? When the old guard mocks you? When your ego tries to whisper, "You deserve better"? This is the cost of greatness—and the reward. You don't need a new title. You need a new posture.

A Challenge to the Reader

I challenge you: **step into servant leadership**. Not tomorrow—**today**. Start with your team, your family, your community. Look someone in the eye and ask, "How can I serve you today?" Then do it again. And again. And again until your legacy is not what you built for yourself—but

CHAPTER 10: The Greatest Among You

who you built up around you.

Daily Habits of Servant Leaders

Servant leaders don't rise by accident—they rise through **discipline**. Wake up and pray: "God, help me serve well today." Keep a gratitude journal. Ask for feedback. Eat last. Listen more. Speak life. Show up early, stay late, and never forget: **you are a leader because someone needs you, not because you need to feel important**. Live these habits, and your leadership will outlive you.

The Commissioning

Now we close not with applause, but with **an anointing**. You've been equipped, stretched, convicted, and ignited. Now go out and lead like Jesus. Not soft. Not passive. But **bold. Unshakable. Fiercely humble**. You were not born to dominate. You were born to serve—and in doing so, lead a revolution that this world cannot ignore.

Prayer of Commissioning

"Father, raise up leaders who walk with humility, lead with wisdom, and serve with fire. Let Your Spirit stir up in them a desire not for praise, but for purpose. May they become warriors of compassion and architects of transformation. Fill their hands with grace and their hearts with courage. Commission them now, Lord—not for comfort, but for calling."

The Final Flame

Now go. Not with fear, but with fire. Carry this message into every corner of your world. The revolution starts with **you**, and the world is watching. Let them see what **greatness really looks like**. Let them see **you**—the greatest among them—**serving**.

CHAPTER 10: The Greatest Among You

30 Days to a Servant-Led Culture: The Challenge

WEEK 1: LAY THE FOUNDATION

Day 1 – Define the Why
Action: Write a personal leadership purpose statement.
Reflect: Why do I lead? What legacy do I want to leave?

Day 2 – Speak Identity
Action: Affirm someone's character, not just their performance.
Reflect: Who needs to hear who they are becoming?

Day 3 – Audit the Culture
Action: Ask your team anonymously: "What's one thing we need to change?"
Reflect: What's being tolerated that shouldn't be?

Day 4 – Model the Mission
Action: Serve someone in a visible, humble way.
Reflect: What message did my actions send today?

Day 5 – Create a Culture Contract
Action: Collaboratively define 3–5 core values with your team.
Reflect: Are our values aspirational or actual?

Day 6 – Tell a Story of Service
Action: Share a real story that reflects servant leadership.
Reflect: What story is shaping our culture?

Day 7 – Pray or Meditate for Your Team
Action: Spend 10 minutes lifting your team up in prayer or focused intention.
Reflect: What burdens are they carrying that I can help

lift?

WEEK 2: BUILD TRUST

Day 8 – Listen First
Action: In your next meeting, speak last. Just listen.
Reflect: What did I hear that I usually miss?

Day 9 – Own a Mistake
Action: Publicly acknowledge a leadership misstep.
Reflect: What did it cost me to be honest—and what did it build?

Day 10 – Celebrate Character
Action: Recognize someone for who they are, not just what they did.
Reflect: What gets celebrated here—and what should?

Day 11 – Ask for Feedback
Action: Ask your team: "What's one thing I could do better?"
Reflect: How did I respond to truth?

Day 12 – Create a Safe Space
Action: Invite someone to share a struggle without fixing it. Just be present.
Reflect: Do people feel safe to be real with me?

Day 13 – Empower a Voice
Action: Give someone the floor who's usually quiet.
Reflect: Who's waiting for permission to lead?

Day 14 – Reaffirm the Vision
Action: Remind your team why their work matters.
Reflect: Are we chasing tasks or living out purpose?

CHAPTER 10: The Greatest Among You

WEEK 3: MULTIPLY LEADERS

Day 15 – Identify a Future Leader
Action: Tell someone, "I see leadership in you."
Reflect: Who am I raising up?

Day 16 – Delegate with Trust
Action: Hand off a meaningful responsibility—and don't micromanage.
Reflect: Do I empower or control?

Day 17 – Coach Through a Challenge
Action: Help someone process a failure with grace and growth.
Reflect: Am I building resilience or fear?

Day 18 – Share the Spotlight
Action: Publicly give credit to someone else.
Reflect: What does my team think I value most?

Day 19 – Create a Mentorship Moment
Action: Spend 15 minutes mentoring someone intentionally.
Reflect: Who's learning from my life—not just my words?

Day 20 – Build a Leadership Ladder
Action: Create a simple plan to help someone grow into leadership.
Reflect: Is leadership development a priority or an afterthought?

Day 21 – Rest and Reflect
Action: Take a Sabbath moment. No work. Just reflect.
Reflect: Am I leading from overflow or exhaustion?

WEEK 4: TRANSFORM THE CULTURE

Day 22 – Rebuild a Broken Bridge
Action: Reach out to someone you've hurt or neglected.
Reflect: What relationship needs restoration?

Day 23 – Create a Ritual of Honor
Action: Start a weekly rhythm of celebrating servant-hearted wins.
Reflect: What rhythms are shaping our culture?

Day 24 – Rewrite a System
Action: Identify one policy or process that doesn't reflect your values—and change it.
Reflect: Where is our system out of sync with our soul?

Day 25 – Invite a Story
Action: Ask someone to share a story of impact or purpose.
Reflect: What stories are shaping our identity?

Day 26 – Create a Culture Wall
Action: Post quotes, values, or stories that reflect your servant culture.
Reflect: What does our space say about our soul?

Day 27 – Lead a Legacy Conversation
Action: Ask your team: "What do we want to be remembered for?"
Reflect: Are we building something that lasts?

Day 28 – Serve Outside the Walls
Action: Organize a team service project in the community.
Reflect: Are we leading for ourselves—or for others?

CHAPTER 10: The Greatest Among You

Day 29 – Commission a New Leader

Action: Publicly affirm and release someone into greater leadership.

Reflect: Am I multiplying or maintaining?

Day 30 – Write the Culture Declaration

Action: Write a bold, 3–5 sentence declaration of the culture you're building. Share it.

Reflect: What kind of movement are we becoming?

Acknowledgments

First and foremost, I want to acknowledge my wife, Donna. Your unwavering faith in Jesus continues to inspire me every single day. The way you stand firm in your faith, no matter the season, is a testimony that has strengthened my own walk and reminded me of what it means to truly live with Christ at the center. This book would not have been possible without your encouragement, your prayers, and your steady belief in me.

To my children—Dynasty, Grace, Brooklyn, and Boston—you are my greatest blessings and the legacy I hope to leave behind. Each of you has taught me something unique about love, perseverance, and purpose. And to my granddaughter, Parker Mae, you are a daily reminder that the next generation is already rising up. May you always know how deeply you are loved.

I also want to recognize my students. You challenge me every day—sometimes in ways you may not even realize. Your questions, your energy, and your perspectives push me to grow as both a teacher and a leader. You remind me why it matters to invest in people, and for that, I am grateful.

This book is the product of faith, family, and the countless lives that have sharpened me along the way. To all of you—I say thank you.

About the Author

Lee Burchett is a teacher, coach, author, and builder of people. With a career that spans from the soccer field to the classroom, Lee has devoted his life to helping others grow, discover their purpose, and step into leadership rooted in service.

He holds an MBA with an emphasis in Sports Business and an M.S. in Leadership, both from Grand Canyon University—a Christian university where servant leadership is a foundational pillar of the curriculum. His time at GCU deepened not only his academic understanding of leadership but also his conviction that true greatness is found in humility, service, and faith.

As a head soccer coach and athletic leader, Lee built programs that turned underdogs into champions, sending players on to compete at the collegiate level. In the classroom, he challenges his students to think critically, act responsibly, and live with integrity. His influence reaches beyond academics, inspiring students to see leadership as an opportunity to serve.

Lee's writing reflects his belief that faith, family, and community are inseparable from leadership. He has lived this truth at home with his wife, Donna—whose unwavering faith in Jesus continues to inspire him—and with his children, Dynasty, Grace, Brooklyn, and Boston, and granddaughter, Parker Mae.

Through *The Greatest Among You*, Lee seeks to ignite a movement of servant leadership—one that transforms businesses, classrooms, athletic programs, and churches by placing people above power and service above status.

You can connect with Lee and discover more of his work at www.vykanlegacy.com

References

Amundsen, S., & Martinsen, Ø. L. (2014). Empowering leadership: Construct clarification, conceptualization, and validation of a new scale. *The Leadership Quarterly, 25*(3), 487–511. https://doi.org/10.1016/j.leaqua.2013.11.009

Barbuto, J. E., & Wheeler, D. W. (2006). Scale development and construct clarification of servant leadership. *Group & Organization Management, 31*(3), 300–326. https://doi.org/10.1177/1059601106287091

Blanchard, K., & Hodges, P. (2003). *Lead Like Jesus: Lessons from the Greatest Leadership Role Model of All Time*. Thomas Nelson.

Brown, M. E., & Treviño, L. K. (2006). Ethical leadership: A review and future directions. *The Leadership Quarterly, 17*(6), 595–616. https://doi.org/10.1016/j.leaqua.2006.10.004

Cameron, K. S., & Quinn, R. E. (2011). *Diagnosing and changing organizational culture: Based on the competing values framework* (3rd ed.). Jossey-Bass.

Clear, J. (2018). *Atomic habits: An easy & proven way to build good habits & break bad ones*. Avery.

Colangelo, J. (2022). *Servant leadership in business*

education. Grand Canyon University.

Collins, J. (2001). *Good to great: Why some companies make the leap… and others don't*. HarperBusiness.

Duhigg, C. (2016). *Smarter faster better: The secrets of being productive in life and business*. Random House.

Edmondson, A. C. (1999). Psychological safety and learning behavior in work teams. *Administrative Science Quarterly, 44*(2), 350–383. https://doi.org/10.2307/2666999

Eva, N., Robin, M., Sendjaya, S., van Dierendonck, D., & Liden, R. C. (2019). Servant leadership: A systematic review and call for future research. *The Leadership Quarterly, 30*(1), 111–132. https://doi.org/10.1016/j.leaqua.2018.07.004

Gallup. (2020). *State of the American workplace*. Gallup Press. https://www.gallup.com/workplace/257578/state-american-workplace-report-2017.aspx

Greenleaf, R. K. (1970). *The servant as leader*. Greenleaf Center for Servant Leadership.

Greenleaf, R. K. (1977). *Servant leadership: A journey into the nature of legitimate power and greatness*. Paulist Press.

Greenleaf Center for Servant Leadership. (2023). *Research and resources*. https://www.greenleaf.org

Harter, J. K., Schmidt, F. L., & Hayes, T. L. (2002). Business-unit-level relationship between employee satisfaction, employee engagement, and business outcomes: A meta-analysis. *Journal of Applied Psychology, 87*(2), 268–279. https://doi.org/10.1037/0021-9010.87.2.268

Heskett, J. L., Jones, T. O., Loveman, G. W., Sasser, W. E., & Schlesinger, L. A. (1994). Putting the service-profit chain to work. *Harvard Business Review, 72*(2), 164–174.

Hunter, J. C. (2004). *The world's most powerful leadership principle: How to become a servant leader*. Crown Business.

Hunter, E. M., Neubert, M. J., Perry, S. J., Witt, L. A., Penney, L. M., & Weinberger, E. (2013). Servant leaders inspire servant followers: Antecedents and outcomes for employees and the organization. *The Leadership Quarterly, 24*(2), 316–331. https://doi.org/10.1016/j.leaqua.2012.12.001

Keith, K. M. (2008). *The case for servant leadership*. Greenleaf Center for Servant Leadership.

Kouzes, J. M., & Posner, B. Z. (2017). *The leadership*

challenge (6th ed.). Jossey-Bass.

Lencioni, P. (2002). *The five dysfunctions of a team: A leadership fable*. Jossey-Bass.

Liden, R. C., Panaccio, A., Meuser, J. D., Hu, J., & Wayne, S. J. (2014). Servant leadership: Antecedents, processes, and outcomes. In D. V. Day (Ed.), *The Oxford handbook of leadership and organizations* (pp. 357–379). Oxford University Press.

Liden, R. C., Wayne, S. J., Zhao, H., & Henderson, D. (2008). Servant leadership: Development of a multidimensional measure and multi-level assessment. *The Leadership Quarterly, 19*(2), 161–177. https://doi.org/10.1016/j.leaqua.2008.01.006

Parris, D. L., & Peachey, J. W. (2013). A systematic literature review of servant leadership theory in organizational contexts. *Journal of Business Ethics, 113*(3), 377–393. https://doi.org/10.1007/s10551-012-1322-6

Schneider, B., Ehrhart, M. G., & Macey, W. H. (2013). Organizational climate and culture. *Annual Review of Psychology, 64*, 361–388. https://doi.org/10.1146/annurev-psych-113011-143809

Sisodia, R., Wolfe, D., & Sheth, J. (2007). *Firms of endearment: How world-class companies profit from passion and purpose*. Wharton School Publishing.

Spears, L. C. (1995). *Reflections on leadership: How Robert K. Greenleaf's theory of servant leadership influenced today's top management thinkers*. John Wiley & Sons.

Van Dierendonck, D. (2011). Servant leadership: A review and synthesis. *Journal of Management, 37*(4), 1228–1261. https://doi.org/10.1177/0149206310380462

Van Dierendonck, D., & Patterson, K. (2015). Compassionate love as a cornerstone of servant leadership: An integration of previous theorizing and research. *Journal of Business Ethics, 128*(1), 119–131. https://doi.org/10.1007/s10551-014-2085-z

Zak, P. J. (2017). The neuroscience of trust. *Harvard Business Review, 95*(1), 84–90.

Biblical Scriptures (NIV unless otherwise noted):

- **Matthew 23:11** – "The greatest among you will be your servant."

- **Luke 22:26–27** – "…the greatest among you should be like the youngest, and the one who rules like the one who serves…"

- **Philippians 2:3–8** – "Do nothing out of selfish ambition or vain conceit…"

- **Micah 6:8** – "What does the Lord require of you? To act justly and to love mercy…"

- **1 Peter 5:2–3** – "Be shepherds of God's flock that is under your care…"

- **Romans 12:10** – "Be devoted to one another in love. Honor one another above yourselves."

- **Galatians 5:13** – "Serve one another humbly in love."

- **Proverbs 22:6** – "Start children off on the way they should go…"

- **Colossians 3:23–24** – "Whatever you do, work at it with all your heart…"

- **2 Timothy 4:7–8** – "I have fought the good fight..."

- **Hebrews 13:7** – "Remember your leaders, who spoke the word of God to you..."

Works Consulted

- Blanchard, K., & Hodges, P. (2003). *Lead Like Jesus: Lessons from the Greatest Leadership Role Model of All Time*. Thomas Nelson.

- Collins, J. (2001). *Good to Great: Why Some Companies Make the Leap… and Others Don't*. HarperBusiness.

- Covey, S. R. (2004). *The 7 Habits of Highly Effective People: Powerful Lessons in Personal Change*. Free Press.

- Damon, W. (2008). *The Path to Purpose: How Young People Find Their Calling in Life*. Free Press.

- Greenleaf, R. K. (1970). *The Servant as Leader*. The Robert K. Greenleaf Center for Servant Leadership.

- Greenleaf, R. K. (1977). *Servant Leadership: A Journey into the Nature of Legitimate Power and Greatness*. Paulist Press.

- Maxwell, J. C. (1998). *The 21 Irrefutable Laws of Leadership: Follow Them and People Will Follow You*. Thomas Nelson.

- Maxwell, J. C. (2005). *360° Leader: Developing Your Influence from Anywhere in the Organization*.

Thomas Nelson.

- Sinek, S. (2009). *Start with Why: How Great Leaders Inspire Everyone to Take Action*. Portfolio.

- Spears, L. C. (Ed.). (1995). *Reflections on Leadership: How Robert K. Greenleaf's Theory of Servant Leadership Influenced Today's Top Management Thinkers*. John Wiley & Sons.

- Tichy, N. M., & Cohen, E. B. (1997). *The Leadership Engine: Building Leaders at Every Level*. Harper Business.

- Vanourek, G., & Vanourek, B. (2012). *Triple Crown Leadership: Building Excellent, Ethical, and Enduring Organizations*. McGraw-Hill.

- Willard, D. (1998). *The Divine Conspiracy: Rediscovering Our Hidden Life in God*. HarperOne.

- Wright, N. T. (2010). *After You Believe: Why Christian Character Matters*. HarperOne.

Suggested Reading

1. *The Servant: A Simple Story About the True Essence of Leadership* by James C. Hunter
A powerful narrative that breaks down servant leadership into practical truths. Easy to read, impossible to forget.

2. *Dare to Lead* by Brené Brown
A bold and brave roadmap for vulnerable, courageous, and connected leadership rooted in empathy and trust.

3. *Jesus on Leadership* by C. Gene Wilkes
A deep dive into how Jesus flipped the leadership script. Essential reading for anyone who wants to lead like the King.

4. *The Road to Character* by David Brooks
A masterclass on humility, moral strength, and building a life of meaning over success.

5. *Strength to Love* by Dr. Martin Luther King Jr.
Timeless, prophetic essays on love, nonviolence, and moral leadership. The heartbeat of a servant revolution.

6. *It's Your Ship* by Captain D. Michael Abrashoff
The story of how one naval captain built a high-performing culture of trust, empowerment, and care—through servant leadership.

7. *Love Works* by Joel Manby

How one CEO led a multibillion-dollar company with love as the core value—and proved it wins in business.

8. *Humilitas: A Lost Key to Life, Love, and Leadership* by John Dickson
A life-changing case for why humility is the most powerful posture a leader can have.

9. *Leading with a Limp* by Dan B. Allender
An honest look at the pain and beauty of leadership—where brokenness becomes strength and weakness becomes wisdom.

10. *Living into Community* by Christine D. Pohl
How gratitude, truth-telling, promise-keeping, and hospitality can shape healthy cultures where people thrive.

Call to Connect

This book is just the beginning of the conversation. Servant leadership is a movement, and I'd love for you to be part of it.

If this book encouraged, challenged, or inspired you, I invite you to connect with me. Share your story, ask your questions, or tell me how you're putting servant leadership into practice—I want to hear from you.

Stay connected here:

- Website: www.vykanlegacy.com

- LinkedIn: [insert link]

- Facebook / Instagram: [insert links if you want]

- Email: lee@vykanlegacy.com

Your journey matters. Together, we can build a generation of leaders who serve first, lead boldly, and leave a lasting legacy.

Coming Soon: *Profit with Purpose*

What if business could be more than profit margins, quarterly reports, and shareholder demands? What if it could be a force for good—a platform to transform lives, strengthen communities, and leave a legacy that money alone could never buy?

In my next release, *Profit with Purpose: A New Blueprint for Business*, I challenge leaders, entrepreneurs, and organizations to reimagine success. This book blends cutting-edge business strategy with the principles of conscious capitalism, showing how companies can thrive financially while also fueling purpose, impact, and long-term sustainability.

You'll discover:

- Why purpose-driven companies outperform their competitors

- How to align mission, culture, and profit for unstoppable growth

- Practical strategies to build organizations people love to work for and support

- Stories of businesses that are proving "doing good" and "doing well" are not opposites, but allies

Profit with Purpose isn't just a business book, it's a call to rewrite the rules of leadership in the marketplace. If *The Greatest Among You* equips you to serve, *Profit with Purpose* will equip you to build.

Stay tuned—the blueprint is coming.

The movement doesn't end here. It begins with you.

Stay connected with Vykan Legacy on **Facebook, Instagram, and LinkedIn**—where leaders are built, culture is forged, and legacies are unleashed.

If *The Greatest Among You* stirred something inside you, take the next step. Dive into *Building Bridges Between Athletics and Community* and keep building a life and legacy that will outlast you.

Lead with courage. Serve with strength. The world is waiting for you.

www.ingramcontent.com/pod-product-compliance
Lightning Source LLC
Chambersburg PA
CBHW040236110526
44582CB00022B/216/J